UP WITH CREATION!

ICR ACTS/FACTS/IMPACTS 1976-1977

Edited by

Duane T. Gish, Ph.D.

and

Donald H. Rohrer

CREATION-LIFE PUBLISHERS

San Diego, California

Up With Creation!

Copyright © 1978

Creation-Life Publishers, Inc.
P.O. Box 15666
San Diego, California 92115

Library of Congress Catalog Card Number 78-55612
ISBN 0-89051-048-2

Cataloging in Publication Data:

Gish, Duane T. 1921 —   ed.
  Up with creation.
  Partial reprints from *Acts & Facts* 1976 & 1977. Third in a series.

1. Creation. 2. Bible and science.
I. Rohrer, Donald H. 1946 —   jt. ed. II. Title.

213   78-55612

CONTENTS

PREFACE

Acts and Facts is the monthly publication of the Institute
for Creation Research. The main section contains articles
of current interest on the creation/evolution controversy.
These include reports of the activities of creationists,
particularly those of the ICR staff, in their efforts to make
known the tremendous scientific case for creation and to
urge educational authorities to present both models of
origins to our students. The activities of creationists have
generated vigorous opposition from evolutionists and
humanists, such as the American Humanist Association,
and some of this opposition is recorded as well. Reports
of events of unusual interest, such as discovery of an
unusual fossil, reports of the space program, cosmological
events or reports, etc., are included from time to time.

Included as an insert with each month's issue of *Acts
and Facts* is an "Impact" article. These "Impact"
articles usually, but not always, deal with some technical
aspect of the creation/evolution question and are generally
written so as to be comprehensible to both scientist and
layman. Topics that have been touched upon include, for
example, thermodynamics, the fossil record, the origin of
life, evidences for a young earth, influence of the teaching

of evolution on the social sciences, interpreting earth history, the decay of the magnetic field of the earth, and many others.

Up with Creation contains most of the articles published in *Acts and Facts* during 1976 and 1977, plus the 24 "Impact" articles published during these two years. Thus the reader is provided in convenient form all of the articles of continuing interest published in *Acts and Facts* during 1976-1977. Similar volumes were published for the years 1972-1973 *(Creation: Acts/Facts/Impacts)* and 1974-1975 *(The Battle for Creation)*.

Chapter 1, Reports from the Battle Front, contains summaries of debates between ICR staff members and evolutionists on many major university campuses, as well as other sites. One of the amazing developments of the creation/evolution controversy is the reluctance of evolutionists in general to debate creation scientists. In spite of this, success has been achieved in arranging debates from time to time. During the debates the creationists always restrict their presentations strictly to science, while the evolutionists often devote much of their time discussing the religious and philosophical aspects of the question.

Chapter 2, The Challenge of Creation on the University Campuses, is the report of the many lectures and seminars by ICR staff members on university campuses.

Chapter 3, The Case for Creation Reaching Out, contains reports of the many lectures, seminars, and other activities of ICR scientists throughout the U.S., Canada, and other countries of the world, as well as reports of the activities of other creation scientists and creation organizations.

Chapter 4, The Challenge of Creation to the Educational Establishment, reports the many activities of the ICR staff and others toward convincing educators that good science, good education, and academic and religious freedoms require that the scientific evidence for both creation and evolution be presented to students throughout their educational training.

Chapter 5, Special Interest Stories, reports significant

events, stories, and developments related to creation/evolution that have appeared in scientific journals, newspapers, popular magazines, and other sources. Certain aspects of ICR activities, as well as those of other creation scientists and creationist organizations, will be found here as well.

Chapter 6, Director's Column, includes selections from the Director's Column, written by Dr. Henry Morris, Director of the Institute for Creation Research, and published periodically in *Acts and Facts.*

The final chapter, Chapter 7, Impact Series 1976-1977, contains the 24 Impact articles published during those years.

The activities of the Institute for Creation Research with its enlarged staff are continuing and expanding. Opposition is growing as well and we can expect a strong, organized effort to develop in the campaign to thwart the efforts of creation scientists to make known the powerfully convincing case for creation. For additional information on the work of the Institute or to receive a free subscription to *Acts and Facts,* write to ICR, 2716 Madison Avenue, San Diego, California 92116.

Chapter 1
Reports from the Battlefront

The Great Debate Continues—1976

ICR DIRECTOR DEBATES CREATION AT FORMER SCHOOL

A creation-evolution debate with unusual emotional overtones took place on Saturday night, November 8, 1975, when Dr. Henry Morris of ICR debated Dr. Richard Bambach, Professor of Paleontology at the Virginia Polytechnic Institute and State University in Blacksburg. An audience of 1100 or more attended the debate, approximately half of whom were Virginia Tech students and faculty.

Dr. Morris had served as Professor and Chairman of Civil Engineering at Virginia Tech from 1957 to 1970, the period during which he wrote *The Genesis Flood* and six of his other books on Biblical creationism. The nationwide impact of his creationist books at the time had generated much opposition locally, as the liberal faculty and clergy of the university community considered them an embarrassment to their image. At least one unsuccessful attempt had been made to get him removed from the faculty. In the meantime, the Civil Engineering Department itself had developed into one of the nation's largest, with an outstanding faculty and one of the university's top graduate and research programs. Another factor contributing to the unusual background of the debate was that Dr. Morris had been one of the founders of Blacksburg's College Baptist Church in 1962, the first fundamental church in the town oriented primarily to reaching the university community for Christ.

The debate was held in connection with a Creation Seminar sponsored by the College Baptist Church on November 5-9. Campus sponsorship for the debate was provided by "Genesis," the student organization associated with this church. The seminar consisted of eight sessions, with question periods following most of them, in addition to three church services on Sunday. Dr. Morris also spoke to the Sunday breakfast meeting of the county's Gideon camp, which he had helped organize in 1958.

The debate format involved a 30-minute presentation by each speaker, with Dr. Bambach first. Then followed two 15-minute presentations by each speaker, with Dr. Morris first in both cases. The unusual format had been requested by Dr. Bambach. In his presentations, the latter contended that (1) biological changes which lead to evolution had been experimentally verified; (2) the known age of the earth was sufficient for almost unlimited evolutionary changes to have occurred; (3) the geological record showed that such changes had indeed occurred. He included a number of the standard arguments and examples in support of these claims, though without documentation.

Dr. Morris showed that (1) "vertical" evolutionary changes from one kind to a more complex kind of organism could *not* be experimentally demonstrated, because of the extreme time spans involved; (2) the creation model facilitates direct prediction of the phenomena actually observed in the organic world more effectively than does the evolution model; (3) the fossil record exhibits systematic and universal gaps between the different kinds of organisms, as predicted from the creation model; (4) the law of increasing entropy precludes development of increasing degrees of complexity in organisms unless it can be demonstrated that there exists a program which directs such growth, and a complex "motor" which converts the sun's energy into the specific types of work required to develop increasingly complex systems; (5) the laws of probability preclude the chance development of even the simplest living system within the durations of time available in the universe. These contentions were all supported either by self-evident observations or else by documentation from recognized evolutionary authorities.

WESTERN MICHIGAN UNIVERSITY DEBATE WITNESSED BY 1500

Nearly 1500 students, faculty, and townspeople crowded into a lecture hall at Western Michigan University in Kalamazoo to witness a debate between Dr. Elizabeth Baldwin, W.M.U. Professor of Anthropology, and Dr. Duane Gish on October 29, 1975. The debate was arranged by Charles Johnson of Campus Crusade for Christ.

At Dr. Baldwin's request, Dr. Gish made the initial presentation. Dr. Gish documented the fact that evolution is no more scientific than creation, and that each is as intrinsically religious as the other. He then presented evidence which convinces creation scientists that the laws of thermodynamics and the laws of probability are incompatible with the modern neo-Darwinian theory of evolution. This was followed by documentation from the scientific literature that the fossil record convincingly contradicts predictions made on the basis of evolution theory but which on the other hand is remarkably `in accord with the predictions based on special creation.

Dr. Baldwin maintained that the lack of transitional forms that characterize the fossil record was due to the fact that there are so many factors operating against the possibility of fossilization that it is astounding that any fossils at all are found. She insisted in any case that some examples of transitional forms are found, citing the example of the so-called mammal-like reptiles.

During the remainder of her time, Dr. Baldwin, assisted by a series of charts and slides, presented the standard textbook story of human evolution. She spent much time discussing evidence which she believes establishes *Australopithecus* as one of the direct ancestors of man, asserting that it is certain he walked upright in the human fashion. She also pointed out a number of features of Neanderthal Man she believes were primitive and which establishes that he was an evolutionary progenitor of modern man.

In Dr. Gish's rebuttal he pointed out that while evolutionists generally admit that any particular evolutionary mechanism or phylogeny is open to challenge, they will not tolerate a challenge to the "fact of evolution," being absolutely dogmatic on this point. In reply to Dr. Baldwin's statement that lack of transitional forms can be explained by the general absence of conditions required for fossilization, Dr. Gish pointed out that it has been estimated, for example, that the Karoo Formation of South Africa alone contains 800 billion vertebrate fossils. He asserted that the available fossil record has become almost unmanageably rich, the only lack being the predicted transitional forms.

Dr. Gish completely undermined Dr. Baldwin's story of human evolution through the introduction of recent evidence apparently unknown to this anthropologist. On her chart, Dr. Baldwin had shown the evolutionary sequence of *Australopithecus—Homo habilis—Homo erectus.* Dr. Gish pointed out that Dr. Louis Leakey had reported that he had found the remains of these three creatures contemporaneous in Bed II of Olduvai Gorge, and had found evidence of a circular stone habitation hut, an artifact of man, below this level in Bed I. This evidence renders untenable the idea that any of these creatures were ancestral to any of the others, or that any were ancestral to man.

Dr. Gish also described the research of Dr. Charles Oxnard of the University of Chicago (see Dr. Gish's Impact article #29, November, 1975) which establishes the fact that *Australopithecus* was not intermediate between man and apes, and that this creature did not walk upright, as Dr. Baldwin had asserted. She seemed to be at a loss to explain this highly significant evidence, evidence which Dr. Gish claimed served to indicate that man, the apes, and monkeys had always been contemporary, and each had been separately created. Dr. Gish also pointed out the fact that anthropologists have established that the alleged primitive features of Neanderthal Man were not due to genetic differences, but were due to arthritis and rickets, and that he is now classified as *Homo sapiens* and not sub-human at all.

2800 HEAR DEBATE
IN SANTA ANA

A capacity crowd of approximately 2800 college-age young people, from numerous Los Angeles-area colleges and universities attended a debate on creation versus evolution on Monday night, November 17, 1975. The debate was held in the large auditorium of Calvary Chapel, in Santa Ana, California. In addition to the large audience in the auditorium, the entire program was broadcast live over one of the local radio stations, so that many additional thousands actually heard the debate. The debate was video-taped for future use in schools and on local television stations. Strange to say, however, none of the Los Angeles area newspapers carried stories of the debate.

Creationist debaters were Dr. Henry Morris and Dr. Duane Gish of the Institute for Creation Research. For the evolution side, the speakers were Dr. Bayard Brattstrom, Professor of Zoology, and Dr. William Presch, Asst. Professor of Zoology—two of the leading evolutionary spokesmen on the campus of the California State University at Fullerton. Both Dr. Brattstrom and Dr. Presch are well-known zoologists and herpetologists, with long lists of biological publications and honors to their credit.

Dr. Brattstrom's talk was primarily a critical attack on the Genesis record of creation, combined with undocumented assertions that evolution was in conformity with the scientific method. Dr. Presch continued the attack on Genesis and stated that evolution had been proved by the experimental formation of new species and by numerous transitional forms in the fossil record.

Dr. Morris showed, with documentation from evolutionary writings, that evolution was not capable of scientific proof and that, in fact, the entropy principle indicated evolution was essentially impossible. Dr. Gish showed that the traditional arguments for evolution (homology, embryology, vestigial organs) were invalid and that the gaps between kinds in the fossil record were universal and systematic.

Comments by numerous students after the debate indicated that the consensus was one of surprise at the unscientific and undocumented nature of the evolutionists' arguments, in contrast with the carefully documented scientific case for creationism. Much of the evolutionary case was religious in emphasis, arguing that all of the world's religions, except Biblical fundamentalism, were evolutionary in philosophy. One speaker said that Genesis 1:1 had been mistranslated by creationists, and that it really should be read as follows: "In the beginning, matter and energy created the gods." Later, in response to a question from the audience, this speaker said that he had no need to believe in God, since he had faith in himself. Although the creationists did not use Biblical or religious arguments in their main presentations, Dr. Morris did show in his rebuttal that the arguments against Genesis were invalid.

DR. GISH DEBATES
MADALYN MURRAY O'HAIR

On Tuesday morning, April 20, from 8:30-10:00 a.m., Dr. Gish participated in a debate on creation vs. evolution with Mrs. Madalyn Murray O'Hair, internationally famous atheist leader, whose law suit led to the banning of prayer and Bible reading from public schools. The debate was held in the studio of radio station KTRH, a 50,000-watt station in Houston, Texas, reaching a large radio audience. The debate was moderated by Ben Baldwin, a Peabody Award winner in broadcasting.

Dr. Gish and Mrs. O'Hair were each initially given ten minutes to present their cases. Dr. Gish presented a summary of the scientific evidence from several fields which supports creation and contradicts evolution. Mrs. O'Hair in her presentation said that she objected to the "simplistic argument that God did it," but her defense of evolution was itself a simplistic argument. She tacitly acknowledged contradictions between evolution theory and scientific facts by the argument that conditions might be different beyond the observable universe or that conditions may have been different in the distant past. She stated her objections to teaching a theory of origins in public schools which involves God as the agent, insisting that an atheistic theory is the only secular theory possible and thus the only theory permissible for public schools.

Dr. Gish replied that Mrs. O'Hair objected to creation being taught in schools because it introduces God as Creator, but that she has no objections to the teaching of her own atheistic religion in public schools. He pointed out that teaching the evidence for both points of view is the only way of reestablishing academic freedom, separation of church and state, and of putting an end to the indoctrination of students in a humanistic, materialistic philosophy and religion.

Mrs. O'Hair and Dr. Gish replied to questions and comments from the moderator and to a question from one of those in the listening audience. Each was then given an opportunity to present a two-minute summation.

Houston listeners have reported that the interchange was a significant victory for creationism and testimony for God. Testimonies have already been received of atheistic and skeptical listeners who were profoundly affected by the broadcast and who have begun reading creationist books as a result.

UNSCHEDULED TALK BY
STANLEY MILLER FEATURES SAN DIEGO DEBATE

Famed evolutionist, Stanley Miller, was persuaded to defend his origin-of-life studies before an overflow crowd attending a creation-evolution debate at San Diego State

University on April 7, but his remarks were unconvincing, failing to help the case for evolution presented by the University's Dr. Benjamin Banta and Dr. Hale Wedberg in their debate with ICR scientists, Dr. Henry Morris and Dr. Duane Gish.

Approximately 1400 overflowed Montezuma Hall for the debate, officially staged by the University under the co-sponsorship of the Zoology Club and the Aztec Christian Fellowship. Dr. Banta is Professor of Zoology and Dr. Wedberg, Professor of Botany at San Diego State. Dr. Miller is the internationally acclaimed bio-chemist at the University of California (San Diego) whose experiments generating amino acids in the laboratory are believed by many to have practically amounted to a laboratory creation of life. Dr. Gish, both in a technical monograph published by ICR, and in frequent lectures, had been an outspoken critic of the evolutionary inter-pretations of these experiments, so that Dr. Miller and his colleague, Dr. Jeffrey Bada (famous for his amino acid "racemization" dating method, also frequently criticized by Dr. Gish) with many of their students attended the debate.

Order of the speakers was determined by coin toss. Dr. Morris stressed the complete absence of any evidence of present-day evolution, the argument for creation from probability studies, and the evidence from the second law of thermodynamics that evolution was impossible. Dr. Banta confined his remarks mainly to a recital of familiar historical facts about the life of Charles Darwin, making no effort to present any scientific evidence for evolution. Dr. Gish showed that the traditional evidences for evolu-tion (homology, embryology, vestigial organs and, es-pecially, the fossil record) do not support evolution at all and are much better evidences for creation. Dr. Wedberg discussed only his own experiments on variations and hybrids in the tobacco plant, insisting that *these* proved evolution(!) Both creationist speakers emphasized that all the facts of science were in perfect correlation with pre-dictions from the creation model. The evolutionist speakers made frequent irrelevant references to God, religion, and the unreliability of the Bible and "truth", but made no attempt to answer any of the scientific arguments given by Dr. Morris and Dr. Gish.

In the question-and-answer period after the debate, a question was posed by Dr. Banta about the origin of life. He called Dr. Miller up from the audience to answer the question and Dr. Miller first charged Dr. Morris with mis-using the second law of thermodynamics and the laws of probability (though without indicating *how* they had been mis-used) and then attacked Dr. Gish for his published criticisms of the evolutionary interpretation of Miller's experiments. Dr. Gish then responded, first by confirming the validity of the arguments from thermodynamics, and then by devastating Miller's interpretation of his own experiments, showing that there was no possible way that his laboratory production of amino acids could have anything to do with the real origin of life, for numerous cited reasons. To the suggestion (applauded heartily by the audience) that he and Miller schedule a formal debate on this single topic, Dr. Gish responded enthusiastically in the affirmative, but Dr. Miller declined.

The general reaction to the debate was expressed by two former graduate students in biology at San Diego State, both of whom remarked independently, that they had been appalled to see at first hand in this way the barrenness of evolution, and strongly convinced of the necessity of special creation.

MASSACHUSETTS DEBATE
HIGHLIGHTS
NEW ENGLAND MEETINGS

Over 900 students and faculty filled every nook and cranny of the 500-seat Mahar Auditorium at the University of Massachusetts on April 28, with several hundred others unable to get in at all, as ICR Director Henry M. Morris debated two evolutionists on the question of whether creation or evolution provides the best scientific model for explaining the origin and history of life. Both sides adhered strictly to a discussion of scientific data, and the two evolutionists, Dr. David J. Klingener, a vertebrate paleontologist, and Dr. Bruce R. Levin, a population geneticist, were very cordial and respectful of the creationist position in their presentation. Both men are Associate Professors of Zoology at the University, the large (25,000 students) and very liberal state university in Amherst, and are widely recognized in their fields. The debate was capably and fairly moderated by Dr. Mulcahy, an evolutionary ecologist at the University.

Several Christian student organizations, under the general guidance of Dr. Ward M. Hunting, Associate Professor of Food Science, had worked together to sponsor the debate. Because of the limited space, most of the Christian students remained outside so the audience was made up predominantly of non-Christians. In spite of this, and the four-hour length of the meeting, the case for creation emerged so clearly as the superior model that the audience gave Dr. Morris a standing ovation at the close. An interesting sidelight of the question session following was when a professor teaching thermodynamics arose to comment that Dr. Morris' use of the entropy law as a refutation of evolution seemed irrefutable and to challenge the evolutionists to answer it. This, they confessed, they were unable to do, and then appealed to anyone in the audience who could answer it. The only response was an irrelevant (though correct) statement by a chemist that amino acids and nucleotides could be generated in the laboratory from simpler molecules.

An attempt had also been under way for over a year to arrange debates at Harvard University and/or Massachusetts Institute of Technology, but no one on these faculties proved willing to debate. Instead, a noon lecture on creationism was given by Dr. Morris in the student union at M.I.T. In New Hampshire, Dr. Morris also spoke to a large and responsive audience at the Plymouth College of the University of New Hampshire, and, in Rhode Island, in a convocation service and two classes at Barrington College.

PRESTON CLOUD
PARTICIPATES IN SANTA BARBARA DEBATE

One of the nation's top geologists, Preston Cloud, was one of the evolutionist debaters challenging Henry Morris and Duane Gish in a tense confrontation at the University of California at Santa Barbara on Monday evening, May 24. Dr. Cloud has been Professor of Biogeology at UCSB since 1968. Before that, he had served as Chief Paleontologist of the US Geological Survey, Chairman of the Department of Geology at the University of Minnesota, and Professor of Biogeology at UCLA. The second evolutionist debater was Aharon Gibor, Professor of Plant Physiology at UCSB. A native of Israel, Dr. Gibhor had received his Ph.D. in Biology from Stanford in 1956.

A capacity crowd of 950 paid $1 admission to the Campbell Hall Auditorium for the debate, with 150 others hearing the debate through speakers set up in various classrooms. The evolutionists had stipulated that no part of the proceeds should go to support creationism, so that all income above travel and promotional expenses was assigned to a charity designated by them. The debate was sponsored by a student organization, the Creation Society of Santa Barbara, and was officially approved as a university program.

As usual, the evolutionists cited no specific evidences for "vertically-upward" evolution at all, but confined most of their talks to attacks on the Biblical account of creation and the flood, and to criticizing passages in books by Gish and Morris which indicated that they had taken the Bible as authoritative on these subjects.

The creationist speakers showed that the scientific data confirmed the predictions from the creation model and contradicted those from the evolution model, with Dr. Morris especially stressing the evidence from the entropy law and Dr. Gish emphasizing the ubiquitous absence of transitional structures in the fossil record. Although Dr. Cloud, as a paleontologist, answered that transitional fossils did exist in the record (e.g., archaeopteryx, the crossopterygian fishes, etc.), Dr. Gish was easily able to show that these were not really transitional forms and contained no transitional structures. Neither evolutionist even attempted to rebut the compelling evidence from the second law of thermodynamics. Dr. Morris received a hearty wave of applause when he pointed out that although the title of the debate dealt solely with the *scientific* aspects of the creation-evolution question, and the evolutionists continually insisted that the issue was one of "science" (i.e., evolution) vs. "religion" (i.e., creation), it was the evolutionists who talked almost entirely about religion and the creationists who had confined their presentation to science.

Approximately half of those in attendance filled out an opinion poll after the debate. Of these, 49% initially had believed in creation, 35% had believed in evolution, and 16% were undecided. After the debate, 55% believed in creation, 33% in evolution, with 12% undecided. Perhaps a more significant factor was that 74% of the creationists reported that their belief in creation had been strengthened with only 1% indicating it had been weakened. Of the evolutionists, 35% said their belief in evolution had been strengthened, but 21% said it had been weakened.

Those who wrote specific comments on their opinion sheets included 33 creationists, 34 evolutionists and 23 "undecideds." Although space precludes reproducing all of them here (indeed, some of the evolutionists' comments were unprintable!), the following were typical: **(Creationist)** "It sounded as if the only persons offering any substantial documented evidence were Drs. Morris and Gish . . . . " **(Creationist)** "Both Dr. Morris and Dr. Gish were very scientific and professional. They really glorified God!" **(Evolutionist)** "I now believe Morris and Gish are morons." **(Evolutionist)** "I was amazed that the creationists presented a more scientific presentation! Evolutionists seemed to stray from topic, while creationists kept strictly to subject." **(Undecided)** "I hope the creationists do not claim their obvious victory in the debate . . . . It is unfortunate that the debate was so uneven, but it results from a selection of prepared creationists and unprepared evolutionists." **(Undecided)** "Creation theory should be given equal credibility in our public schools." **(Evolutionist changed to Creationist)** "Dr. Gibor and Dr. Cloud's approach to the whole debate too emotional and an insult to science itself. They were much more dogmatic than the creationists."

3500 HEAR KANSAS
CREATION DEBATE

Approximately 3500 people filled the Hoch Auditorium at the University of Kansas on Friday, September 17 to hear Dr. Duane Gish and Dr. Henry Morris defend creationism against two leading evolutionists, Dr. E.O. Wiley and Dr. Marion Bickford. This is believed to be the largest crowd in recent times to attend a creation-oriented meeting of any kind. The debate and rebuttals, with questions from the audience afterward, lasted 3½ hours, with practically all of the audience remaining throughout the first 3 hours at least, intently interested in the debater's arguments and rebuttals. Dr. Lewis McKinney, Professor of History of Science at the University, was moderator for the debate, which was sponsored by the Creationist Club at Kansas University and had received extensive publicity throughout the state.

Dr. Bickford is Professor of Geology at the University of Kansas and a specialist in geochronology. Dr. Wiley is Assistant Curator at the Kansas Museum of Natural History and a specialist in ichthyology. Both men were courteous in their critiques of creationism and were careful to limit their discussions to scientific matters, as did Dr. Gish and Dr. Morris.

The first speaker, Dr. Morris, defined the evolution and creation models and then demonstrated the impossibility of "vertical" evolution by probability arguments and by the Second Law of Thermodynamics. Dr. Gish stressed the universal absence of transitional forms in the fossil record showing that evolution had not occurred in the past.

For the evolutionists, Dr. Wiley devoted his arguments

mainly to criticizing the ICR book *Scientific Creationism,* especially its treatment of flood geology. Dr. Bickford confined his remarks primarily to criticizing the young earth concept, arguing that such phenomena as the Grand Canyon and radiometric measurements require an old earth.

In the first rebuttal, Dr. Wiley argued that the gaps in the fossil record could be explained in terms of recent concepts of mutation, in which random changes in "controller genes" produce major changes in organisms by simultaneously affecting many structural genes. He also rejected the entropy argument, claiming that entropy had no relation to complexity, so that a world of increasing entropy had no bearing on whether organisms were increasing in complexity.

Dr. Morris showed that Dr. Wiley was quoting out of context and distorting the arguments in his critique of *Scientific Creationism.* He then documented the fact that entropy indeed *was* related to complexity and that some leading evolutionists are now admitting that they do not yet know how to harmonize the contradictory concepts of entropy and evolution. He also pointed out that neither evolutionist had attempted to give any scientific evidence at all in support of evolution itself! Dr. Bickford had argued for an old earth and Dr. Wiley against flood geology, but neither of these topics were germane to the question being debated—namely whether creation or evolution was a better explanation of the scientific data. However, Dr. Morris did show briefly that there actually was evidence of catastrophism in all the geologic strata.

Dr. Bickford acknowledged much evidence of catastrophism but also detailed further radiometric evidence of an old earth, insisting that the assumptions were justified and the results consistent. He also suggested that the formation of crystals negated Dr. Morris' entropy argument(!)

Dr. Gish, in the concluding rebuttal, showed that the evolutionary mechanism proposed by Dr. Wiley, who had admitted the gaps in the fossil record, was even less likely to produce new and higher kinds of organisms than natural selection. The complete absence of incipient or transitional features in the fossils remains an overwhelming problem to the evolution model.

In addition to the debate itself, Dr. Morris and Dr. Gish gave a total of ten lectures to various classes and other meetings on campus at the University of Kansas. The student response in all of these classes, and the faculty response in most of them, was very encouraging.

UNIVERSITY OF MARYLAND
DEBATE

On Thursday afternoon at 3:00 p.m. on October 14, over 1200 students and faculty of the University of Maryland gathered in the ballroom of the Student Union to witness a debate between ICR scientist Dr. Duane Gish and evolutionists Dr. Geerat J. Vermeij, Associate professor of Zoology, and Dr. Isidora Adler, Professor of Chemistry and Head of the Geochemistry Division, both of the U. of M. Dr. David Lay of the Department of Mathematics served as moderator. Students reported that this was the largest attendance for a university function they had seen except for sporting and social events.

Dr. Vermeij, blind and reportedly understanding seven languages, led off the debate. He stated that if evidence for evolution cannot be found in the fossil record then there is no evidence for evolution. He then gave the textbook story of evolution, relating various types of organisms to the geological column, maintaining that this constitutes evidence for evolution. He asserted that there were transitional forms between lobefinned fishes and amphibia. He then attempted to describe a mechanism for evolution which would account for the fact that very few transitional forms are found and that the fossil record consists mainly of gaps. He also cited an example of a fish that was transplanted from the Gulf of California to the Salton Sea that resulted in the production of many anomalous forms, maintaining that this was evidence of evolution.

Dr. Gish then took the platform and documented the case for creation from the laws of thermodynamics, supposed evolutionary mechanisms versus probability laws, and the fossil record. He also quoted Dr. Margaret Grene, one of the world's foremost philosophers of science, that evolution theory itself has become a religion demanding dogmatic acceptance.

Dr. Adler's main theme was that he wanted to help blunt the tendency of students today to turn from science to mysticism. He asserted that there was no conflict between religion and science (as he understood each). He then described the big-bang theory of the origin of the universe and described evidence for this theory. He mentioned the alleged discovery of organic molecules in space and suggested that they may have been produced by the action of ultraviolent light and simpler molecules.

In his rebuttal, Dr. Gish stated that he too saw no conflict between real religious truths and the facts of science, but that he did see conflicts between religious truths and the theories of some scientists, including the theory of evolution. He then emphasized the admission of some evolutionists that the fossil record produces no transitional forms, and reemphasized the fact these same evolutionists feel forced to propose incredible theories, such as Goldschmidt's "hopeful monster" theory, and Bourne's evolution of apes and monkeys from man theory because of contradictions between these facts and the current evolutionary theory. He used slides to illustrate that, contrary to Vermeij's claim, there are no transitional forms between fish and amphibia. He also refuted Vermeij's claim that the evidence for creation is based solely on negative evidence against evolution, while at the same time asserting that there is nothing wrong with using negative evidence since this is a method commonly used by scientists.

In Dr. Vermeij's rebuttal, while asserting that nobody accepts Goldschmidt's "hopeful monster" mechanism nonsense, he then claimed that there may be some instances where something like this could occur. He maintained that evolution theory is not static but is subject to change. Neither Dr. Vermeij nor Dr. Adler made any attempt to refute Dr. Gish's arguments against evolution based on the Second Law of Thermodynamics.

CAPACITY CROWD AT
CHICO STATE UNIVERSITY DEBATE

The 1400-seat Laxson Hall on the campus of Chico State University, Chico, California, was filled to capacity on the evening of November 19 to witness the debate between evolutionist Michael Erpino and Dr. Duane Gish. Dr. Erpino, who holds a Ph.D. in biology from the University of Wyoming, is a professor of biology at Chico State University. The debate was moderated by Dr. Arnold Oettell, a clinical psychologist of Chico.

Erpino, in his initial presentation, announced that he would clear up some misconceptions about evolution, present evidence for evolution, and point out scientific errors in the Bible. Among those who do not understand evolution, Erpino included the general public, French scientists, anthropologists, and molecular biologists. He maintained that arguments against evolution based on chance are spurious since natural selection is not a chance process.

Erpino cited embryological recapitulation and homology (similarity in structures and organs) as evidences for evolution. He claimed that foot, back, and eye problems, and imperfections in the female birth canal are evidences for incomplete evolution and evidences against an omniscient Creator. He maintained that the fossil record demonstrates a change from simple to complex as expected on the basis of evolution.

Erpino then gave several explanations for the gaps in the fossil record.

Erpino's examples of scientific errors in the Bible included the report that the sun stood still on the occasion of Joshua's long day (the earth rotates rather than the sun rotating around the earth), the creation of Eve from Adam's rib (man and woman should then be identical according to Erpino), and the alleged contradiction between the creation accounts in Genesis—Chapters 1 and 2.

In his initial presentation, Gish argued that evolution theory is no more scientific than creation, and each is as intrinsically religious as the other. He then presented the scientific case for creation based on the laws of thermodynamics, probability considerations, and the fossil record. He maintained that natural laws based on thermodynamics and probability demonstrates the impossibility of the molecules-to-man evolutionary hypothesis, and that the absence of transitional forms in the fossil record is exactly as expected on the basis of creation but contradictory to expectations based on evolution theory. He argued that evolution has been hypothesized, but never observed.

In his rebuttal, Erpino maintained that the production of new species of grasses is evidence of evolution in action. He also made some attempt to blunt Gish's argument based on the fossil record.

Gish, in his rebuttal, pointed out that evolution is a chance process, since, although natural selection is not a chance process, ultimately, all of evolution is due to mutations, which are chance events. He pointed out that the idea of embryological recapitulation (the belief that the embryo resembles successive evolutionary ancestors during its development) has been thoroughly discredited by embryologists. He further pointed out that even Sir Gavin de Beer, British biologist and evolutionist, has admitted that the evidence from the study of homologous structures is contradictory to expectations based on evolution. He emphasized that evolutionists such as Erpino are forced to attempt to explain away the gaps in the fossil record, while on the other hand, the gaps are directly predicted on the basis of creation.

Gish pointed out that our physical problems are not due to the imperfections of creation, but were suffered subsequent to creation because of man's sin and rebellion against God. He maintained that Erpino's argument that there are scientific errors in the Bible is based on mis-understandings. He explained why there are no errors in the account of Eve's creation or of Joshua's long day. He finally showed that the creation accounts in Genesis are not contradictory.

LARGE AUDIENCE
WITNESSES DEBATE

An overflow crowd in excess of 3,000 attended the creation-evolution debate held at Calvary Chapel in Costa Mesa, California, on the evening of Friday, October 1. The evolutionist position was argued by Dr. Gary Lynch, neurobiologist, and Dr. George Miller, physical scientist, both professors on the Irvine campus, University of California. The creationist position was defended by Prof. Harold Slusher and Dr. Duane Gish.

Dr. Lynch maintained that paleontologists are not trying to prove evolution, but practice their science in a strictly pragmatic sense. He pointed out that one of the most important characteristics separating man from other animals is the brain. He then showed a chart listing the primates (prosimians, monkeys, apes, and man) with their dental characteristics. He claimed that these dental characteristics showed systematic differences along an ascending scale from prosimians (modern prosimians include lemurs, tarsiers, and shrews) to man, and that this, therefore, demonstrates that there was an ascending evolutionary process beginning with prosimians and ending with man.

Dr. Miller devoted his initial presentation to a description of the carbon-14 radiometric dating method. This is the dating method radiochronologists use to date objects with ages of a few thousand years, it is also used to estimate the age of older objects (with increasing uncertainty) up to perhaps 50,000 years.

Dr. Gish in his initial presentation described the nature of the fossil record of plants, animals, and of the primates, including man, which shows the abrupt appearance of the many different kinds of organisms, without known ancestors or transitional forms.

Prof. Slusher first described the basic contradiction between the Second Law of Thermodynamics and evolution theory, from the origin of stars to the origin of life. He maintained that on the basis of established scientific laws and principles no complex natural system could have generated itself. The highly complex universe and its multitude of incredibly complex living things, therefore, could only have been produced by an omnipotent, omniscient Creator independent of the natural universe and of the natural laws which He had created. Prof. Slusher then attacked the assumptions on which all radiometric dating systems are based, maintaining that, due to the erroneous nature of these assumptions (particularly assumptions concerning initial conditions), these dating systems produce apparent ages much older than the real ages. He then described several excellent physical processes that indicate a young age for the earth.

The initial constructive arguments were followed by 10-minute rebuttals by each debater. Reaction to the debate was overwhelmingly favorable by those in the audience who were hoping for a victory by the creationists.

The Great Debate Continues—1977
HEATED SCHOOL DEBATE
IN DALLAS TELEVISED

"We chopped their heads off in California; we chopped their heads off in Arkansas; we will chop their heads off in Indiana, and—look out—here comes the axe in Dallas!" These were the opening comments of evolutionist Ken Gjemere as he set the tone for the emotional outbursts that characterized a formal televised panel debate on creation and evolution in Dallas on February 24.

The occasion leading to the confrontation was the recent decision by the Dallas School Board to adopt the Creation Research Society textbook *Biology: A Search for Order in Complexity* as a supplementary textbook for classes in the Dallas schools. Evolutionists have threatened to initiate legal action to reverse the action of the board and the controversy has received heated attention in recent weeks in the Dallas news media. In order to present both sides to the public, the "Americans United for Separation of Church and State" arranged the debate panel in the Dallas Public Library. Over 300 people from the community jammed the 200-seat auditorium.

The format consisted of a 5-minute presentation by each of four expert witnesses on each side—a scientist, attorney, theologian, and educator. Each side had an "advocate" to introduce the presentations of his side, and to question the opponents. The creationists all spoke first.

The creationist advocate was Dr. Haddon Robinson, Professor of Practical Theology at Dallas Seminary. Dr. Harold Slusher, of ICR and the University of Texas (El Paso) presented scientific arguments for creation; Jody Dillow, a doctoral candidate at Dallas Seminary, stressed the non-sectarian nature of the scientific creation model, together with the religious implications of the humanism and atheism supported by evolution; attorney Tom Newberger showed that the adopted textbook would not be construed by the courts as supporting a sectarian religion; and finally, Richard Bliss, of ICR, stressed the pedagogical effectiveness of a two-model approach to the study of origins.

The evolutionists' advocate, Gjemere, began his questioning with the unique outburst noted above, following which he waved a book already adopted by the state (published by Allyn and Bacon) and hysterically complained that even this book, with its three pages of very inadequate discussion of creation, was intolerable. His questioning concentrated on Professors Bliss and Slusher, but related more to their personal affiliations and to possible ties between creationist groups than it did to their arguments. He did question the factual content of the "two-model" approach, but Bliss responded that this approach dealt with many more facts, not being limited to only those scientific data which could be interpreted to favor evolution.

The first evolutionist to speak was Dr. Virginia Currey, a member of the state board of education. Her argument was a diatribe charging that the creationists were a political movement, that the biology textbook was merely propaganda, and that the devil himself couldn't have devised a better plan. Rev. Wilford Bailey, a Methodist pastor, said the textbook was biased and placed "Christian evolutionists" in a bad light. Neither Dr. Curry nor Rev. Bailey would answer Advocate Robinson's questions.

The evolutionist scientist, Dr. Jagger, a biology professor at the University of Texas (Dallas) stated that all biology professors at major universities would reject the book, and then argued that crystals disproved Professor Slusher's argument for creation based on the second law of thermodynamics. Slusher immediately responded to show the scientific irrelevancy of these remarks.

The summations by Advocates Robinson and Gjemere were in marked contrast. Dr. Robinson showed in eloquent and stirring fashion the scientific and educational superiority of the two-model approach adopted by the school board. Mr. Gjemere's summation consisted mostly of threatening court action and repeating his head-chopping promises. The audience applause indicated overwhelming support for the creationists.

DUO OF DEBATES AT UNIVERSITY OF OREGON

On Thursday evening, January 20, on the campus of

the University of Oregon, Eugene, Dr. Duane Gish debated Dr. Arthur J. Boucot, Professor of Geology at Oregon State University and adjunct professor at the Museum of Natural History, University of Oregon. The subject of the debate was "Fossil Records Support the Evolution of Life." On Friday evening, Dr. Gish debated Dr. Paul Simonds, Professor of Anthropology at the University of Oregon, the subject being "Fossil Records Support the Evolution of Man." Dr. Gish also presented lectures during the day on Friday on the origin of life and supposed evolutionary mechanisms. Miss Judy Pollock and Karsten Masaeus assisted in arrangements for the debates, and Jon Schultz served as moderator.

Dr. Boucot, a graduate of Harvard University specializing in Silurian-Devonian brachiopods, biogeography, and paleoecology, in contrast to most evolutionists Dr. Gish has debated, did not seem deeply committed either philosophically or scientifically to evolution theory. His attitude might best be characterized as 25% agnostic and 75% committed to the view that evolution theory offers a reasonable means of interpreting the meaning of the fossil record. He admitted that no transitional forms between the higher categories, such as those between phyla, classes, orders, and families, had yet been found, and the same was true for at least 99% of the categories below the level of the family. He maintained however, that there was evidence to indicate that some gradations have occurred at the species level, and that this had led most geologists to accept evolution theory as an adequate explanation for the origin of all life forms.

Dr. Gish emphasized that evolutionists have in fact, intensely searched for these expected transitional forms for over a century. He pointed out that appeals to the adequacy of the fossil record were not valid, since the available fossil record was more than adequate to provide vast numbers of transitional forms if they had existed. He then documented in detail the systematic absence of transitional forms between all higher categories of plants and animals, such as phyla, classes, orders, and families. These, creationists maintain, are the created kinds, none of which arose from one another or from any lower form.

On Friday evening, Dr. Simonds began by maintaining that the chimpanzee was man's closest cousin. He pointed out structural similarities between man and chimpanzee. He maintained that some chimps can be taught to use language, that chimps use a simple tool, they hunt in groups as does man, and they organize into a society as does man. He then described the anatomy of the skull, face, dentition, and postcranial skeleton (particularly the pelvis) of apes, monkeys, and men.

Simonds maintained that these characteristics in the "man-apes," as he called them (Australopithecus), indicated that these creatures walked upright and that their dentition and certain facial characteristics indicated that they were intermediate between an ape-like creature and man.

Dr. Gish began his presentation by describing various factors which have affected the study of human origins, such as the influence of preconceived ideas in conjunction with the scanty nature of the evidence, the very considerable natural variability within a species, and the overlap in certain features between ape and man. He pointed out that due to the powerful influence of preconceived ideas, evolutionists accepted an outright hoax, the famous "Piltdown Man" (a doctored-up modern ape's jaw and recent human skull), and a pig's tooth ("Nebraska Man"), as man's subhuman ancestors. He then described the complete lack of transitional forms between insectivores (the supposed ancestors of primates) and the primates, and a similar lack of transitional forms between the so-called lower primates and monkeys and apes.

Gish used the published research of Dr. Charles Oxnard and Sir Solly Zuckerman, both evolutionists, to document the fact that Australopithecus (the central figure in Simond's human evolution story) did not walk upright and that he was not intermediate between ape and man. Sir Solly, who has done far more research on Australopithecus than any other scientist, concludes that Australopithecus was a pongid (Ape) and not a hominid (a man-like creature). This evidence demolished much of Simond's scheme.

SLUSHER AND GISH IN
CREATION EVOLUTION FORUM AT UTEP

On Thursday evening, February 17, Dr. Harold Slusher, Professor of Physics on the UTEP Campus, and Dr. Duane Gish of I.C.R. presented the case for creation at an evolution-creation forum held in the Union Theater of the University of Texas (El Paso). The case for evolution was presented by Dr. Peter Chrapluy, Professor of Biology, UTEP, and by Dr. Walter Whitford, Professor of Biology at New Mexico State University (Las Cruces). Dr. Robert Dinegar, Chemist at the University of California Los Alamos Laboratory and an ordained Episcopalian priest, offered comments primarily as a theologian. The forum was sponsored by the UTEP University United Ministries, with Dr. Frank Williams of the Religion Department acting as moderator. The forum had been inspired through the efforts of Dr. Thomas Barnes, Professor of Physics at UTEP and President of the Creation Research Society executive board.

Every seat in the 450-seat auditorium was filled and several hundred more people filled all available space in the foyer and adjacent areas. Fortunately Dr. Seth Edwards, creationist, geologist, Professor of Education, and in charge of instruction in audio-visuals, had set up speakers to accommodate an overflow crowd. Each of the four main speakers was given 30 minutes each to present his case, and these were to be followed by a short presentation by Dr. Dinegar.

Dr. Gish, the initial speaker, after pointing out that evolution theory is no more scientific than creation, documented the relationship between evolution theory and the philosophy of secular humanism by quoting from several sources, including literature of the American Humanist Society. He then documented the impossibility of evolution based on probability considerations. He finally used the scientific literature extensively to support his contention that the fossil record contradicts evolution but supports creation.

Dr. Whitford, the second speaker, cited several examples of what he considered as evidence for evolution, such as mutations, natural selection, shift in populations of peppered moths, the Miller-Urey experiments, the comparative blood chemistry of chimpanzees and man. He stated that not all evolutionists deny the existence of God, but all do deny that God created by special creation.

Dr. Chrapluy, the third speaker, defined evolution as change with time, and then pointed out examples of changes that took place in the automobile, the airplane, etc., to establish that indeed change with time is a fact. He then further defined Darwinian evolution as change brought about by a struggle for existence and survival of the fittest through natural selection. He pointed to comparative biochemistry as support for evolution. He claimed that there were 100 vestigial organs in the human body. He suggested that the Genesis account should not be taken literally, but only symbolically. He finally claimed that evolution is a fact, only the mechanism is in dispute.

Dr. Slusher, the next speaker, first mentioned that we had heard a lot that evening about minor variations within kinds but no evidence whatever of change of one kind into another, which is what evolution is really supposed to be about. He then described the Second Law of Thermodynamics and the fundamental contradiction between this law and the theory of evolution. He finally described a number of physical processes that indicate that the universe is young rather than billions of years old.

Dr. Dinegar closed out the formal discussion. He maintained that there were two creation accounts in Genesis. He stated that it was unfortunate that some have forced the issue of creation and evolution into an either/or situation and that the two could be compatible.

Dr. Slusher and Dr. Gish were given an opportunity to reply to Dr. Dinegar. They pointed out that evolution is, according to the theory, a process that utilized millions of mistakes, which by chance somehow were beneficial, while uncounted other mistakes were harmful, resulting in misfits, dead-ends, and suffering. Such a process is hardly compatible with an omniscient, omnipotent God. The effect the theory had had on the moral climate they maintained, has been very bad. Students have been led to believe they are merely mechanistic products of a mindless universe and have acted accordingly.

Unfortunately, because of the format which excluded rebuttals, Slusher and Gish were unable to offer rebuttals to arguments advanced by the evolutionists. During the interaction with the audience which closed out the evening, however, questions from the audience did give Slusher and Gish further opportunity to develop their case.

TEXAS UNIVERSITY DEBATE
DRAWS OVERFLOW CROWD

A heated creation-evolution debate attracted a more-than-usually involved (at times rude and unruly) crowd to the Texas University Student Union Ballroom on March 24, as Dr. Duane Gish and Dr. Henry Morris of ICR debated Dr. Larry Gilbert and Dr. Alan Templeton, of the Texas University Department of Zoology. The *Daily Texan,* student newspaper estimated the overflow crowd at more than 2,000, almost all of whom were University students. Large numbers of others were turned away when they could not even get into the adjacent halls for standing-room.

The evolutionists followed a strategy of ridicule and personal attack combined with much discussion of "horizontal" changes within genera and species of insects as "proof" of evolution. They repeatedly misapplied and distorted creationist writings, and stirred up their large gallery of student followers, so that it eventually became the most discourteous and unruly crowd the ICR scientists had yet encountered in a public debate.

Dr. Morris and Dr. Gish refrained from responding to the personal attacks and religious slurs. They concentrated

instead on showing that the horizontal changes emphasized by the evolutionists had no relevance to the grand
vertical changes required by true evolution, and that the
universal gaps in the fossil record and the universal law of
increasing entropy demonstrated that "vertical" evolution
neither had occurred nor could occur.

The moderator was Dr. Burt Judd, also of the Zoology
faculty, and cosigner of the recent Humanist Association
appeal to school boards not to allow creation in the
schools. In the question period, the first one called upon
was Dr. Irwin Speer, of the Botany Department. He made
a highly inflammatory and slanderous attack on the
honesty and intelligence of Dr. Morris for using the
entropy argument against evolution (though, of course,
offering no answer to the argument!) Dr. Templeton, in
dealing with the final question, accused Dr. Gish of dis-
honesty in misquoting Dr. Preston Cloud of the University
of California at Santa Barbara. Dr. Cloud had himself
made the same accusation in *The Humanist* magazine for
January-February 1977. Dr. Gish responded by reading
directly from the original article by Dr. Cloud (*Geology,*
Vol. 1. p. 123, 1973), showing that he had neither misquoted nor misunderstood Dr. Cloud, also pointing out
that when he had used the same quote in an actual campus
debate with Dr. Cloud at the University of California at
Santa Barbara in May, 1976, the latter had not claimed
then that he was being misquoted.

The debate was under the official sponsorship of the
University, through several student organizations (Natural
Sciences Advisory Council, Ideas and Issues Committee,
University Interaction Committee). Grace Covenant
Church of Austin helped with some of the expenses. Tracy
Stark, a geology student, organized and led in the
promotion of the meeting.

Although the nature of the evolutionists' approach and
the emotionally-charged crowd made real communication
difficult, many students did afterwards express much
appreciation for the gracious and informative manner in
which the case for creation had been presented.

NORTHWESTERN UNIVERSITY DEBATE
HIGHLIGHTS MIDWEST CREATION WEEK

Approximately 75 events were scheduled at over 50 locations during the ICR Midwest Center Creation Emphasis Week which began on the evening of March 31 and ended on the evening of April 7.

One of the highlights of the week, during which thousands heard the case for scientific and Biblical creationism, was the debate held on the campus of Northwestern University before an audience of over 1500. Participants were evolutionists Drs. Michael Ruse and Donald Weinshank, professors at the University of Guelph, Ontario, and Michigan State University, respectively, and Drs. Morris and Gish.

During the debate, the main thrust by Dr. Weinshank was an attack on several articles published in the Creation Research Society Quarterly which he considered to be poor science. Both Drs. Weinshank and Ruse invoked the thoroughly discredited embryological recapitulation theory as support for evolution. Ruse claimed that evolution fits the standards of a scientific theory while creation does not.

Morris and Gish presented documentation that neither creation nor evolution satisfies the criteria of a scientific theory and that evolution is as religious as creation. They then presented the scientific case for creation based on the laws of thermodynamics, probability considerations, and the fossil record.

SECOND SAN DIEGO STATE DEBATE
DRAWS OVERFLOW CROWD

A crowd estimated at 1500 overflowed a 1000-seat auditorium at San Diego State University on April 26 for an important debate featuring ICR Scientists Henry Morris and Duane Gish against two San Diego State geneticists, Frank Awbrey and William Thwaites. A similar debate had been held the previous April with two other evolutionists from the same university, and many had felt the evolution case had not been adequately presented and that another debate should be held. Dr. Awbrey and Dr.

Thwaites had heard the previous debate and, in the intervening year, had studied the tapes of the debate and the
ICR literature, so that they were much better prepared.
In fact, both Dr. Gish and Dr. Morris agreed that these
two men constituted the best-prepared and most effective
evolutionist debaters they had yet encountered.

Most of their presentations, however, consisted of
attempting to overcome the probability argument against
the chance development of complex systems and the argument based on gaps in the fossil record, as they had been
presented the previous year by Dr. Morris and Dr. Gish.
They also maintained that chemical similarities proved
man to be closely related to chimpanzees and that, in
general, these and other types of similarities supported
the same relationships between various animals as had
previously been deduced from the fossil record of evolution. Recent computer studies were cited which had been
able to simulate on a probabilistic basis the same types of
groupings, branchings, and extinctions characterizing the
fossil record. Their main argument for intermediate forms
centered on recent studies which indicated the primitive
bird Archaeopteryx to have had many reptilian characteristics.

However, the basic and definitive creationist arguments were not answered. Dr. Morris, in the first affirmative, had documented that "vertical" evolutionary changes had never been observed and that "horizontal" changes were irrelevant. He had also shown that the second law of thermodynamics made vertical evolution essentially impossible, unless it could be demonstrated that the evolutionary process was directed by a previously designed program and energized by an energy-converting motor to convert solar energy into the highly specific work required by the increasing organization of the evolutionary biosphere. The evolutionists, as usual, were unable to answer the second-law argument, and so tried to sidestep it by claiming (incorrectly) that the creationists were using a form of the second law which they had invented themselves.

Dr. Gish documented the universal and systematic gaps in the fossil record, and also emphasized the marvelous complexity of living things, using as examples the amazing structures of the woodpecker and the bombardier beetle. The probability arguments cited by the evolutionists had attempted to show that random changes such as mutations could eventually become significant, but ignored the requirement that such mutations be *cumulative* to a tremendous degree before they could produce such highly-adapted systems as these animals, or before they could develop even the simplest living system from non-living chemicals.

The arguments based on similarities in chemical and other characteristics of organisms can, of course, be explained better in terms of creation by a common designer than by evolution from a common ancestor. Furthermore, the differences between organisms, usually ignored by evolutionists, are much more numerous and significant than the similarities. The evolutionist debaters attempted to explain the ubiquitous gaps between living kinds and in the fossil record by rapid changes in small populations, but this is an argument based strictly on the lack of transitional forms. Whether Archaeopteryx was a bird or reptile, for example, does not obviate the universal absence of transitional structures (e.g., half-scales, half-feathers; half-legs, half-wings) in both living organisms and fossils.

Dr. Gish and Dr. Morris both stressed that the array of similarities and differences, the gaps in the fossils, the tremendous complexities of living systems, and the basic laws of science, are all *exactly* as expected and predicted from the creation model, and can only be made to fit the evolution model by secondary explanations.

5000 ATTEND UNIVERSITY OF MINNESOTA DEBATE

What is believed to be the largest attendance on record for a creation-oriented meeting was recently experienced in Minneapolis.

The 5000-seat Northrup Auditorium on the campus of the University of Minnesota was filled to capacity on the evening of Friday, April 29, to witness the debate between evolutionist Dr. Sam Kirkwood and Dr. Duane Gish. Dr. Kirkwood is a Professor of Biochemistry at the University of Wisconsin. Dr. Gish took the affirmative in debating the question "Resolved: the theory of special creation is superior to the theory of evolution as an explanation for the scientific evidence related to origins."

Dr. Gish, in his initial 60-minute presentation, first expressed his desire that the debate would be held at a high academic level. He then presented the case for creation based on a consideration of the laws of thermo-dynamics, probability considerations, and the fossil record. Much to Dr. Gish's disappointment, Dr. Kirkwood devoted the first 15-20 minutes of his initial presentation mainly to a personal attack on Dr. Gish. He questioned the ability of evolutionists whom Dr. Gish had cited, and the quality of the articles Dr. Gish quoted (all of which were from leading scientific journals).

Dr. Kirkwood presented what he considered to be con-clusive evidence from astronomy and radioactive dating methods for a very old earth. He spent considerable time attacking Dr. Gish's use of the Second Law of Thermodynamics, stating that the combustion of hydrogen and oxygen to form water, and the crystallization of water provide some of the many spontaneous increases in complexity. Although this sort of discussion demonstrated that Dr. Kirkwood did not have the slightest idea what problem the Second Law of Thermodynamics poses for the spontaneous evolutionary origin of biological order, he confidently asserted that Dr. Gish, not he, would have to answer to God for a misuse of the Second Law.

Dr. Kirkwood, after stating that he thought that neither Dr. Gish nor he had any authority to discuss matters in paleontology, attacked Dr. Gish's use of the fossil record, appealing to the poverty of the fossil record as one means of explaining the gaps, and challenging Dr. Gish's analysis of the hypothetical fish to amphibia transition.

In the rebuttal period Dr. Gish responded to Dr. Kirkwood's analysis of the Second Law of Thermodynamics and its relation to the origin of biological order and his attempt to reconcile the fossil record with evolution. While denying the authenticity of the coexistence of human footprints with dinosaur footprints in the Paluxy River bed of Texas, Dr. Kirkwood had asserted that there were valid footprints of fish in the fossil record. In his rebuttal, Dr. Gish replied that, first of all, no fish, living or fossil, had ever been found which had the required anatomy to walk, and, secondly, it would indeed be incredible to find footprints of fish in the fossil record in as much as fish don't have feet!

The debate closed with questions from the audience directed alternately to each debater. The intense interest of the audience in the debate was indicated by the fact that upwards of 75% of the audience remained through the entire question period, which ended at 11:00 p.m., four hours after the start of the debate.

Dr. Henry E. Fritz, chairman of the History Department of St. Olaf College, served as moderator of the debate. The debate was co-sponsored by the Twin Cities Creation-

Science Association and Campus Crusade for Christ. On Saturday, Prof. Richard Bliss, ICR Director of Curriculum Development, and Dr. Gish conducted a workshop for teachers, planned and sponsored by the Twin Cities Creation-Science Association.

ICR SCIENTIST DEBATES AT U.C.L.A.

Dr. Duane Gish returned on May 10 to his alma mater, the University of California at Los Angeles, where he had received his B.S. degree in chemistry in 1949, to debate Dr. Henry Hespenheide, an assistant professor of biology at U.C.L.A. Dr. Hespenheide received his Ph.D. in population biology from the University of Pennsylvania. The moderator was Dr. Everett C. Olson, well-known biologist and paleontologist, author of numerous articles and books on paleontology and evolution and Professor of Paleontology and Biology at U.C.L.A. Dr. Olson, although an evolutionist himself, performed in a completely neutral manner and was generous in his comments about Dr. Gish and his presentation.

Dr. Hespenheide identified himself as a Christian who believes it is unnecessary and unwise to accept the Genesis account of creation as literal. He expressed his belief that God used evolution as His method of creation. He set forth the usual textbook assumptions on which evolutionary hypotheses are based and claimed that all the data were consistent with these hypotheses, citing evidence from biogeography (distribution of animals) in support. Very little other actual scientific evidence to support evolution was given by Dr. Hespenheide. He also stated that if special creation is true then the actual world was either a big joke or a lie since it gave so much evidence for evolution.

Dr. Gish presented the scientific case for creation based on the laws of thermodynamics, the laws of probability, and the fossil record, using slides to illustrate the latter. He maintained that all of the critically important evidence was contradictory to evolution theory but consistent with creation.

In his rebuttal Hespenheide suggested that Gish's arguments based on the Second Law of Thermodynamics were invalid because all that is needed to create order in a system is a flow-through of energy. Gish had anticipated this argument and had offered a refutation in his presentation. In Gish's rebuttal he rejected Hespenheide's explanation for the lack of transitional forms based on the poverty of the fossil record as totally inadequate. He pointed out the inconsistency of attributing a wasteful, inefficient, cruel, meandering evolutionary process to an omnipotent, omniscient God. He further pointed out that in contrast to the idea that this world gave evidence for evolution by natural processes, it actually gave so much evidence that it has been created that the Bible states (Romans 1:20) that man is without excuse. He cited in support the fact that scientists were able to discover from the study of fossil trilobites that these creatures, now extinct, had had perfect undistorted vision, acknowledging that these eyes gave every evidence that they had been designed by a physicist, but still insisted that their origin had been due to the blind, chance processes of evolution.

The debate, witnessed by about 1200 students and faculty, had been arranged by Dan Cosgrove, a U.C.L.A. student, and was sponsored by the Evolution Inquiry Association, a student organization.

FULLER THEOLOGICAL SEMINARY STUDENTS AND FACULTY WITNESS SPECIAL CREATION VS. THEISTIC EVOLUTION DEBATE

The First Congregational Church of Pasadena provided the site of the debate on May 17 between creationist Duane Gish and theistic evolutionist Jerry Albert, research biochemist on the staff of Mercy Hospital of San Diego and graduate Ph.D. in biochemistry from Iowa State University. The debate, witnessed by about 400 students, faculty, and friends of Fuller Theological Seminary was sponsored by student organizations of Fuller and had been arranged by Terry Mathis, a student at the seminary.

Dr. Gish, the first speaker, first compared both the

Genesis account of creation and New Testament creation references to the theory of evolution to document his conviction that it is impossible to reconcile one with the other. He also pointed out that if God were at any point of time or space necessary or involved in the origin of the universe, its origin was miraculous and beyond scientific study. If not, then one could not say God had created the universe. It is contradictory, therefore, for someone like Dr. Albert to say that he believes in both creation and an evolutionary process that is scientifically testable. He then presented the scientific case for creation. Dr. Gish contended that theistic evolutionists use poor science (evolution theory) to support an inconsistent, false interpretation of the Bible.

Dr. Albert related that he had resolved the contradiction between the theory of evolution and the Bible by assuming that the Genesis account of creation is not to be taken literally. He accepts the total evolutionary viewpoint, even the evolutionary origin of life, maintaining that God had created matter with an inherent ability to evolve. He maintained that evolution is a fact, with only its mechanism in question. He cited facts about zoogeography (animal distribution), comparative biochemistry, and the genetic code common to all animals as evidence for evolution. He also stated that a theory did not necessarily have to be true to be useful.

In Gish's rebuttal he stated his amazement at Albert's statement that a theory does not necessarily have to be true to be useful, especially in the context of a creation-evolution debate between Christians. An atheist would agree that evolution theory would be useful even though it were untrue because it removes God from geology, biology, and all the natural sciences, but that is hardly a tenable position for a Christian. Gish also maintained that Albert's attempt to explain the lack of transitional forms in the fossil record was based on invalid assumptions and was in any case forced by the fact that the evidence predicted on the basis of evolution theory simply is not found.

In his rebuttal, Albert stated that the creation account of Genesis was written to be understandable by primitive people rather than to be accurate history. He maintained that statements by evolutionists cited by Gish which Gish used to document that evolution theory is not a scientific theory were merely directed at certain aspects of theory. He challenged creationists to cite evidence of new research by creationists which supports creation. The debate closed with questions from the audience.

ORIGIN OF LIFE DEBATE
AT U.C. BERKELEY

On the evening of May 19 before about 400 students and faculty of the University of California at Berkeley, Dr. Duane Gish of ICR debated Dr. Harold Morowitz, a molecular biophysicist, author of several textbooks on thermodynamics, and professor on the Berkeley campus. Dr. Gish received his Ph.D. in biochemistry from this university in 1953. The debate had been arranged by Neil Thomason, a Ph.D. candidate in philosophy at Berkeley who is writing his thesis on the evolution-creation controversy.

Dr. Gish, the initial speaker, used Dr. Morowitz's own calculations to point out first of all that the improbability of the existence (and thus its origin by chemical and physical processes) of a relatively simple form of life is $10^{-10^{11}}$ (one over one followed by 100 billion zeroes!) He contended nothing could overcome such impossible odds even if actually non-existent integrative forces existed in the chemical world and therefore, Gish maintained, life could only come from life. He then presented evidence based on proven principles of chemical thermodynamics and kinetics and the laws of probability which, he contended, renders a mechanistic, naturalistic origin of life absolutely impossible. He cited evidence from experiments conducted by evolutionists themselves that ordered arrangements in chemically synthesized protein and DNA molecules are impossible to achieve. He pointed out that Morowitz had stated in a 1972 publication that wherever a planetary surface and an energy flow existed, organic molecules should arise but that, in fact, the Viking probe of Mars had shown, as predicted by creation scientists, that not only was there no life on Mars but its surface was completely devoid of organic molecules in spite of the presence of carbon, nitrogen, oxygen, and hydrogen atoms. This is powerful evidence, Gish contended, from a truly naturalistic setting, that an evolutionary origin of life is impossible.

Dr. Morowitz opened his presentation by asserting that one reason he was opposing Dr. Gish's position was that he felt creation scientists sought to inhibit legitimate scientific inquiry. In answer to Gish's statement that all hypotheses on the origin of life were outside the limits of legitimate testable empirical science Morowitz asserted that since life is based on physical and chemical processes we should be able to reconstruct its origin, and that present failure to do so is only due to our current lack of knowledge. He sought to refute Gish's argument based on probability considerations by asserting that although the combinations of numbers involved in dialing a long distance telephone call exceed 10^{23} (a hundred billion trillion) he had succeeded in dialing such a number perhaps a hundred times successively. Morowitz claimed that all that is needed to create molecular order is a flow-through of energy in an open system and the requisite atomic species. He cited experiments by origin-of-life chemists in which significant quantities of various organic chemical molecules were produced as support for his theory.

In the discussion that followed, Gish maintained that the experiments cited by Morowitz were nothing but exercises in organic chemistry in which these organic chemists employed traps to isolate their products to save them from destruction. Gish insisted that evolutionists are caught between the horns of a dilemma since any form of energy required to form organic molecules also causes their destruction at a rate far in excess of their formation, but if, on the other hand, the products were trapped out and removed from an energy source that would completely end the process because further progress would require energy—either way you're dead. Gish also expressed his utter amazement at Morowitz's reply to Gish's probability arguments. Gish contended that Morowitz's example actually supported Gish's assertion that a deliberate, planned, and executed action by an intelligent being is required to overcome such fantastic odds, and that if a monkey had done the dialing instead of Morowitz the results would have been vastly different.

Morowitz reasserted his confidence that development of future scientific knowledge would provide an adequate basis for reconstructing an evolutionary origin of life. He also reasserted that Gish separates molecular structure from function, and that future developments in non-equilibrium thermodynamics will supply the needed information to reconstruct an evolutionary origin of life. In reply to a question from a student, Morowitz expressed his belief that the material of creation scientists like Gish should be excluded from textbooks and the classroom because it was, in his opinion, bad science. Gish was quick to assert that he felt his position was solidly based on excellent science and that Morowitz had placed himself in the position of inhibiting legitimate scientific inquiry, a position he supposedly opposes.

CREATION-EVOLUTION
DEBATE AT ARIZONA STATE

On the evening of May 2 on the campus of Arizona State University, Tempe, Dr. Duane Gish debated evolutionist Dr. Fred Plog, archaeologist and cultural anthropologist of Arizona State. The 350-seat auditorium in the Life Sciences Building was filled to capacity, with an additional overflow crowd of about 100 listening in an adjoining area.

In Dr. Gish's presentation of the case for creation he compared the predictions based on the general theory of evolution (the "fish-to-Gish or frog-to-Plog" theory, as he put it) to those based on special creation. He then compared these predictions to the available scientific evidence, asserting that in this comparison the creation model is far superior to the evolution model.

Dr. Plog, whose expertise was admittedly restricted to cultural anthropology, dealt mainly in generalities, although asserting that domesticated varieties of corn and what he believed to be evidence for evolution in the predecessors of modern man constituted evidence for evolution. The rebuttals by each side included a period of cross examination.

Dr. Gish also gave an afternoon lecture on the origin of man on the ASU campus and spoke at area churches on Sunday. The meetings had been arranged by several creationist students on the ASU campus.

97% OF NEVADA PROFS DECLINE INVITATION TO DEFEND EVOLUTION IN DEBATE

It proved much more difficult than anticipated to obtain evolutionists to debate ICR scientists Henry Morris and Duane Gish at a creation/evolution debate scheduled for the University of Nevada in Reno on October 4. At least 39 evolutionist faculty members were personally invited by local science teacher James Macres and Inter-Varsity Christian Fellowship program chairman, David Terenzoni, to participate, but only one—Dr. Mike Kendall, Professor of Anatomy on the bio-medical faculty—finally took part in the actual debate. At one time or another eight of these men had agreed to debate, but all except Dr. Kendall withdrew after being given a copy of Dr. Morris' book, *The Scientific Case for Creation,* to read for background information.

Since there was only one debater for the evolutionists, the debate finally involved only Dr. Kendall debating Dr. Morris, before a crowd of 800 people, with many others listening over Radio Station KNIS.

The debate was co-sponsored by the I.V.C.F. and the University. Dave Terenzoni acted as moderator, and the audience was orderly and appreciative.

Dr. Kendall spoke first, stressing the traditional circumstantial evidences for evolution, using slides to illustrate many similarities in organisms in their chemistry, anatomy, embryology, etc., interpreting these as evidence of common ancestry. He stressed that the main driving force of evolution was "adaptation" to fill unoccupied niches. He cited the familiar "family trees" of the horse and of man. Surprisingly he also used embryological recapitulation as evidence of evolution.

Dr. Morris showed that the creation model provided a better framework than the evolution model for explaining the array of similarities and differences in living organisms, the phenomena of the fossil record, and the known laws governing the nature of possible changes. He particularly stressed the ubiquitous gaps between kinds, both in the living world and in the fossils, the testimony of the second law of thermodynamics for creation and against evolution, and the high degree of improbability of the chance origin of even the simplest form of life.

In his rebuttal, Dr. Kendall stated that although entropy implied increasing disorder, the second law also involved "enthalpy", which served to increase order in an open system. As evidence of transitional forms of the fossil record, he referred to the crossopterygians, lungfishes, and labyrinthodonts as intermediate between fish and amphibians, to the therapsids and insectivores as transitions between reptiles and mammals, and *Archaeopteryx* as the link between reptiles and birds.

Dr. Morris, in his rebuttal period, documented the fact that embryological recapitulation is no longer accepted by evolutionary embryologists, and that the lungfishes, insectivores, *Archaeopteryx, et. al.* were not genuine transitional forms as alleged. He further stressed that neither enthalpy nor any concept yet suggested by evolutionists had been able to reconcile evolution and the second law of thermodynamics, nor to explain how systems of high complexity can develop by chance.

CREATION SCIENTISTS FACE EVOLUTIONISTS IN HISTORIC DEBATE AT UTRECHT, HOLLAND

Every seat was filled in the 1100-seat Congress Hall of

the great Jaarbeurs Square in the center of Utrecht, Holland, for the creation-evolution debate between three Dutch evolutionists and three American creationists. This was the first major debate held on this question in Holland, and perhaps the first for continental Europe. The intense interest in this subject was attested by the fact that most of those attending (each of whom paid the equivalent of $6.30) stayed until the very end of the day's proceedings.

The creation scientists participating in the debate were Dr. Donald Chittick, Professor of Chemistry at George Fox College at Newberg, Oregon; Dr. Harold Slusher, Assistant Professor of Physics at the University of Texas, El Paso, and Professor and Chairman of Geoscience at Christian Heritage College; and Dr. Duane Gish of ICR. Dr. Chittick's opponent was Mr. Cees Laban, a geologist with the Geological Service of Holland; Dr. Slusher's opponent was astronomer and scientific journalist Mr. Carl Koppeschaar; and Dr. Gish was opposed by Dr. M. Sluijser, biologist at the Dutch Cancer Institute. The moderator of the debate was Dr. W.J. Ouweneel, a geneticist and one of the leaders of the creationist movement in Holland.

The debate was organized and sponsored by Evangelische Omroep (Evangelical Broadcasting) of Utrecht under the direction of Dr. J.A. van Delden. Evangelische Omroep has 200,000 supporters in Holland and, in addition to radio, presents a 2½-hour program each Thursday evening on the nationwide government-operated television network, the sole TV network in Holland. The debate was recorded on video-tape and will be broadcast by Evangelische Omroep as part of their TV series on creation versus evolution, several episodes of which have already been broadcast.

At the request of many visitors from Germany who wished to attend the debate and who are more fluent in English than Dutch, the entire proceedings were in English.

After opening remarks by the moderator, Dr. Chittick

and Dr. Sluijser presented brief descriptions of the creation and evolution models, respectively. Mr. Koppeschaar then was given 25 minutes to present the evolutionist's theory of the origin of stars and planets and the age of the universe. Dr. Slusher was given 25 minutes to present the evidence against a naturalistic evolutionary origin of the universe and the evidence demanding a supernatural origin and the evidences of a young age for the universe. These discussions were followed by a 20-minute exchange between the two debaters involving rebuttals and cross-examination. After a 25-minute intermission, a similar exchange of views took place between Dr. Chittick and Mr. Laban, and, after lunch, the same format was used for the debate between Dr. Sluijser and Dr. Gish.

In the exchange between Mr. Koppeschaar and Dr. Slusher, Koppeschaar related the standard textbook theory of the origin and evolution of the universe, beginning with its "Big Bang" origin and continuing through the suggested evolution of the stars and planets in an expanding universe. He pointed to the observation of dark globular clouds of dust and gas as evidence that stars are still forming today.

Slusher emphasized that all of our common experience tells us that an explosion such as the "Big Bang" would never generate order. He pointed out that the expansion from the explosion would have to stop long enough for stars and galaxies to form, and then somehow the expansion would have to begin all over again. The gas pressure during the postulated collapse of a gas and dust cloud to form a star, Slusher pointed out, would exceed gravitational forces by 50-100 fold, rendering a naturalistic formation of a star impossible. Finally Slusher demonstrated that the origin of the universe by a mechanistic evolutionary process involving the spontaneous conversion of a totally disordered isolated system into a highly ordered system is in absolute violation of the Second Law of Thermodynamics. He contended that the origin of the universe by natural processes would have been physically impossible and that a supernatural origin is the only possible alternative. He also described natural processes that would put an upper limit on the age of the universe many orders of magnitude less than the billions of years postulated by evolutionists.

In his presentation, Dr. Chittick described the evidences for a young age for the earth and a catastrophic view of earth history, pointing out flaws in the assumptions used in radiometric dating systems.

Mr. Laban presented the standard evolutionary theory of geological ages and the fossilized remains of creatures associated with them. He described radiometric dating systems, maintaining that their use established absolute ages for the geological periods, which could only be arranged in relative order before these dating systems became available.

Dr. Sluijser opened his presentation by asserting that creationists present no evidence for their creation model but merely attack evolution. He used the variations among the finches of the Galapagos Islands as evidence for present-day evolution and showed slides of trilobites, *Archaeopteryx,* and dinosaurs as evidence of evolution in the past. He declared that *Australopithecus* was a man-like ape ancestral to man and that similarities between the DNA and proteins of man and apes established that men and apes had evolved from a common ancestor. He also used the theory of embryological recapitulation as evidence for evolution.

Dr. Gish first attacked evolutionary theories on the origin of life, pointing out that rates of destruction of chemical compounds by ultraviolet light and other energy sources so vastly exceed rates of formation that no detectable quantities of such products could ever be produced on the hypothetical primitive earth. He pointed out that probability calculations demonstrate that random chemical and physical processes could never, even in 500 billion years, produce the highly ordered and precisely arranged protein, DNA, and RNA molecules necessary for life.

Gish then presented evidence that the theory of embryological recapitulation has been proven to be false by modern embryologists. He showed that the possession of similar structures and organs by different animals does not prove descent from a common ancestor, since such homologous structures are found to be governed by entirely different genes.

Concerning human origins, Gish noted that the combination of the jaw of a chimpanzee and the skull of a modern man (Piltdown Man), the tooth of a pig (Nebraska Man), and certain pathological specimens of modern man (Neanderthal Man) had been used to construct evolutionary ancestors of man in the past. He pointed out that many evolutionists are now asserting that Australopithecus was an ape rather than the ancestor of man. These include Lord Zuckerman, a famous anatomist who has done extensive research on the origin of man, who proclaimed that if man had evolved he did so without leaving a trace of a transitional form in the fossil record. In his closing remark which brought a warm response from the audience, Gish, in contrast to Sluijser's statement, "to reject evolution is like standing at Cape Canaveral and believing the earth is flat and the moon is made of green cheese," a rational scientist standing there could indeed proclaim, with the Psalmist "The heavens declare the glory of God and the firmament shows His handiwork."

In the exchange between Sluijser and Gish, Sluijser attacked Gish's probability argument by asserting that he had calculated the probability that Gish would be on that particular spot in the world at that particular time and, according to these calculations, it was impossible for him to be there. Gish was quick to point out that his being there was not due to random chance processes but that he was there because he had been invited and had used deliberate processes to get there. Response from the audience showed that they realized that Sluijser had strengthened Gish's probability argument by unwittingly demonstrating that random chance processes could never accomplish events that would require deliberate actions by an intelligent being.

The debate was followed by written questions from the

audience. The proceedings closed by a brief statement from each debater and the moderator. The audience reacted very positively to the statement of Dr. Gish that academic and religious freedom and an adequate education and good science demand that the evidence for both creation and evolution be presented in schools and universities. Dr. Sluijser read the statement published in *The Humanist* that was signed by many scientists and which opposed the teaching of creation. When Dr. Slusher, in his closing remarks, referred to this statement and asserted that truth is not determined by a majority vote, the majority of the audience again, by their applause, indicated agreement. The creationists pointed out if they attempted to supply a mechanism for creation, as demanded by Sluijser, they would only be attempting to present a better theory of evolution. The whole burden of their case is to demonstrate that the origin of the universe and of life demands a supernatural creation because a study of natural science demonstrates that a naturalistic origin is impossible.

The evolutionists at all times were gracious in their conduct, and the entire debate was held in a friendly atmosphere. It is believed that this debate will open a new era in academic circles in Holland. The Evangelische Omroep, with its outstanding leadership, is well-equipped to provide leadership to the creation movement in Holland in the new era.

2000 AT COLORADO STATE U. DEBATE

Nearly 2000 students, faculty and others from as far away as Pueblo, Colorado, and Laramie and other cities in Wyoming, were present in Moby Gym on the Colorado State University campus in Ft. Collins for the debate between evolutionists Dr. Michael Charney and Dr. Charles Wilbur and creationists Prof. Harold Slusher and Dr. Duane Gish on Friday evening, October 7, 1976. The debate was organized by Rev. Marvin Lubenow, pastor of the First Baptist Church in Ft. Collins.

Dr. Charney, just recently retired, was Professor of

Anthropology at C.S.U. and a world-renowned authority in forensic science and author of papers on human evolution theory. Dr. Wilbur is Professor of Zoology at C.S.U. and is also an internationally known expert in forensic science and ecology. Moderator for the debate was Professor Michael McCulloch, Assistant Professor of Philosophy and Director of the University Honors Program. The debate was sponsored by the University Honors Program, Campus Crusade for Christ, Intervarsity Christian Fellowship, the Navigators, Campus Ambassadors, and Corbett Hall Fellowship.

Dr. Gish, the initial speaker, described the evolution and creation models as understood by creationists, and described what should be expected on the basis of each model concerning present natural laws and processes and the fossil record. After pointing out that neither creation nor evolution are valid scientific theories, he described the evidence from the fossil record which he asserted contradicted expectations based on evolution but which supported creation.

Dr. Wilbur, the second speaker, claimed that creation was a religious term which closed off debate from the start. He asserted that one must look to earth history as the only source of evidence concerning origins, the crucial evidence being the geological record, the interpretation of which must be provided only by experts in the field. He then briefly described the standard textbook interpretation of earth history and evolution. He stated that man must control his future evolution and that he was confident that man would do just as good a job at it as he had done in influencing human events up to the present.

Prof. Slusher contrasted evolutionary theories on the origin of the universe to the Second Law of Thermodynamics, pointing out that these theories clearly violate this fundamental natural law. He maintained that an explosion, as postulated by the "Big Bang" hypothesis of the origin of the universe, could never generate order. He pointed out that theories on the origin of stars contradict physical processes. He then gave evidences that establish an upper limit on the age of the universe far short of the billions of years postulated by evolutionists.

Dr. Charney in his presentation first deplored the action of one of his colleagues, (Dr. Stephen Stack, Professor of Biology) who published an emotional letter in the campus newspaper opposing the debate and creationism in general. Charney referred to this attitude as "cavalier", and stated that the fact that 2000 people were in attendance at the debate was evidence enough that such a debate was appropriate and that there were questions that demanded answers. He then showed a chart published in one of the *Time-Life* publications on human evolution, pointing out that this contradicted the Biblical account of man's origin. He then gave a detailed account of human anatomy and of the numerous physical difficulties suffered by man, such as back trouble. He claimed this demonstrated incomplete evolution and not creation by an omniscient Creator.

The initial discussions were followed by ten minute rebuttals by each debater. Slusher's rebuttal was especially telling, eliciting responses on several occasions from the audience. Gish pointed out that an appeal to material means only could explain the structure and function of a watch, for example, but could tell us nothing about its origin. He asserted that man's ills were due to conditions which occurred since creation, and were most often due to man's abuse of his own body. Wilbur asserted that gaps in the fossil record were due to incompleteness of the record, partly because professors hadn't made their students work hard enough! Charney stated that there was no such thing as a missing link but that the entire record of life was a continuum. He insisted, in contrast to Gish's assertion to the contrary, that there were transitional forms documenting human evolution.

The debate was followed by questions from the audience. An all-day creation seminar was held at the First Baptist Church on Saturday with Drs. Slusher and Gish. Dr. Gish spoke at all services on Sunday at First Baptist.

Chapter 2
The Challenge of Creation on the Campus

1976

MORRIS IS N.S.F. LECTURER
AT ALASKA COLLEGE

Students and faculty at Sheldon Jackson College in Sitka, Alaska, heard a special series of lectures and discussions on the theme of scientific creation from ICR Director Henry M. Morris on November 13-14, 1975. Dr. Morris' lectures were sponsored by the Biology Department of the college with funds provided by a National Science Foundation grant designed to expand science education at the two-year college. Sheldon Jackson is Alaska's oldest continuously operating school, having been established as a Presbyterian mission school in 1878. No longer under church auspices, the college still has as its primary goal the provision of a college education to the Eskimo, Aleut, and Indian peoples of Alaska. Sitka, in southeastern Alaska, was the first territorial capital of the Russians who colonized Alaska. In charge of arrangements was Mrs. Mary Jo Nutting, of the biology faculty at the college.

MORRIS IS STALEY LECTURER
AT CEDARVILLE

ICR Director Henry M. Morris served as Cedarville

College's Fourth Annual Staley Distinguished Lecturer to the faculty and students at Cedarville College in Cedarville, Ohio, on January 13-15. Theme of the lectures was "Scientific Biblical Creationism." Cedarville College, with 1,165 students, is the largest of the nine colleges and seminaries affiliated with the General Association of Regular Baptists. As a liberal arts college, it recently received full accreditation by the North Central Association of Schools and Colleges. Dr. Robert Gromacki, Head of the Bible Department, was in charge of arrangements for the Staley Lectures.

CREATIONISM AT THE CITADEL

Dr. Lane Lester, ICR Extension Scientist for the Southeast, spoke March 1, 1976, to an audience at The Citadel in Charleston, South Carolina. This was the first time in recent memory that the case for creationism has been presented at the famous military college. The audience was primarily composed of cadets, but also included Citadel faculty members and students from The Medical University of Charleston and Charleston College.

Dr. Lester gave his slide-illustrated lecture, "Scientific Creationism", in which he compared the evolution and creation models, and then discussed the evidence from biology. The following question period was enlivened by both friendly and hostile questions. The lecture was sponsored by the Religion Council of The Citadel and the coordinator of arrangements was Captain Thomas Moore, director of recruiting.

INTEREST IN CREATION HIGH IN ALBERTA

The large crowds which attended creation-evolution lectures by Dr. Gish on university campuses and at city meetings in Edmonton, Red Deer, and Calgary in the province of Alberta testified to the intense interest in the creation-evolution controversy in that province. On Sunday evening, March 14, a standing-room-only crowd packed out the Memorial Centre in Red Deer, and several hundred more were turned away at the door. Dr. Gish presented a slide-illustrated popularized lecture on the scientific case for creation. That morning he spoke at the morning service of Central Baptist Church in Edmonton, and in the afternoon had presented the scientific evidence for creation to an audience of 400 at the German Pentecostal Church.

On Monday afternoon Dr. Gish presented a lecture on creation, evolution, and genetics at the University of Alberta in Edmonton. About 700 students and faculty filled the Student Union Building Theatre to capacity. In his lecture Dr. Gish concentrated on several scientific papers published during the last year in which evolutionists, while refusing to abandon faith in evolution, proposed radical departures from the long-held neo-Darwinian theory of slow, gradual evolutionary changes. They acknowledged that one reason they feel this is necessary is because of the absence of ancestors and of transitional forms in the fossil record. Creationists, over the protests of most evolutionists, have long emphasized the extreme difficulty these facts pose for evolution theory, while supporting in a remarkable way predictions made on the basis of creation. Some evolutionists are even proposing that natural selection, which has long been held in almost religious reverence by evolutionists, has exerted no significant effect in evolution. Again, creationists have been asserting all along that natural selection could never accomplish what evolutionists have claimed for it. Dr. Gish emphasized the superiority of the creationist explanation for all of the real hard facts of genetics and the fossil record.

A telephone survey among students the day following the lecture revealed a decidedly positive response to Dr. Gish's lecture. A large number of students majoring in biology and genetics had attended. The lecture was recorded on television for later rebroadcast.

On Monday evening Dr. Gish presented a slide-illustrated lecture to 500-600 students, faculty, and townspeople on the University of Calgary campus. This well received lecture was also followed by a one and one-half hour question-and-answer session.

2,000 HEAR ICR SCIENTIST AT UNIVERSITY OF PUERTO RICO

Over 2,000 students and faculty crowded into an auditorium on the campus of the University of Puerto Rico in San Juan on Friday afternoon, March 25, 1976, to hear Dr. Gish present a slide-illustrated lecture on the scientific case for creation. He cited papers by evolutionists to show that evidence for evolution from embryology, vestigial organs, and homology has been discredited, and that such natural laws as those from thermodynamics and probability contradict evolution theory. He then illustrated the fact that the fossil record contradicts predictions based on evolution but is remarkably in agreement with predictions based on creation.

His lecture was very well received, and based on reports by U.P.R. students, the effect of the lecture on this campus could be called electrifying. On Monday, groups of students all over the campus were discussing the lecture. Some classes devoted the entire period to discussing the lecture. The intense interest was also reflected by the fact that over 500 students and faculty on this campus asked to be added to the ICR mailing list.

Most university students in Puerto Rico speak English, but since a significant number do not, an interpreter was used for Dr. Gish's lectures on the campuses. Dr. Paul Lopez, professor of natural science, served as interpreter in San Juan, while Dr. Carlos Lugo, professor of English, served as interpreter at Mayaguez. Both are excellent interpreters, and necessity for their use did not seem to diminish the effectiveness of the lectures.

Dr. Gish spoke to a capacity audience of nearly 300 on Thursday morning on the campus of the College of Agriculture and Mechanical Arts at Mayaguez on the west coast of Puerto Rico, reached by air, which provided a good air view of this beautiful island. The reception was very good, and the lecture was followed by a question-and-answer period. In the afternoon Dr. Gish spoke to about 50 professors in the natural sciences at the University of Puerto Rico. His address was cordially received and was followed by questions and answers.

On Thursday evening Dr. Gish spoke to an overflow audience of 300 or more on the Medical Campus of the University of Puerto Rico. This slide-illustrated lecture was warmly received and was followed by a question-and-answer period of about one hour.

On Friday afternoon Dr. Gish spoke at the regular faculty meeting of Universidad Mundial (World University), a private university with an emphasis on philosophy rather than the sciences. Much interest was expressed in the religious and philosophical aspects of the question of origins.

UNIVERSITY OF NORTHERN COLORADO SEMINAR DRAWS 800

About 800 faculty, students, and local residents attended the Friday evening session of a weekend seminar on scientific creationism held April 8-9, 1976, on the campus of the University of Northern Colorado in Greeley. At the Friday evening meeting, Dr. Gish presented his slide-illustrated lecture on Creation, Evolution, and the Fossil Record. The lecture was followed by a showing of the film "Footprints in Stone." After the film questions from the audience were received by Dr. Gish and Professor Slusher.

On Saturday before about 350 students and faculty, Professor Slusher presented lectures on the origin of the universe, evidences for a young earth, and on radiometric dating methods. Dr. Gish presented lectures on creation, evolution, and the laws of science, and on the origin of man. The lectures were enthusiastically received by most of those in attendance.

Earlier on Friday Dr. Gish had presented lectures in four classes, including classes on evolution and geology. A number of the faculty were present who are currently teaching evolution in various subjects. They engaged Dr. Gish in discussions and questions, offering Dr. Gish further opportunities to buttress his case for creation.

The seminar and lectures on campus are expected to create a considerable stir on this campus which earlier had seen pros and cons on the evolution/creation question discussed in the campus newspaper. It is expected that the rapid decline one professor had noted for the acceptance of evolution by students in his class (from 90 per cent in 1968 to 48 per cent in the fall quarter of 1975) will be followed soon by an additional serious decline.

ALMOST 900 HEAR ICR SCIENTIST ON U.C. DAVIS CAMPUS

Between 800-900 students, faculty, and local residents heard Dr. Gish give a lecture in Freeborn Hall on the campus of the University of California, Davis, on Monday evening, May 3, on "Creation, Evolution, and Recent Research in Genetics." In this well-received lecture Dr. Gish reviewed several papers published by evolutionists during the last year or so which suggest rather radical departures from the current neo-Darwinian explanation of evolution. These included papers by those who tacitly admit that the sudden appearance of many different kinds of plants and animals without ancestors and intermediate forms is difficult if not impossible to understand on the basis of the modern neo-Darwinian theory of evolution.

Dr. Gish emphasized the embarrassing (to evolutionists) lack of ancestors and transitional forms by citing several publications by evolutionists containing such admissions and by illustrating a few examples using slides. He pointed out that this evidence is just as predicted on the basis of creation but has been a perennial puzzle to evolutionists.

The meeting was sponsored by the Navigators, and had been arranged by Bob Witmer and Gid Adkisson of the Navigators Davis staff. The Davis campus was the site of Dr. Gish's first lecture on a college campus approximately four years ago. That lecture was attended by an overflow crowd of about 600 in a smaller auditorium, including

Dr. G. Ledyard Stebbins, world-famous evolutionist, and other faculty members. That lecture was followed by an impromptu debate between Gish and Stebbins.

ICR SCIENTIST LECTURES ON GEORGIA CAMPUSES

Dr. Gish presented the scientific case for creation on the campus of the Medical College of Georgia, Augusta, on the evening of April 13, and on the campus of Georgia State University, Atlanta, on the afternoon of April 14. Of the 2,500 students in medicine and allied health sciences at the Medical College, about 300 attended Dr. Gish's lecture, where he was introduced by Dr. Lois Ellison, Provost of the Medical College. The lecture, which was sponsored by the Student Council of the Medical College, had been arranged through the efforts of Dennis Jones, a junior medical student.

At Georgia State University, Dr. Gish's lecture was critiqued by a panel of three evolutionists, including Mr. James Satterfield, a zoologist; Dr. Carol Hill, an anthropologist; and Dr. Robert Blakely, a physical anthropologist. After Dr. Gish's response to the panel, an interchange between Dr. Gish, the panel, and the audience followed. This lecture, which was attended by about 400 students and faculty, had been arranged by Cilia Reed and Maurice Sikes, students at the university. A report of the lecture appeared in the *Atlanta Journal,* one of Atlanta's largest papers.

ICR SCIENTIST SPEAKS ON COLLEGE CAMPUSES IN KANSAS

On Thursday evening, April 22, Dr. Gish presented the scientific case for creation to a capacity audience of 500 students, faculty, and townspeople on the campus of Wichita State University. The meeting was jointly sponsored by the Mid-Kansas Branch Chapter of the Bible-Science Association and the Forum Board of WSU. Arrangements for the meeting had been made by Dr. Paul Ackerman, WSU professor of psychology and Mrs. Ellen Myers, president and secretary, respectively of the Mid-

Kansas Bible-Science Association, and Phillip Jensen, a WSU student. This was the first public venture of the Wichita creationist organization, and all were grateful for its outstanding success.

COLLEGE PROFESSOR NOTES
PRECIPITOUS DECLINE IN
ACCEPTANCE OF EVOLUTION

An article in the February 25, 1976, issue of the *Mirror,* the campus daily of the University of Northern Colorado, Greeley, reports a drastic decline in the number of students indicating their belief in evolution. Since 1959, history professor Dr. Dane A. Arnold has conducted a survey of the students in his World History I class concerning their acceptance of evolution theory. In 1968 the survey showed that 90 per cent of the students accepted evolution theory, but by the fall of 1975 the percentage had dropped to 48 per cent. Arnold, an ardent evolutionist, is very concerned about the drop and has determined to double the amount of time he spends in his class promoting the theory of evolution.

Dr. Michael J. Higgins, an assistant professor and former student of Arnold, and Dr. James Wanner, an anthropology instructor, have both noticed an increasing number of papers and essay tests rejecting evolution and substituting the Biblical version of creation. A number of professors on the campus have suggested various reasons for the drop in support for evolution, including a reaction against science in general and a return to fundamentalism caused by the insecurity of the time.

These professors expressed dismay at this turn of events, and some felt that if the trend to fundamentalism continued, it would lead to mental slavery and a turn inwards including selfishness, lack of concern for social problems, and isolationism. Fortunately, the article also included the observations of Rev. Durant Van Oyen, pastor of the Fellowship Christian Reformed Church, who welcomed the trend as meaning that more and more people are coming under the lordship of Jesus Christ and are relating their total lives to God.

Those in the creation movement would heartily agree with Rev. Van Oyen and would further suggest that the trend back to belief in creation and consequent acceptance of the lordship of Christ has been greatly assisted by the Institute for Creation Research, the Creation Research Society, the Bible-Science Association, and other creationist organizations. This appears to be positive proof that the program of the Institute for Creation Research, which has been largely directed toward reaching students on university and high school campuses, is producing significant results.

ICR SCIENTIST SPEAKS ON
UNIVERSITY OF MISSOURI CAMPUSES

Panel discussions followed lectures by Dr. Gish on the Kansas City and Columbia campuses of the University of Missouri on September 20 and 22, 1976, respectively. In his lecture on the Kansas City campus in Pierson Hall, attended by about 400 students, faculty, and townspeople, Dr. Gish presented the scientific case for creation, emphasizing the laws of thermodynamics and probability and the evidence from the fossil record. Following the lecture, comments and questions came from a panel of evolutionists consisting of Dr. Richard Wilson, professor of biology at Rockhurst College, Dr. Frank Millich, Professor of Chemistry at U.M.-K.C., and Dr. Paul Hilpman, professor of Geology at U.M.-K.C. Dr. Omar Conrad, professor of Geology at Penn Valley College, was moderator.

Dr. Hilpman suggested that the earth and the stars are in a process of evolution or change, and also attempted to explain the gaps in the fossil record. Dr. Millich argued that laboratory experiments have made some progress toward suggesting how life may have evolved. Dr. Wilson argued for the validity of evolutionary mechanisms. Dr. Gish offered rebuttals to these suggestions by the panel, and further exchange followed. The evening's discussion was conducted in a congenial spirit and all panelists agreed that the case for creation should be presented in our educational system.

A similar congenial panel discussion followed Dr. Gish's lecture on the main campus of the University of Missouri at Columbia. Panel members appeared to be divided on the creation-evolution question. Dr. David Shear, associate professor of biochemistry at U.M.-C, and Dr. Tom Freeman, professor of geology at U.M.-C., offered suggestions in defense of evolution theory. Dr. Olan Brown, a microbiologist and assistant director of the Dalton Research Center at U.M.-C. supported Dr. Gish's arguments against evolution on the basis of probability laws, while Dr. Robert Marshall, professor of food science and nutrition at U.M.-C. appeared to be either neutral or favorable to Dr. Gish's position. Dr. Terry Ten Brink, professor of educational psychology, was program chairman, while Dr. David Rodabaugh, associate professor of mathematics and member of the Missouri Association for Creation, served as moderator.

DR. PARKER SPEAKS AT
WASHINGTON STATE UNIVERSITY

On Sunday afternoon, November 14, 1976, Dr. Gary Parker of the ICR staff spoke to about 300 students at Washington State University in Pullman. Although no one willing to offer a formal defense of evolution could be obtained, Dr. Parker took questions from the floor concerning embryological development, "pre-biological" chemistry, continental drift, the age of fossils, and the evidence of a global Flood. Interest seemed high, and many students stayed for individual conversations with Dr. Parker. Young Life, the Navigators, and Inter-Varsity Christian Fellowship promoted the meeting, which was arranged by the Onecho Bible Church near Colfax, Washington.

Dr. Parker spoke at the morning worship service of the Onecho Church and at a youth group meeting in the evening. The members of the Onecho Bible Church have continuing interests in witnessing to WSU students, and in obtaining a fair hearing for creation in their local school system. The church saw Dr. Parker's creation-science talks as one appropriate means toward both of these goals.

1977

ICR SCIENTIST ON EMPORIA
STATE COLLEGE CAMPUS

Dr. Duane Gish spent two days on the campus of Emporia Kansas State College, Emporia, Kansas. On Monday evening, February 14, Dr. Gish participated in an evolution-creation forum with Dr. John Peterson, evolutionist, biologist, and Dean of the School of Liberal Arts and Science at EKSC. On Tuesday evening, Dr. Gish sat on an evolution-creation panel with five members of the EKSC faculty, including Dr. Thomas Bridge, geologist, Dr. Samuel Dicks, historian, Dr. David Dumas, philosopher, Dr. H. Michael LeFever, biologist, and Dr. Dallas Roark, theologian. Dr. Robert Smalley, Professor of Chemistry, was the moderator for all sessions.

On Monday evening each participant had about one hour to present his case. The program was videotaped by the college. Dr. Peterson, whose specialty is fungi, identified himself philosophically as an atheist. He professed ignorance of the physical sciences and of paleontology, but accepted what his evolutionist colleagues in these fields had to say. He cited evidence for changes in microorganisms, such as mutations and resistance to antibiotics, and the great diversity among the fungi as evidence for evolution.

Dr. Gish reviewed evidence from such fields as thermodynamics, probability, and the fossil record in building his case against evolution, maintaining that this evidence is much more readily correlated and explained by special creation than evolution and that, in fact, this evidence establishes that the universe could not have arisen by natural processes. He pointed out that neither creation nor evolution are scientific theories and that each is as religious as the other. He maintained, however, that on the basis of all of the scientific evidence available, special creation was far more credible than evolution.

On Tuesday evening each panel member had an opportunity to express his views on the importance of the acceptance of one theory or the other on his particular discipline. Dr. Bridge (geologist) spoke for a few minutes without saying much except to the effect that in earlier times man ascribed the origin of the universe and living things to a mystical fairy godmother type of operation but now is seeking a rational explanation. Dr. Dicks discussed several philosophical aspects of the creation-evolution question.

Dr. Roark presented in concise and clear terms the moral and spiritual contrasts involved in accepting the materialistic concept of evolution and the God-centered concept of special creation. Dr. Gish reviewed the effect that the theory of evolution has had in education, scientific research, philosophy and religion in general, and views regarding the Bible in particular.

These brief presentations were followed by an interaction between panel members and then by an interaction between panel members and the audience. Dr. Gish also presented two lectures each on Monday and Tuesday afternoons on the EKSC campus and spoke at all services on Sunday at Bethel Baptist Church, Rev. Duane Atkins, pastor. The meetings on the campus were sponsored by the EKSC Forum Committee and had been arranged by Campus Crusade for Christ with Dave Arendale of the CCC staff acting as coordinator.

BLISS SPEAKS TO STUDENTS ON UCLA CAMPUS

The *Evolution Inquiry Association* of UCLA sponsored a lecture by Prof. Richard Bliss on the subject of scientific creationism on Tuesday, March 9, 1976. Bliss spoke on a general creation theme and emphasized the inadequacy of the geologic record, as well as the inconsistency of evolution in light of the Second Law of Thermodynamics. The room capacity of 80 students was crammed with over 120 interested people wanting to hear this one-hour lecture. Bliss stayed over to answer questions on specific topics from interested graduate students. This was first in a series of lectures that will culminate in a debate between Dr. Duane Gish of ICR and Dr. Henry Hespenheide on May 10.

BLISS SPEAKS TO 300 AT USC

On March 15, 1977, 12:30 in Bovard Hall at the University of Southern California, what was heralded as "The Great Half Debate" turned out to be a lecture by Prof. Richard Bliss on the fossil record and thermodynamics. Bliss spoke for one hour and fifteen minutes on his topic and opened the floor to written questions afterward. Students questioned him for one-and-one-half hours after the session on specific points of scientific interest. The afternoon attendance at USC was about 300 students and interested faculty members.

Chapter 3
The Case for Creation Reaching Out

1976

Nearly 400 people filled the chapel of First Baptist Church of San Jose for the fourth Annual Bay Area Creation-Science Seminar conducted by the institute for Creation Research. Dr. Clarence Sands, pastor of this large church, introduced the speakers, Dr. Clifford Wilson, noted Australian Biblical archaeologist and author of many books, including the best-seller *Crash Go the Chariots,* and Dr. Duane Gish, Associate Director of ICR. The meetings began on Friday evening, January 30, and continued throughout the day on Saturday.

Dr. Wilson spoke on Genesis in the light of archaeology, the results of archaeological research on the period from Moses to Solomon, and on the great impact the Dead Sea Scrolls have had on Biblical scholarship. He gave numerous examples of archaeological findings which demonstrate the historical accuracy of the Scriptures and that without exception the writings of the Bible were indeed the product of the times that were contemporary with the events they report rather than having been written many centuries later.

In his slide-illustrated lecture on the Dead Sea Scrolls, Dr. Wilson gave a fascinating account of the discovery and content of these ancient scrolls. He detailed in particular the content of the scroll which contained the Book of Isaiah. A comparison of modern manuscripts of this book to this ancient manuscript, dated between 100 and 200 years B.C., demonstrates the remarkable manner in which the ancient text has been preserved as far as accuracy is concerned. The Essenes, who left these scrolls, were strongly messianic, as an examination of their writings reveals.

Dr. Gish gave slide-illustrated lectures on creation, evolution, and the fossil record, and on human origins, as well as a lecture on creation, evolution, and the laws of science. He also participated in a spirited personal discussion with several students who attempted to offer explanations for the absence of transitional forms in the fossil record. A professor from one of the local colleges related that he had abandoned the teaching of evolution, having come to the realization that evolution is a false theory and that creation is much more in accord with all of the evidence. He reported that several other faculty members on the staff of the college were creationists.

CONVENTION WORKSHOP FEATURES
CHICAGO MEETINGS

The annual convention of the Chicago Greater Sunday School Association on April 1, 1976, featured an all-day workshop on "Creation Science" conducted by Dr. Henry Morris of ICR. Over 100 pastors, educators, scientists, and other Christian leaders of the Chicago area participated in the five and one-half hour session.

In addition, while in Chicago during that week, Dr. Morris spoke to capacity crowds at the Medinah Baptist Church, the Brentwood Bible Church, the Westchester Bible Church, the Marquette Manor Baptist Church, and the Ashburn Avenue Baptist Church (the latter church also hosting an all-day seminar on April 3).

The week of the meetings was organized by ICR's Midwest Center, headquartered in Wheaton, Illinois. Dr. Morris addressed a special breakfast meeting of the officers, committee members, and guests of the Center. Another special meeting was held for the students at the Wheaton Christian High School.

AMERICAN SCIENTIFIC AFFILIATION
CHAPTER HEARS DR. MORRIS

"Scripture, Science, and Creation" was the theme of a one-hour message given by ICR Director Henry M. Morris to the Chicago chapter of the American Scientific Affiliation on the night of March 30, 1976. This chapter is A.S.A.'s largest and had a record turnout for the meeting, indicating the high degree of interest among its members in the issue. Many long-time leaders in A.S.A. (Russel Mixter, Donald Boardman, James Buswell, Gerald Haddock, Paul Wright, Richard Aulie, and others) were present. Executive Secretary William Sisterson was in charge of arrangements and Dr. Buswell was moderator. A stimulating one-hour question-and-answer session followed the message.

Dr. Morris stressed the Biblical and scientific difficulties with the framework, gap, and day-age theories of the Noahic Deluge, pointing to the necessity of reinterpreting the scientific data within the framework of recent creation and a global cataclysmic flood. Although most members of A.S.A. do not agree with this conclusion, the message received a courteous hearing and sincere interest, with several expressing full support. Dr. Morris himself has been a member of A.S.A. for thirty years and a Fellow in the organization for about twenty years.

SCIENTIFIC SOCIETY
HEARS CREATION LECTURE

Dr. Henry M. Morris, Director of ICR, served as Sigma Xi Lecturer for a regular meeting of the University of Southern Mississippi Sigma Xi Club following its initiation banquet on May 4, 1976. Sigma Xi is the national scientific honor society, stressing scientific research. Dr. Morris had been elected to Associate Membership in the Society while a student at Rice University in 1939, and had been elected to full membership (awarded for significant research contributions) in 1943.

At the USM meeting, Dr. Morris lectured on the theme "Scientific Creationism." A lively discussion followed, and much interest was generated in this subject on the campus. Dr. B.J. King, Associate Professor of Biology and Vice-President of Sigma Xi on the campus, was in charge of the meeting.

SANTA ANA SEMINAR SETS ATTENDANCE RECORD

Approximately 3,000 enthusiastic young adults crowded out the main auditorium and the auxiliary hall (with closed-circuit TV monitors) for the opening sessions of the Santa Ana (California) Creation Seminar on Friday night, May 21, 1976. Many of these were students or recent graduates of the colleges and universities in the Orange County area. Meetings were held at the Calvary Chapel, an outstanding non-denominational church pastored by Rev. "Chuck" Smith. Sessions continued through Saturday.

This was the largest attendance to date for a creation seminar, more than doubling the previous record set in Miami a year previously. Sales of creationist books also set a record for a single seminar. Much of the credit for the record interest was due to the church and its pastor.

Speakers for the seminar were ICR scientists Duane Gish and Henry Morris. Dr. Gish and Dr. Morris had also participated in a creation/evolution debate held at this church six months previously, and met a number of converts who had been influenced to become Christians largely through the debate.

CREATION CONFERENCE IN ENGLAND

Mr. David C.C. Watson, one of ICR's correspondents in England, sent information on the Conference on Creation and Origins to be held at Hayes Conference

Centre, Swanwick, Derbyshire, England, April 20-23, 1976. Speakers and subjects include Dr. Ferran Davies (Aberystwyth): "Creation, Evolution, and Botany;" Dr. Arthur Jones (Birmingham): "Creation, Evolution, and Zoology;" John Hoad, M.Sc. (Manchester): "Thermodynamics and Evolution;" Dr. David Lyon (Bradford): "Darwinism and Society;" Dr. Jack Milner (Derby): " 'Good and Bad Science'—and the Relevance of Scripture for Science;" Dr. Vern Poythress (Cambridge): "Jesus Christ as Eschatological Scientist;" Dr. John Reynolds (London): "Man: the Image of God;" David Tyler, M.Sc., M. Inst. P. (Derby): "What Can We Learn From Radiocarbon Dating?"

U.S. creationists are pleased to learn that creationist scientists in Britain are supporting vigorously the scientific evidence for creation.

ICR STAFF SCIENTISTS IN
PHILADELPHIA SEMINAR

Dr. Harold Slusher and Dr. Duane Gish were the speakers at a Friday evening and Saturday seminar on scientific creationism presented at the Reformed Episcopal Church in Philadelphia. Registrants for the seminar numbered about 350. This was the first seminar in scientific creationism presented in the Philadelphia area, and plans are under way for an expanded effort and a permanent local creationist organization. The seminar had been arranged by John C. Brandenburg and by David Livingston.

On Thursday evening Dr. Gish spoke to an audience of about 600 on the campus of Bucks County Community College, just north of Philadelphia. A panel of four faculty members, including a biologist, a geologist, a mathematician, and an historian, responded to Dr. Gish's presentation. This interchange was followed by questions directed to Dr. Gish and the panel from the audience. Prof. Eugene Ferri of Bucks County Community College had made arrangements for this meeting.

ICR STAFF SCIENTIST
ADDRESSES NSTA MEETING

Dr. Duane Gish of ICR was an invited panelist recently at one of the sessions of the National Science Teachers Association meeting in Philadelphia on Saturday, March 20. He was one of three participants in the session on *Creation and Evolution: An Update*. Other panelists were Robert J. O'Neil, Instructor at Strake Jesuit College Preparatory, Houston, Texas, and Rev. J. Guy Morin, Science Department Chairman at Don Bosco High School, Ramsey, New Jersey. The session was moderated by Jesse M. Harris, Director, Science-Health, Dallas Independent School District.

Each panelist was given 15 minutes for an initial statement, and then, following interaction with the audience, each panelist presented a five-minute summation. Rev. Morin, the first speaker, assumed the position that the Biblical account of creation was written to reveal the Who and the *why* of creation, but not the *how* of creation. He emphasized that the Bible is not a textbook on science, while stating that he believed that there was geological, paleontological, and biological evidence supporting evolution, although he maintained evolution was no more than a theory.

O'Neil tentatively suggested that perhaps God had used some sort of an evolutionary process in creation, thus leaving open an evolutionary approach to origins.

In his initial presentation Dr. Gish emphasized that neither creation nor evolution is a valid scientific theory, although one or the other must be the true explanation of origins. Concerning the non-testability and non-falsifiability by evolution theory, Dr. Gish cited several recent papers by evolutionists themselves frankly admitting that evolution theory cannot be tested nor falsified. Citing several recent papers, Dr. Gish documented the fact that the fossil record fits the predictions based on creation but contradicts predictions based on evolution.

Dr. Gish also pointed out that some evolutionists are

now stating their belief that natural selection has had no significant effect on the course of evolution. The concept of natural selection has been held in almost religious reverence by evolutionists since Darwin's time and was the concept that gained acceptance of the Darwinian theory by the majority of scientists.

About 175 science teachers filled the room to overflowing. Each received a revised copy of Dr. Gish's paper, *Creation, Evolution, and Public Education.*

ANNUAL MISSOURI SEMINAR FEATURES KANSAS CITY MEETINGS

The third annual Creation Science Seminar of the Missouri Association for Creation was held on September 18 in Kansas City, Missouri, at the Blue Ridge Baptist Temple. Speakers included Dr. Duane Gish and Dr. Henry Morris of ICR, Dr. David Rodabaugh and Dr. John Lasley of the University of Missouri, Dr. David Menton of Washington University and Dr. Stephen Jones of Drury College. Approximately 300 registrants attended the seminar.

Dr. Gish and Dr. Morris also spoke at several colleges in the Kansas City area, including Calvary Bible College, Maplewoods Community College, and Penn Valley Community College. On Sunday, September 19, Dr. Morris was guest preacher at the Kansas City Baptist Temple and Red Ridge Baptist Church, while Dr. Gish spoke at the Blue Ridge Baptist Temple and the Grace Baptist Temple. Dr. Morris was guest speaker on the call-in "Encounter" program on Radio Station KCCV.

SANTA ANA CHURCH HOSTS CREATION CONFERENCE

A five night Creation Bible Conference featuring five different ICR speakers, attracted large and enthusiastic crowds—largely of college and young adult age—at southern California's famed Calvary Chapel, one of the nation's largest churches, located adjacent to Costa Mesa in Santa Ana (Charles "Chuck" Smith, Pastor), on September 27-October 1. Speakers were Dr. Duane Gish, Professor Richard Bliss, Dr. Clifford Wilson, Dr. Henry Morris, and Professor Harold Slusher.

Attendance for the first four nights averaged approximately 1500 each night. For the final session, an overflow crowd exceeding 3000 attended the debate on dating and human origins featuring Drs. Gish and Slusher on the creationist side (see article in next month's issue).

Calvary Chapel had already sponsored a previous creation-evolution debate and a weekend ICR seminar in 1975. In addition, Dr. Morris had conducted a special day-long "college briefing Bible-science seminar" at the church's Lake Arrowhead conference center on August 31, 1976, and Pastor Henry Morris III spoke to Calvary Chapel's Bible Institute at the same conference center on October 12-13, speaking on the exegesis of Genesis One.

OHIO SEMINAR REACHES THOUSANDS

One of the most effective creation seminars in ICR's history was held in the Columbus, Ohio area on October 8-11, sponsored by the Grace Brethren Church of Worthington. Speakers were ICR scientists Duane Gish and Henry Morris.

Over 1300 attended the opening sessions of the seminar on Friday night. This number exceeded the 100-seat capacity of the church's main auditorium, so that Dr. Morris and Dr. Gish conducted duplicate sessions in the chapel along with those in the auditorium. More than half this number continued through the all-day sessions on Saturday. In addition, Dr. Morris brought the Sunday message at all three morning services of the church (one of the two largest Grace Brethren Churches in the country) to a total of well over 2,000, and Dr. Gish spoke at the evening service.

Another feature of the Columbus seminar was a Monday night meeting in the Student Union Theatre on the Ohio State University campus, sponsored by the Fellowship of Christian Athletes. Both Dr. Gish and Dr. Morris brought lectures at this meeting, which was originally scheduled as a debate until the sponsors found it impossible to obtain qualified evolutionists on the faculty to participate.

Additional outreach opportunities in Ohio's capital city area included luncheon addresses by Drs. Morris and Gish to scientists of the famous Battelle Research Institute, a morning workshop for science teachers in the Columbus schools (see article elsewhere in this issue), a session with the students and teachers at the area's Christian schools, three radio programs, one television program, feature articles in Columbus' two newspapers, a public high school assembly, and services in two other Brethren churches.

In charge of all these arrangements was Dick Mayhue, associate Pastor of the sponsoring church, and Director of the Worthington Bible Institute. Pastor Mayhue had been saved while in San Diego in the Navy through the Scott Memorial Baptist Church (as had the other Associate Pastor, John Willett), just before the founding of Christian Heritage College, and had been an audit student in Dr. Morris' first Apologetics course at the College in 1970. Both Pastors Mayhue and Willet later graduated from Grace Theological Seminary (as did the Church's pastor, Jim Custer), studying under ICR Advisory Board member, John Whitcomb, co-author with Dr. Morris of *The Genesis Flood*. Worthington's Grace Brethren Church was founded in 1964 by David Hocking, now pastor of the denomination's largest church, the First Brethren Church of Long Beach, California, a church which had also sponsored a very successful ICR seminar in 1973.

FIRST IOWA SEMINAR HAS LARGE REGISTRATION

The Institute for Creation Research's first Creation Seminar in Iowa was held on November 12-13, with 700 paid registrants participating, making it one of the most successful such meetings to date. Speakers for the seminar were Dr. Duane Gish and Dr. Henry Morris.

All meetings were held in the Walnut Ridge Baptist Church of Waterloo, of which Dr. Mark Jackson is pastor. The church's college pastor, Bruce McDonald, was in charge of arrangements.

Many other churches cooperated, and a large number of registrants came from other parts of the state. At least 200 were college students and faculty from the University of Northern Iowa in Waterloo.

COLORADO SPRINGS SEMINAR

A creation seminar was held at Mesa Hills Bible Church of Colorado Springs, Rev. Erwin Ericson, pastor, on Friday evening and Saturday, October 22 and 23. An overflow crowd of 350-400 necessitated the use of closed-circuit TV to accommodate the overflow. The speaker, Dr. Gish, presented a lecture on Friday night on the evidence for creation from the fossil record preceding the showing of the film "Footprints in Stone." On Saturday, Dr. Gish presented lectures on alleged evolutionary mechanisms, the origin of life, the origin of man, and the Christian view on abortion.

1977

SAN ANTONIO HOSTS SEMINAR

The first creation seminar in San Antonio, the nation's tenth-largest city, was held on January 14-16, sponsored by a special committee organized by Robert T. Jensen, M.D. Speakers were the ICR Director and Associate Director, Dr. Henry Morris and Dr. Duane Gish. Paid registrations exceeded 500. The opening session was held on the Trinity University campus, under the co-sponsorship of Inter-Varsity Christian Fellowship. Diligent, but unsuccessful, attempts had been made to find faculty members willing to participate in a creation-evolution debate. However, student groups from many central Texas colleges and universities attended the seminar.

Other sessions were held at the Trinity Baptist Church near the campus. On Sunday, Dr. Morris and Dr. Gish brought messages in seven different San Antonio churches, representing six denominations, with excellent response in each. Dr. Gish also spoke on two radio stations preceding the seminar.

CREATION SEMINAR HELD
IN BIRMINGHAM

ICR scientists Duane T. Gish and Henry M. Morris were speakers at a Creation Seminar held in Birmingham, Alabama, on January 28-30. The seminar was sponsored by the Shade's Mountain Independent Church, and the opening session on Friday night attracted an attendance of 600. On Sunday, Dr. Gish spoke in all services at the large Briarwood Presbyterian Church. Dr. Morris also was guest on a popular local call-in radio program hosted by Dave Campbell. Jim Haley, Associate Pastor of the Shade's Mountain Church, was in charge of arranging and promoting the seminar.

SLUSHER AND GISH IN WICHITA SEMINAR

Drs. Harold Slusher and Duane Gish were the speakers in a series of meetings and a weekend seminar in Wichita, April 14-16. These meetings were arranged and sponsored by the Mid-Kansas Branch of the Bible-Science Association. Dr. Paul Ackerman, Wichita State University Professor of Psychology, is president and Mrs. Ellen Meyers is secretary of this organization.

A joint lecture by Drs. Slusher and Gish on the Wichita State campus on Thursday evening was followed by a three-hour debate over a local radio station between the creationists and evolutionists Dr. Bussjaeger and Dr. Potts, biologists and professors at Kansas Newman College and Friends University, respectively. In spite of the fact that Slusher and Gish presented practically all of the empirical evidence that was presented during the debate, Bussjaeger and Potts insisted the creationist position was largely theological, while their position was scientific.

The Friday evening and Saturday seminar was held at Calvary Bible Church, Rev. Walter Peterson, brother of composer John Peterson, pastor. Drs. Slusher and Gish also spoke in area high schools.

SECOND MIAMI CREATION SEMINAR
ATTRACTS WIDE INTEREST

Over 1800 people overflowed the auditorium of Miami's large Northwest Baptist Church for the opening session of another outstanding Miami Creation Seminar on March 18-19. In addition to large numbers of students from area schools, many scientists and educators also attended. Featured speakers were Dr. Duane Gish and Dr. Henry Morris of ICR, with Dr. Rush Acton, Dr. Mary Stanton, and Dr. Harlan Wyborny also participating. The seminar was co-sponsored by the Miami Christian College and a committee of business and professional men under the leadership of Dr. Acton, Associate Professor of Anatomy and Orthopedic Surgery at Miami University Medical School, and Mr. John Chalfant, a businessman whose organizational and promotional activities were an important key to its success.

In addition to the seminar sessions, all of the speakers participated in one or more of four popular Miami radio talk shows. Channel 10 gave significant and favorable television news coverage. On Sunday, March 20, Dr. Morris brought messages at the Southwest Community Church and the Granada Presbyterian Church. Dr. Gish spoke at both morning and evening services at the Island Community Church in the Florida Keys.

Many people young and old, both in the seminars and church services, testified of the life-changing impact which they had experienced from the meetings.

WORD OF LIFE CONFERENCE
FEATURES ICR SPEAKERS

The annual spring Bible Conference at the famed Word-of-Life headquarters beside beautiful Schroon Lake in New York, held during the week of May 23, featured ICR scientists Henry Morris, Duane Gish, and Harold Slusher as speakers. The 300 students at the one-year Word-of-Life Bible Institute (many of whom plan to come to Christian Heritage College to complete their education) plus many outside guests were in attendance. Other speakers included Jack Wyrtzen, Word-of-Life founder, and Wendell Kempton, president of the Association of Baptists for World Evangelism.

ICR SCIENTIST AT ST. LOUIS
CREATION SEMINAR

Dr. Duane Gish gave lectures on alleged evolutionary mechanisms, and evidences for a young earth at the St. Louis Creation Seminar of the Missouri Association for Creation held on Saturday, May 7, in the facilities of Calvary Heights Baptist Temple. The seminar, attended by approximately 200 registrants, many of whom were teachers, also included lectures by Dr. Glen Wolfram of the Research Laboratories of Pet Foods, Greenville, Illinois, Dr. David Rodabaugh, Professor of Mathematics at the University of Missouri, Columbia, and Dr. David Menton, Professor of Anatomy of the Washington University Medical College, St. Louis.

The meetings were moderated by Rex Hess, M.S., anatomist and electron microscopist at Washington University Medical College, and president of the Missouri Association for Creation. Creationists in Missouri are urged to join this outstanding creationist organization. The home office is at 7334 Colgate, St. Louis, MO 63130.

BLISS SPEAKS TO EIGHT GROUPS IN FLORIDA

Richard Bliss, Director of Curriculum Development at ICR, spent several days in Florida during the month of August speaking to a variety of groups on the topic of creationism. All arrangements were made by Rev. C.E. Winslow of Bradenton. Bliss spoke to both the Bradenton and Sarasota Kiwanis clubs, stressing the creation model as a curriculum imperative for public schools, universities, and colleges. Bliss was well received by the members of both clubs and was strongly encouraged to continue with the ICR efforts in public education. He also spoke to the Calvary Baptist Church and First Church of Nazarene in Bradenton as well as the Grace Baptist Church of Sarasota. Interested persons in these places volunteered their services to help with creation efforts in education and all showed surprise at the inroads that both atheism and humanism had made in the public schools.

During this time Professor Bliss was invited to speak on the Pat Colmenares "Pulse" show, WVTV—13 in Tampa, as well as a two-hour radio interview and call-in on the top-rated, Lowell Schumaker program on WQSA. WKZM radio also interviewed Bliss on a radio segment related to Scripture and science.

PARKER AT NATIONAL YOUTH SCIENCE CAMP

On July 3, 100 outstanding science students, two high school graduates chosen by each state's governor, heard Dr. Gary Parker present "A Scientific Case for Creation" at the National Youth Science Camp hosted annually since 1963 at beautiful Camp Pocahontas by the State of West Virginia.

Only about five of these select young people acknowledged ever having heard a creationist before. At the end of his talk, Dr. Parker received a standing ovation— and responded to some perceptive and penetrating questions reflecting the scientific expertise of these award-winning students.

LECTURE TO MARINE SCIENTISTS
INCLUDED IN GULF COAST MEETINGS

Two weeks of mid-summer lectures on the Gulf Coast by Dr. Henry Morris reached hundreds of Christian leaders in the south and also provided opportunity for a special creationist presentation to an important group of researchers and educators in the marine sciences. Record attendances marked the twice-daily messages by Dr. Morris at the annual Coast Bible Conference in Biloxi, Mississippi, on August 7-13. The Conference also featured John Sproules, Chairman of the Department of Greek at Grace Seminary, and was attended by pastors and church leaders from several southern states. James Raiford, Dean of Faculties at Southeastern Bible College in Birmingham, was director of the Conference.

On August 14-18, Dr. Morris also spoke in Tampa, Florida primarily as the Bible Conference speaker at the Bayside Community Church of that city, Rev. William Lay, pastor. His messages were on "Science in the Psalms."

The marine scientists meeting was at the Gulf Coast Research Laboratory in Ocean Springs, Mississippi, on August 12. This Laboratory is state-supported and provides the marine research and graduate training in the marine sciences for all the state's colleges and universities. The meeting was arranged and chaired by biologist Robert Allen, and Dr. Morris' discussion was well received.

ICR STAFF SCIENTIST SPEAKS
AT BELL LABORATORY

Dr. Gish spoke to about 250 engineers and others at the Holmdel, New Jersey, laboratory of Bell Laboratories on Tuesday, August 16. Audiences at the Murray Hill and Whippeney laboratories of the Bell Laboratories witnessed the lecture via a video simulcast. Dr. Gish presented the scientific case for creation in his slide-illustrated lecture. Following the lecture Dr. Gish answered questions via a three-way hook-up with the three laboratories. The lecture was arranged by Ed Underwood.

ICR SCIENTISTS AT CREATION CONVENTION

Dr. Lane Lester, ICR representative in the Southeast, Prof. Richard Bliss, and Dr. Duane Gish were among the speakers at the Fifth Annual Creation Convention held at the Philadelphia College of the Bible August 14-17. The convention was sponsored by the Bible-Science Association of Caldwell, Idaho.

Dr. Gish gave the keynote address on Sunday evening. His address was entitled "Challenges by Evolutionists to the Neo-Darwinian Interpretation of Evolution". He also spoke on Monday evening on "Human Origins". Prof. Bliss conducted a workshop on Tuesday afternoon on teaching two models of origins in public schools. Dr. Lester gave a lecture on Monday afternoon on "Cell Design." Nearly 300 attended the convention. David Livingston, Director of Associates for Biblical Research, was in charge of arrangements.

Chapter 4
The Challenge of Creation to the Educational Establishment

DR. GISH SPEAKS
TO ARKANSAS BIOLOGY TEACHERS

Dr. Gish spoke to the biology section of the Arkansas Educational Association annual meeting in Little Rock on Tuesday, November 25, 1975. The report which appeared the next day in the Arkansas *Gazette* related that Dr. Gish "held rapt" his audience of science teachers. He especially emphasized the fact that the concept of creation cannot be excluded from the classroom on the basis of the false assumption that it is less scientific than evolution theory, asserting that a sound educational process, academic freedom, and separation of church and state can be obtained only when the evidence supporting both concepts is taught. He then presented the scientific case for creation.

The reception to Dr. Gish's lecture was very cordial, and interest was expressed in arranging for an ICR scientist to speak to all of the science teachers at next year's meeting.

The following is an excerpt from an article in the

Arkansas *Gazette*:

Hits 'Brainwashing' In the Schools

Nevertheless, today evolution is being widely accepted as the only scientific explanation for origins, and even as established fact, while creation is excluded as a mere religious concept, he said.

"This rigid indoctrination in evolutionary dogma, with the exclusion of the competing concept of special creation, results in young persons being indoctrinated in a nontheistic, naturalistic, humanistic religious philosophy in the guise of science," Gish contended. "Science is perverted, academic freedom is denied, the educational process suffers, and constitutional guarantees of religious freedom are violated."

Presentation of both the evolution and creation models in the classroom would allow students to evaluate the strengths and weaknesses of each. "This is the course true education should pursue rather than following the present process of brainwashing students in evolutionary theory."

ALABAMA PASSES CREATION RESOLUTION

Notice has been received that the Alabama legislature has recently passed a "creation resolution," encouraging the teaching of creation as a scientific alternative to evolution in the public schools of Alabama. The resolution was patterned after the suggested resolution proposed by ICR *(Acts & Facts,* "Impact" No. 26). The resolution does not **require** the teaching of creation, but does encourage the teachers in the state to realize that such teaching is permitted and recommended by the representatives of the citizens of the state.

COLUMBUS SCHOOLS OPEN TO CREATION

The public schools of Columbus, Ohio widely recognized as one of the nation's most effective school systems, are among the leaders in acknowledging the validity and importance of teaching scientific creationism along with evolution as a scientifically viable alternative model of origins. Credit for this advance is largely due to Mrs. Marilyn Redden and Mr. Paul Langdon, President and Vice-President, respectively, of the Columbus Board of Education, both of whom have actively supported the principle of equal teaching of the two models.

The most recent effort in this direction was a one-day seminar on Scientific Creationism sponsored by the Columbus Board of Education for specially-selected biology teachers—one from each of the city's eighteen schools with biology programs. ICR scientists Henry Morris and Duane Gish were the two leaders for the workshop. Since it was held on a Friday, the school district paid for substitute teachers for those attending. Mr. Robert E. McNemar, Director of Science and Mathematics for the Columbus Education Center, coordinated the program. Mr. Paul Langdon, who is also an official of the Battelle Memorial Research Institute, arranged for the meeting to be held in the Battelle facilities. The Battelle Institute is one of the nation's top private scientific research organizations.

After the morning sessions, many of the Battelle scientists joined the biology teachers for the luncheon addresses by Dr. Gish and Dr. Morris. Mrs. Redden and Mr. Langdon also were present for this session and were enthusiastic in their endorsement of the subject matter presented.

Mrs. Redden writes: "In talking with teachers individually, I found that they were anxious to see and use the new materials. If I can do anything to help, please do not hesitate to call on me." Mr. Langdon writes in similar vein: "Doctors Duane Gish and Henry Morris, in their recent presentation. . . to the science teachers of the

Columbus Public Schools . . . suggested the study of the creation model along with the evolution model . . . applied to what one is able to observe in science, not a study of theology or the Bible . . . I know that the science teachers and others are looking forward to the use of such a book, and I believe this is the best approach to the question when handled in the public schools.''

In addition to the biology teacher's seminar, Dr. Morris was guest speaker on the Columbus School District public service radio program, with Dick Coldren as host. The program was taped in the studios of Station WCBE ("Columbus Board of Education") for later broadcast on many area radio stations, and dealt with the teaching of scientific creationism in the schools.

Arrangements have been made through the Columbus Board of Education to provide each of the 200 science teachers in Columbus a copy of the ICR books *Scientific Creationism* (Public School Edition) and *Origins: Two Models*. A 1971 resolution, sponsored by Mr. Langdon and approved unanimously by the Board, had stipulated the teaching of both creation and evolution as scientific theories in the public schools, with the provision of appropriate classroom materials to facilitate this. Mr. Langdon at that time had arranged for each science classroom to have a copy of the Creation Research Society textbook, *Biology: A Search for Order in Complexity*.

BLISS SPEAKS TO SCIENCE
TEACHERS IN TWO STATES

Professor Richard Bliss, Director of Curriculum Development at ICR recently had the unusual opportunity of speaking to state conventions of public school science teachers in two adjacent states, urging them to teach creation as a valid scientific alternative to evolution in the schools of their respective states. In September, Professor Bliss addressed the Oklahoma Science Teachers, meeting in Tulsa. In November, he spoke to the Arkansas Science Teachers Association in Little Rock.

On both occasions, Mr. Bliss discussed the "Two-

Model" approach to the teaching of origins, instructing the teachers in the use of the ICR instructional materials now available for this purpose. Response in both cases was excellent. At Little Rock, over 75 per cent of the teachers at the convention attended the creation lectures, leaving 25 per cent to be divided among the seven other sectionals being offered at the same time.

Professor Bliss also spoke in several churches and other meetings while in the Tulsa and Little Rock areas, including a television interview on the "Good Morning Arkansas" program.

AN UPDATE ON THE TEACHING
OF CREATION IN CALIFORNIA

By John R. Ford, M.D.,
California State Board of Education*

In April 1974 the California State Board of Education voted unanimously to include the following statements in the social science framework:

Part of humankind's long intellectual history has been grappling with the question of human origins. In virtually every culture, whether ancient or modern, accounts of human origin have been part of the system of beliefs held by the people of that culture.

In the Judeo-Christian tradition, which has been the most influential religious factor in Western civilization, human origin has been explained as an act of divine creation as described in the Book of Genesis. The development of scientific theories of origin in the nineteenth century both added to the variety of explanations of human origin and encouraged a re-evaluation of earlier explanations. For some the conflict of beliefs caused by the scientific theories has been sharp enough to force them to choose between their system of belief and the evolu-

*Note: The above article was published in *Origins* (Vol. 3, No. 1, p. 46) and is reprinted here with permission of the author and publishers. Dr. Ford has, for many years, been the chief spokesman on California's State Board of Education for teaching creation in the public schools as a scientific alternative to evolution.

tionary explanations offered by science. Others have found it possible to accept scientific accounts of human evolutionary development while still holding to a belief in divine creation. Still others believe that the concept of divine creation is scientifically valid.

These various views of human origin, together with various approaches to the relationship between religious belief and scientific theory, must be seen as part of the intellectual and cultural diversity of our society. These representative views of origin are studied in the social sciences because they make significant contribution to human systems of belief and values.

Although this framework was adopted in April 1974, it was not printed until January 1976. Because of a similar issue in Tennessee at that time (See ORIGINS 2:96-97), and because of the strong anti-creation sentiment in the scientific community, it was felt the first step should be to place the topics of human origins and the early history of mankind in the social science texts. This was also done to avoid the complication of legal charges from evolutionary scientists.

Significant advances towards including creation in the elementary textbooks of California have been made. A number of books that were eventually adopted for the social sciences in 1975 contained some creation concepts, and a number of evolutionary ideas formerly stated as facts in science texts are now presented only as theories.

Because of the unprecedented two-year delay in the printing of the social science framework, and because of the urgency of including creation theory along with evolution, the State Board of Education adopted the following statement as an addendum to the social science framework.

The State Board of Education had determined that the appropriate place for discussing the subject of origins is in the Social Science classroom, K-12. Books on the approved matrix for Social Science do not include an adequate study of the various views of human origin. Notwithstanding, when the matter of origins is studied in Social Science classes, various alternatives should be pre-

sented appropriately.

This directive was distributed throughout all the school districts of the State of California to be added to the social science framework, thus informing the school districts that the Board does expect creation to be included in the teaching of the history of early man.

A definite victory has been won by the creationists in having materials on creation printed in the textbooks, and in notifying all school districts in the State of California that they are expected to teach alternate views when dealing with the subject of origins.

BLISS MEETS WITH STATE
AND LOCAL EDUCATORS IN OREGON

Four event-packed days were the result of efforts by an enthusiastic group "Citizens for Better Education" in Portland. The local Board of Education in Portland was contacted by the citizens group to hear Richard Bliss on the question of a two-model approach to the origin of life. Bliss stressed that it was a curriculum imperative and also a very fine instructional approach. The school officials seemed very interested in this approach and indicated that their curriculum committee would review the material— *Origins: Two Models* for possible purchase as supplementary materials within the school district. Bliss also had an opportunity to meet with the State Board of Education in Salem, Oregon. The State Superintendent of Schools, his assistant, and the Secretary of the State Board of Education listened to a presentation of how a two-model approach could be implemented and why it is imperative to place this in context with process and inquiry teaching techniques. Bliss was also interviewed on the local news for Channel 12 television. A twenty-minute tape was made the following day at the same studio and Sunday, February 27, he spoke to an overflow crowd at the Hinson Memorial Baptist Church.

PROF. RICHARD BLISS
SPEAKS TO SCHOOL PERSONNEL IN THREE STATES

Richard Bliss, Director of Curriculum Development at ICR, visited several school districts during April 20 through May 4. Among these was the Hillsborough County School District in Tampa, Florida. Bliss explained the educational value of using a two model approach to the members of the board of education and indicated that it could be an acceptable solution to a very significant problem in education. He also appeared on radio station talk shows and was interviewed for one-half hour on Channel 40 T.V. in Sarasota. The interviewers in both instances showed a great interest in two models as the only scientifically fair approach to the study of the origin of life.

Bliss was also invited to speak to school board members and educators in West Bend, Wisconsin. Over one-hundred and twenty-five interested persons listened to his emphasis on the imperative nature of a two-model approach. He explained that this was a mandate to all professional educators. He also held a workshop for teachers in Minneapolis, Minnesota.

FLORIDA SCIENCE TEACHERS HEAR BLISS

In an important meeting, Dick Bliss of ICR was well received as he spoke to the Florida State Science Teachers Association, meeting in Tampa on October 21-22. He spoke to three sessions of the convention, emphasizing both the responsiblities and the benefits of teaching the two models of origins in the public schools. In addition to presenting scientific evidence for creation, Bliss presented data proving that students learn more and think more incisively when both creation and evolution are studied in the classroom.

While in Florida, Bliss also spoke to Tampa's Bayshore Community Church and to the Samoset Baptist Church of Bradenton.

Chapter 5
Special Interest Stories

**EVOLUTIONIST DECLARES:
APES EVOLVED FROM MAN!**

Duane T. Gish, Ph.D.
Associate Director - ICR

Dr. Geoffrey Bourne, Director of the Yerkes Regional Primate Research Center of Emory University, an Australian-born, Oxford-educated American cell biologist, anatomist, and now considered to be one of the world's leading primatologists, has declared his belief that apes and monkeys are the evolutionary descendants of man! This is, of course, the exact opposite of what evolutionists have been saying ever since Darwin.

Bourne's views apparently were stated recently to news reporters, and came to our attention through an article in *Modern People,* Vol. 8, April 18, 1976, p. 11. Bourne, in a personal communication, has confirmed the accuracy of the report. He felt forced to adopt this flip-flop theory because of the reports in recent years by Richard Leakey and others (see ICR "Impact" article No. 11, *Acts and Facts,* February, 1974) which claim that fossils of man have been found which pre-date man's supposed ape-like ancestors. According to Bourne's analysis of these reports, individuals that looked very much like modern man were in existence at the same time *Australopithecus* and *Homo erectus* were running around. Both of these latter species had massive eyebrow ridges and snouts which resemble apes more than men.

According to previous theories (and most evolutionists still hold to this view), some as yet unidentified common ancestor of ape and man gave rise to *Australopithecus,* which evolved to *Homo erectus,* which in turn evolved into modern man. But, as noted above, Richard Leakey in recent years has claimed he has found the fossils of man which pre-date many australopithecines and which pre-date the fossils of *Homo erectus* by as much as one to two million years (he says). If, as Leakey believes, man is as old or older than *Australopithecus* and *Homo erectus,* neither can be ancestral to man. That leaves man with no known ape-like ancestor.

Bourne's astounding solution to this dilemma is that evolutionists have been mistaken all along in their belief that man had evolved from an ape-like ancestor. The truth, he says, is that apes, monkeys, and lower primates have evolved from man.

Bourne claims that evidence from embryology supports his theory. A theory widely held by evolutionists and almost universally taught in biology textbooks and other texts that deal with evolution theory is the idea that during embryological development, organisms recapitulate their evolutionary ancestry, resembling their evolutionary ancestors during various stages of development. Thus, a human embryo is supposed to resemble successively a fish, an amphibian, a reptile, and an ape during its development.

This is actually a thoroughly discredited theory and has been abandoned by most embryologists (see B. David-heiser, *Evolution and the Christian Faith,* Presbyterian and Reformed Publishing Co., Philadelphia, 1969, pp. 240-255). Bourne, however, claims that an ape fetus looks like a human fetus during its early stages of development. It is in the later stages of gestation, he says, that the unborn ape starts developing typical ape-like characteristics. Bourne is quoted as saying, "This means the development of an ape infant recapitulates his origin; he goes from a human-like creature to an ape-like animal in the fetus." Again, this is the exact opposite to what evolutionists have said in the past.

Who is right? Is man the evolutionary offspring of ape-like creatures as has been taught for over 100 years, or are apes and monkeys really the evolutionary offsprings of man, as Bourne postulates? And if Bourne is right, then **who was the ancestor of man?** It seems that if evolutionary scientists can use the same evidence and come up with two theories as diametrically opposed as these, then something must be wrong with the basic presuppositions under which they are operating.

The abrupt appearance of all of the lower primates, such as the lemur-like creatures, monkeys, and apes, in the fossil record without ancestors or transitional forms, as well as the abrupt appearance of man with no fossil evidence of ancestors, strongly support the concept of the direct special creation of all of these creatures (see D.T. Gish, *EVOLUTION? The Fossils Say NO!,* 2nd Edition, Creation-Life Publishers, San Diego, 1973, pp. 85-103).

HUMANISTS ATTACK CREATIONISTS
Aim is Directed at all Major School Districts

The American Humanist Association, under the inspiration and leadership of its president, Bette Chambers, has launched a drive against efforts of creationists to convince educational authorities to teach the scientific evidence for creation in public schools. The American Humanist Association, whose members include atheists, agnostics, and free thinkers of various kinds, has, in their literature, described humanism as a nontheistic religion.

A sponsoring committee headed by Bette Chambers has secured the signatures of 179 scientists, educators, and religious figures to a statement which they say is being sent to all major school districts in the United States. The statement, along with several articles attacking the concept of creation, were published in the January/February 1977 issue of *The Humanist,* published for the American Humanist Association and the American Ethical Union.

After asserting that evolution has been well established scientifically and has therefore been "accepted into humanity's general body of knowledge by scientists and other reasonable persons who have familiarized themselves with the evidence," the statement maintains that creationism is a purely religious view. It is further asserted that since evolution is the only scientific, non-religious explanation for origins it is the only view that should be expounded in public school courses on science. The statement then reads:

"We, the undersigned, call upon all local school boards, manufacturers of textbooks and teaching materials, elementary and secondary teachers of biological science, concerned citizens, and educational agencies to do the following:

—Resist and oppose measures currently before several state legislatures that would require creationist views of origins be given equal treatment and emphasis in public-school biology classes and text materials.

—Reject the concept, currently being put forth by certain religious and creationist pressure-groups, that alleges that evolution is itself a tent of a religion of "secular humanism," and as such is unsuitable for inclusion in the public school science curriculum.

—Give vigorous support and aid to those classroom teachers who present the subject matter of evolution fairly and who often encounter community opposition."

The claim of these humanists and their allies that evolution is science and not religion may be refuted out of the mouths of evolutionists themselves. Thus Norman Macbeth has asserted flatly that Darwinism is not science *(American Biology Teacher,* November 1976, p. 496). Marjorie Grene states that "It is a *religion of science* that Darwinism chiefly held, and holds men's minds," *Encounter,* November 1959, p. 48). She further states (p. 49) that "The modified, but still characteristically Darwinian theory has itself become an orthodoxy, preached by its adherents with religious fervor, and doubted, they feel, only by a few muddlers imperfect in scientific faith."

That evolutionism is an integral part of the non-theistic religion of humanism is attested by literature produced by the humanists themselves. A pamphlet released by The Humanist Community of San Jose (California), a chapter of the American Humanist Association, quotes the following statement by Sir Julian Huxley, British biologist, evolutionist, and atheist:

> I use the word "Humanist" to mean someone who believes that man is just as much a natural phenomenon as an animal or plant; that his body, mind, and soul were not supernaturally created but are products of evolution, and that he is not under the control or guidance of any powers.

Humanism is thus an atheistic religion with evolution as its basic dogma. Evolutionists have devised a theory of origins that cannot be verified by either observation or test, and is thus not science. They have subtly interwoven this hypothesis into their non-theistic religion and have clothed the whole with a mantle they *call* "science." Evolutionists are peddling this package as pure science while vigorously denying the student's right to hear the creation alternative. As a result our young people are being indoctrinated in a materialistic, mechanistic philosophy. Many are being convinced that they are nothing more than a mechanistic product of a mindless universe.

In spite of these facts, creationists are not maintaining, as the statement falsely charges (apparently a scare tactic), that evolution theory is unsuitable for inclusion in public school science curricula. Creationists insist that wherever origins are discussed, either in science or in social science curricula, both models of origins should be considered.

That the American Humanist Association should assume leadership in the campaign against the creationists is most appropriate. Creationists have long emphasized that evolution is a dogma spawned primarily by a materialistic, atheistic philosophy. This action by the American Humanist Association is eloquent testimony to the truth of this assertion.

This campaign is also eloquent testimony to the effectiveness of the creationists in exposing the weaknesses and fallacies of evolution theory while at the same time establishing the tremendous scientific case for creation. Cracks in the neo-Darwinian Jericho are widening, and evolutionists are becoming alarmed. They are responding with lavish application of scientific authoritarianism, vulnerable scientific arguments, and all the pressure they can muster.

Evolutionists control our educational and scientific establishments. They dominate most publishing facilities and the news media. They have the use of many millions of dollars of tax money each year, while creationists have no public funds available but are totally dependent on the financial support of interested individuals. Creationists, however, have one tremendous advantage. They have the truth on their side.

The Creation Research Society was founded in 1963 beginning with just ten members. The Bible-Science Association was founded a year later, and the Institute for Creation Research was founded barely seven years ago. No one would have dared to dream what has been accomplished in the few years since. Furthermore, with

God's help, what has been accomplished in this past decade will seem puny compared to what will be accomplished in the next decade or two as a whole new generation becomes aware of the scientific case for creation and contributes a rapidly growing number to the ranks of informed convinced creationists.

THE HUMANIST TO PUBLISH
ARTICLE BY DR. GISH

The editor of *The Humanist,* the bimonthly publication of the American Humanist Society, has informed us that the article Dr. Duane Gish wrote in response to the January/February issue of *The Humanist* will be published in the November/December issue of *The Humanist.*

The January/February issue of *The Humanist* was devoted to the creation/evolution controversy, especially as it relates to the public school system, and contained a number of strongly anti-creationist articles.

In response to a request from Dr. Gish, Dr. Paul Kurtz, the editor of *The Humanist,* graciously consented to the publication of a reply by Dr. Gish. Because of previously established priorities, the article was restricted to 1500-2000 words. Copies of this forthcoming issue may be obtained by sending $2.00 to *The Humanist,* 923 Kensington Avenue, New York 14215. Copies of the January/February issue may be obtained for $2.50.

ATTACK ON CREATIONISTS AT
HUMANIST ASSOCIATION CONVENTION

The American Humanist Association continues its attack on creationists which was launched in the pages of its publication *The Humanist* in the January 1977 issue. That issue of *The Humanist* announced the issuance of a statement to all major school boards in the U.S. that endorsed evolution theory as an accepted principle of science and urged these boards to reject efforts to include the evidence for creation in their educational programs. Included also in this issue was an article by Dr. Preston Cloud, University of California-Santa Barbara geologist, which was an attack on creationists, particularly the ICR staff.

On Saturday evening of April 30, at the 36th Annual Conference of the American Humanist Association, Dr. Cloud gave a public address "In the Beginning," which the AHA announced as a "hard-hitting attack on the Book of Genesis and the Creationist movement." Creationists should be pleased that their efforts have been successful enough to draw the ire and concerted opposition of members of this atheist-agnostic organization. They can be certain that organized resistance to their efforts (to curtail the exclusive teaching of an evolutionary humanistic religion in public schools and to reestablish a balance in our public educational system by presenting in an unbiased manner the evidence for both theories of origins) will greatly increase as further victories are won.

HELP US RESPOND TO THIS ATTACK

The Institute for Creation Research will supply free of charge a packet of material to all parents and other individuals who will personally present this material to their local school board. This material will document the scientific, educational, philosophical, legal, and Constitutional basis for teaching both models of origins, creation and evolution, in public schools.

GOVERNMENT AGENCY
REVEALS EVOLUTIONIST BIAS

According to recent newspaper accounts, a distinguished anthropologist has been "denied a federal research grant because his subject challenges the Darwinian theory of man's descent from prehuman ape ancestry." Dr. Anthony Ostric, a professor at St. Mary's College of Notre Dame University, is threatening legal action against the National Endowment for the Humanities because this government agency has repeatedly turned down his research proposal, which would include gathering evidence from libraries, museums, anthropological expeditions, and prehistoric sites, with the purpose of reappraising the evidence related to man's "Bio-psychic and socio-cultural development."

His proposal has been rejected on the grounds that it "never clearly stated what were the possible alternatives to the application of evolutionary principles to human cultural developments." (Mention of creation as an alternative, no doubt, would have disqualified his proposal on the grounds that it was "religious"). Nevertheless, as Dr. Ostric asks, "How can scientists speak with certainty of a missing link between prehuman ape ancestors and us when they are unable to show even a single link?"

SCIENTIFIC AMERICAN ARTICLE MENTIONS ICR AND MISQUOTES DR. MORRIS

The increasing importance of creationism in the academic world was recognized by the nation's most widely read science journal, *Scientific American,* in its lead article for April 1976, "The Science Textbook Controversy," by Dorothy Nelkin, a professor at Cornell University. It referred to the increasing number of creationist scientists and organizations, although the only ones mentioned by name were Dr. Morris and the Institute for Creation Research. Several excerpts from Dr. Morris' writings were quoted or misquoted, though without specific credit in most cases.

Dr. Morris wrote a "letter to the editor" in response to the article, and the *Scientific American* editors indicated they would probably publish it. However, it was *not* included with the several letters on the article, with a reply by Nelkin, published in the July issue, so it may not be published after all. Since a number of readers of *Acts and Facts* have inquired about these items, Dr. Morris' letter to the *Scientific American* editors is reproduced below:

May 3, 1976

Editor, *Scientific American*

As one of the "scientific creationists" mentioned in Dorothy Nelkin's article ("The Science-

Textbook Controversies,'' April, 1976), as well
as a long-time appreciative reader of *Scientific
American,* I would like to clarify certain points
in her exposition. With regard to my challenge
to BSCS Director, William B. Mayer, to participate in a creation/evolution debate, Ms. Nelkin
wrote that I had ''proposed that the winner of
the debate would be determined by the applause
from the audience.''

This misleading information could only have
have been obtained from Dr. Mayer, since the
letter containing this challenge was a personal
letter written to him. The actual paragraph stated
(see enclosed photocopy of the original letter):
''A decision as to the winner could be made,
either by a panel of impartial judges or by
audience applause. If you would prefer, we can
simply present arguments without any formal
decision as to the winner.'' The purpose was to
give Dr. Mayer full freedom to decide how, or
whether, a ''winner'' of the debate should be
determined.

Of course, Dr. Mayer declined the challenge
anyway, even though he had made numerous
untrue statements about the Creation Research
Society (of which I then was president), as well
as biased and distorted statements about scientific creationism in general, in his BSCS Newsletter
of November, 1972. Evolutionists insist on being
recognized as careful scientists and having their
philosophy promoted as confirmed scientific
fact, but they quickly become careless and emotional when dealing with creationist scientists
and their arguments. Evolutionists still insist that
creationists are religious fundamentalists, incapable of proposing serious scientific objections
to the ''naturalistic religion'' (J. Huxley) of
evolution. It does seem that Ms. Nelkin, despite
her commendable attempt to be analytical and

fair, has fallen into the same patronizing routine.

Although Dr. Mayer refused to defend evolution in a formal debate on its *scientific* merits, many other evolutionists have not been so fearful. In the past three years, over 35 such debates have been held on major university campuses, with qualified scientists on both sides of the debate, and with audiences totalling at least 40,000 students. The creationists never discuss the Book of Genesis, although the evolutionists frequently try to do so. In every case, the response from these student audiences indicated enthusiastic agreement that creationists do have respectable scientific arguments and evidences, which depend in no way at all on the Bible or on religious beliefs.

If the current generation of establishment evolutionary scientists persist in their refusal to take creationism seriously, at least we know that the next generation will be different. The heavy hand of humanistic evolutionary dogma has hindered real scientific advance for too long, and thousands of students are becoming aware of this unhealthy situation.

Henry M. Morris
Director, Institute for Creation Research

ICR MIDWEST CENTER INAUGURATED

A regional center to promote the activities and program of ICR, known as the ICR Midwest Center, has recently been established with offices in Wheaton, Illinois. Its first general meeting, a breakfast with Dr. John Moore, held at Wheaton Christian High School on November 22, 1975, was attended by almost 100 people. Over 250 others heard Dr. Moore at classes at the Wheaton Evangelical Free Church and at the Wheaton Bible Church.

Dr. Moore explained in some detail why he takes the

Biblical account of creation literally, versus the commonly accepted Christian views of theistic evolution and progressive creationism. The basis of this comparative discussion consisted of data from the fields of genetics, taxonomy, and the fossil record. He also showed that the historical evolutionary geologic column doesn't actually exist anywhere and therefore the pressure to accept the column as a proof of evolution can be ignored as far as any compelling scientific evidence is concerned.

Harvey Chrouser, Chairman of the Physical Education Department of Wheaton College, was Master of Ceremonies and took a firm stand for Biblical creationism in his remarks. Paul MacKinney, David D'Armond, and Robert Van Kampen each made brief remarks concerning their areas of responsibility as officers of the ICR Midwest Center. Mrs. Lorayne Schaffer reported on the Milwaukee area creationism seminars which she had helped organize, and shared some "how to" tips gained from her experience. Mrs. Schaffer will lead in organizing future seminars in the region.

Response to the initial mailing from the Center was encouraging. Over 240 homes, churches, and groups responded, with many offers to help in various areas of responsibility. If others in this region are interested in helping to promote seminars, teaching creation in schools, encouraging creationist literature distribution, etc., the address of the ICR Midwest Center is P.O. Box 75, Wheaton, Illinois 60187, and phone number 312-668-1790.

"WILL THE ANTICIPATED ALIGNMENT OF PLANETS IN 1982 CAUSE PHYSICAL UPHEAVALS ON EARTH?"
By Henry M. Morris, Ph.D.

Answer: An interesting phenomenon of the 1970's has been the spate of best-selling books on topics of a quasi-scientific nature—books on unidentified flying objects, extraterrestrial astronauts, demon exorcism, astrological omens, the Devil's Triangle, Bigfoot, scientology, transcendental meditation, psychokinesis, etc. Some or all of these concepts are deeply involved in occultism, and some in plain deception.

However, one such topic of considerable public concern has been proposed as a serious scientific study, with little if any overtones of this kind. This is the so-called "Jupiter Effect," according to which all nine planets in the solar system will be aligned on the same side of the sun in roughly a straight line in 1982. This theory, advocated by two scientists, John Gribbin and Stephen Plagemann in a book published in 1974, says that the combined gravitational pull of all nine planets on the sun will cause tidal forces on the sun which will create an unusually large number and intensity of sunspots.

This effect will in turn cause a solar eruption which will so interact with the earth's atmosphere as to change its rate of rotation. The latter phenomenon, finally, will trigger devastating earthquakes and volcanic activity all over the earth.

This theory of the "Jupiter Effect" (so named because Jupiter is the planet of greatest mass) has not been taken seriously by scientists, but has been appropriated by a number of Bible teachers as proof that the Great Tribulation will begin soon. The Bible, especially the book of Revelation (6:12; 11:13; 16:18, 20), does predict that many great earthquakes will occur on the earth in this future period of judgment. The sun also will burn more intensely (Revelation 16:8), and there will be other physical convulsions on the earth.

However, the Scriptures do not indicate that these catastrophes will be caused by an alignment of planets, or any other naturalistic cause, but rather by the direct activity of the holy angels. There is no way to calculate the date of the coming of Christ (Matthew 24:36; Mark 13:32), and calculating the date of the Tribulation, which is directly connected with the coming of Christ, amounts to an attempt to do just that.

Furthermore, there is no sound scientific basis for the idea that the hypothetical Jupiter Effect will amount to anything significant. An astronomer, Jean Meeus, has shown that the four major planets (Jupiter, Saturn, Uranus, and Neptune) will not be aligned in 1982 at all, but will span an arc of one-sixth of the sky. He has also calculated that the total tidal effect on the sun would be 2.7 million times smaller than the tides raised by the moon on the earth. There is no evidence that such minute gravitational effects would generate sunspots, nor that these would produce earthquakes on the earth even if they did.

It is interesting that the authors calculated 179 years as the interval between such alignments of the nine planets. If so, however, it is noteworthy that the anticipated devastating earthquakes have not been experienced on these imaginary cycles. Since they have not occurred on past alignments, there is no reason to fear them in 1982.

ICR REPORT FOR 1975

All of us at ICR are continually amazed at the many doors of opportunity opened by God in recent years for this unique ministry. Though our limited staff and resources make it impossible for us to accept more than a small fraction of these opportunities, we are grateful for what has been accomplished. A statistical list may be cold and impersonal, but the numbers do represent many minds and many lives that have been strengthened in Christ. With this in mind, the following is a brief summary of the major activities at ICR during 1975.

Teaching, Speaking, Debating, etc.
(H. Morris, Gish, Slusher, Lester, J. Morris)

Creation-evolution debates: 12

Creation-evolution lectures at colleges: 127 (at 65 different colleges and universities)

Creation seminars (each involving five to ten lectures): 22 cities (in 15 different states and 5 foreign provinces)

Messages in churches: 115

Lectures in high schools: 75

Lectures at scientific meetings, educational meetings, etc.: 15

Summer Institutes (each involving 30 hours of lecture): 3
Weekly radio broadcasts ("Science, Scripture, and Salvation"):52
Other radio and television broadcasts: 60
Teaching ten courses (45 lecture-hours each) at Christian Heritage College

Writing and Publication

Publication of *The Troubled Waters of Evolution* (H. Morris)
Publication of *Introducing Scientific Creationism into the Public Schools* (H. Morris)
Third printing of revised edition of *EVOLUTION: The Fossils Say NO!* (Gish)
Second printing of *Scientific Creationism* (ed. by H. Morris)
Second printing of *Many Infallible Proofs* (H. Morris)
Publication of ICR monthly magazine *Acts and Facts*
Articles published in other journals: eight
Completion of writing for *The Genesis Record* (H. Morris)
Completion of writing for *Noah's Ark: the Search Goes On* (LaHaye and J. Morris)
Completion of writing on two technical monographs
Continued progress on writing of history textbook, earth science textbook, two technical monographs, audio-visual materials, teaching modules on creationism, evolution-creation handbook, etc.

Research

Field research at two sites of anomalous fossil footprints
Continued contact with officials, as well as other efforts, in connection with Noah's Ark project
Field research at contact planes of two locations of out-of-order geologic formations
Continuing review of current scientific literature for new information relevant to Bible-science correlation

In September, Lane Lester, Harold Slusher, and John

Morris became (unsalaried) regional extension scientists for ICR (along with Stuart Nevins, Richard Bliss, and Earl Hallonquist), leaving Dr. Gish and Dr. Morris as the only full-time scientific staff members, along with approximately ten (full-time equivalent) support personnel (not including the staff at Creation-Life Publishers), all of whom are vital for the efficient operation of ICR.

Dozens of letters and calls received weekly testify of people won to Christ or strengthened in their Christian faith and witness through the ICR literature and teaching ministries. We are thankful to the Lord for the privilege of serving in this way, and thankful also to the many friends who have helped make it possible through their prayers and gifts.

ICR ANNUAL REPORT
1976 AN OUTSTANDING YEAR
By Henry M. Morris

It is hard to summarize the many 1976 activities of the Institute for Creation Research in a brief report. Although a mere listing of statistics may not seem very inspirational, the facts and figures are exciting when translated into the thousands of lives that have been touched. In any case, some of the statistics are as follows.

I. *Books Sponsored and Completed in 1976*
　　1. Albert Hyma and Mary Stanton, *Streams of Civilization,* 420 pages, (also teacher's guides for public and Christian schools).
　　2. Henry M. Morris, *The Genesis Record,* 716 pages.
　　3. Richard Bliss, *Origins: Two Models, Evolution and Creation,* 59 pages, (also teacher's guides and transparency sets for public and Christian schools).
　　4. Henry M. Morris and Martin E. Clark, *The Bible Has the Answer* Revised and Enlarged Edition, 392 pages.
　　5. Tim F. LaHaye and John D. Morris, *The Ark on Ararat,* 287 pages.
　　6. Henry M. Morris and Duane T. Gish, *The Battle for Creation,* 322 pages.

    7. Marlyn E. Clark, *Our Amazing Circulatory System,* 66 pages.

II. *Other Writing Ministries*
1. Monthly newsletter, *Acts and Facts,* published and sent to approximately 50,000 each month.
2. Weekly radio transcripts printed and sent on request. (Approximately 150 sent out each week.)
3. Approximately 15 newspaper and periodical articles.
4. Approximately 70,000 copies of previous ICR books *(Many Infallible Proofs, Evolution: The Fossils Say No, Scientific Creationism, The Troubled Waters of Evolution, Adventure on Ararat,* and others) sold in 1976.

III. *College and University Meetings*
1. Creation-Evolution Debates: 18 (including San Diego State University, University of California at Santa Barbara, University of Massachusetts, University of Illinois, Kansas University, University of Maryland, etc.).
2. Other lectures: 85 (at 48 different colleges and universities).

IV. *Creation Courses, Workshops, etc.*
1. Course in Scientific Creationism (6 sem.-hrs. credit) offered twice at Christian Heritage.
2. Summer Institutes on Scientific Creationism (2 sem.-hrs. cr.) held at Ozark Bible College and Christian Heritage College.
3. Night course in *Bible and Science* (2 sem.-hrs. cr.), held at Van Nuys Christian College.
4. Teachers' Workshops on Creationism: 8 (30 lectures).
5. Lectures at Scientific Meetings: 9.

V. *Creation Seminars*
1. Number of locations: 24 (in 15 states).
2. Number of lectures: 112.

VI. *Other Meetings*
1. Churches: 75 (in 22 states).
2. High schools, youth groups, etc.: 30.

VII. *Radio, Television, etc.*

1. Weekly ICR Program, "Science, Scripture and Salvation," now heard on 61 stations in 28 states, plus shortwave overseas to over 100 countries.
2. Guest speaker (Morris) for week of "Chapel-of-the-Air" broadcasts.
3. Radio debate between Dr. Gish and Madalyn Murray O'Hair.
4. Forty other radio appearances.
5. Ten television appearances.
6. Appearance in movie "In Search of Noah's Ark" (J. Morris, Bliss, H. Morris).
7. Cassettes of messages and lectures distributed: approximately 10,000.

In addition, the ICR staff has spent many hours in personal counseling and in answering letters from all over the world. There is no way of calculating how many have heard the message of creation and its implications. The largest single audience, 3500, was at the Kansas debate, but there have been at least 30 other meetings where the attendance was over 1000, not to mention the unknown thousands reached via radio, television, newspaper, books, etc. The spiritual impact, as well as the educational and scientific impact, of the ICR ministry is a cause of real thanksgiving to God for such blessing.

ALBERTA LECTURES BY WILSON DRAW HUGE CROWDS

A one-week tour in late February across Alberta Province by Dr. Clifford Wilson drew a total of over 12,000 people, representing the largest creationist project ever undertaken in the province, so far as known. The tour was sponsored by the Creation Science Association of Alberta and included meetings in eight cities. The largest crowd, estimated at 3,000, was in Edmonton, with 2900 at Prairie Bible Institute in Three Hills and over 2,000 in Calgary.

3,000 people pictured here at the Jubilee Auditorium in Edmonton, Alberta, to hear Dr. Clifford Wilson.

Dr. Wilson, an Australian archaeologist and author (best known for his *Crash Go the Chariots)* spoke mainly on archaeological confirmations of the Old Testament and on refutations of the "chariots of the gods" idea.

RADIOHALOS INDICATE RAPID CREATION

In a recent article,[1] some of the very significant work of Robert Gentry on radiohalos is reviewed, together with comments on its significance by various well-known scientists. Gentry has been working at the Oak Ridge Laboratories of the Atomic Energy Commission for many years, and has unquestionably become the top experimentalist in this field.

One of the most significant of Gentry's discoveries has been the fact that "halos" produced by the radioactive decay of the element polonium occasionally exist in nature independently of its parent elements uranium and thorium. Since polonium has a very short half-life, this phenomenon

[1]Stephen L. Talbot, "Mystery of the Radiohalos", *Research Communications Network*, February 10, 1977, Newsletter #2, pp 3-6.

seems to require an almost instantaneous crystallization of the rocks in which they are found, simultaneously with the snythesis or creation of the polonium atoms. Otherwise the polonium would have disappeared and no halos could have been produced and preserved. The data, in other words, seem to require an instantaneous creation of the earth's primordial crust.

The scientists who were willing to comment on the significance of these data were unequivocally opposed to the rapid creation explanation, but were unable to offer any alternative.

THE RETURN OF HOPEFUL MONSTERS
By Henry M. Morris, Ph.D.

This is the title of a remarkable recent article by Stephen Jay Gould in the June-July issue of *Natural History*. Dr. Gould is Professor of Geology and Paleontology at Harvard and is one of the world's current leaders of evolutionary thought. Along with a number of other modern evolutionists, Gould has recognized the failure of neo-Darwinism (slow and gradual evolution by small beneficial mutations preserved by natural selection) and has been advocating what he calls "punctuated equilibria" (rapid evolution in small populations followed by stability in large populations) to explain the universal gaps in the fossil record.

But now, in trying to imagine a mechanism for this rapid evolution, Gould is actually predicting a refurbishing of Richard Goldschmidt's long-ridiculed "hopeful monster" mechanism. Goldschmidt was an outstanding geneticist who, realizing that mutations normally produce monsters, nevertheless believed that occasional small genetic changes could generate *hopeful* monsters, by which, for example, a bird could suddenly be produced from a reptile's egg! Says Gould: "As a Darwinian, I wish to defend Goldschmidt's postulate that macroevolution is not simply microevolution extrapolated and that major structural transitions can occur rapidly without a smooth series of intermediate stages." (p. 24).

Of course, both Goldschmidt and Gould were driven to such an extremity as hopeful monsters by the intractable facts of the fossil record, which they have been honest enough to acknowledge. As Gould says in another article: "The extreme rarity of transitional forms in the fossil record persists as the trade secret of paleontology.—We fancy ourselves as the only true students of life's history, yet to preserve our favored account of evolution by natural selection we view our data as so bad that we never see the very process we profess to study," *(Natural History,* May 1977, p. 14).

The creationist, however, does not have to invent such bizarre explanations for the gaps in the fossils. The creationist *predicted* the gaps! They provide positive evidence for the creation model.

CREATION SOCIAL SCIENCE AND HUMANITIES SOCIETY

The Creation Social Science and Humanities Society (C.S.S.H.S.) has been incorporated by members of the Mid-Kansas Branch Chapter of the Bible-Science Association as a new arm in Creationism, paralleling the work of the Creation Research Society. The C.S.S.H.S. is educational and will promote and disseminate information on the implications of the Bible creation model of origins for the social sciences and humanities, with emphasis on the development of these disciplines in accordance with the rapidly emerging and increasingly well established scientific models of Biblical creation.

The C.S.S.H.S. will publish a Quarterly journal directed toward teachers and students of the social sciences and humanities, especially books, monographs, and other writings, and sponsor speakers, seminars, and research projects, related to its educational purpose.

Dr. Paul D. Ackerman, who has served as chairman of the Mid-Kansas Branch Chapter of the Bible-Science Association since the summer of 1975, and was one of its founding members, has been elected president of the new organization. Dr. Ackerman is assistant professor of psychology at Wichita State University. Articles, book reviews and other contributions are invited for the forthcoming C.S.S.H.S. Quarterly, and should be sent to the C.S.S.H.S., Attn. Dr. Ackerman, 1429 N. Holyoke, Wichita, KS 67208. Inquiries regarding further details on the work of the C.S.S.H.S., membership, etc., should be sent to the same address.

CHRISTIAN HERITAGE COLLEGE HAS RECORD ENROLLMENT

Beginning only its eighth year of operations, Christian Heritage College (the research division of which is ICR) registered its largest enrollment to date, with a total of 437 students signed up for its first module of classes beginning on August 29, 1977. Of these, there are 149 students from outside California, coming from a total of 22 different states and 8 foreign countries.

To accommodate the record enrollment, the temporary administration building had to be converted back to its originally-intended use as a dormitory. The offices of the Institute for Creation Research have been moved to temporary quarters until completion of the College's beautiful new Educational and Research Building, scheduled for occupancy about October 1.

Dr. Henry Morris, Academic Vice-President of the College as well as ICR Director, brought the annual Convocation message on Sunday, August 28, speaking on the theme: "The Battle for the Mind."

ARCHAEOPTERYX DESTROYED AS LINK

Evolutionists for many years have insisted that Archaeopteryx was a transitional form between reptile and bird. Although Archaeopteryx had wings, feathers identical to the feathers of modern birds, a bird-like skull, and perching feet, evolutionists maintain that he had many reptilian features. In fact it is said by many present day evolutionists that if Archaeopteryx had not been feathered he would be classified as a reptile.

A recent discovery, however, has demolished Archae-opteryx as a transitional form.

Science-News (Vol. 112, Sept. 24, 1977, p. 198) announced the discovery of the remains of an undoubted true bird some "60 million years older" than Archae-opteryx (which the article terms a "winged dinosaur!"). This assessment was made by Dr. James A. Jensen of Brigham Young University. Prof. John H. Ostrom of Yale University was quoted as saying that "It is obvious that we must now look for the ancestors of flying birds in a period of time much older than that in which Archae-opteryx lived." Ostrom thus concedes that Archaeopteryx was not the ancestor of birds.

Time and time again, evolutionists have cited Archae-opteryx as *the* example of a transitional form. Now Archaeopteryx has been destroyed as a transitional form. Evolution becomes more and more untenable as scientific evidence accumulates.

Chapter 6
Director's Column

The following are selected from the Director's Columns published periodically in Acts and Facts. This column is written by Dr. Henry M. Morris, Director of ICR.

THE ILLOGICAL THEOLOGICALS

It is inexcusable for revolutionary scientists to accept evolution as a scientific fact, when all the *facts* of science conflict with evolution and support creation, but at least we can understand their desire to find a naturalistic origin for everything. They feel it to be the peculiar mission of science to explain all physical reality without God. Though we disagree with this idea, we can comprehend it.

But what can we say about those theologians who are

evolutionists? Why should those whose specialty is "the study of God" (for that is what "theology" means) attempt to explain things without God (for that is what evolution purports to do)? Is this strange behavior occasioned because "they love the praise of men more than the praise of God" (John 12:43)?

They apparently suppose that evolution may be God's method of creation, but this is a serious charge to bring against God. Evolution is the most wasteful, inefficient, cruel way that one could conceive by which to create man. If evolution *is* true, we certainly should not blame God for it!

The famous scientist-philosopher, Bertrand Russell, had some incisive comments to make about such evolutionist theologians in his well-known atheistic book, *Religion and Science:*

> Religion, in our day, has accommodated itself to the doctrine of evolution, and has derived new arguments from it. We are told that "through the ages one increasing purpose runs," and that evolution is the unfolding of an idea which has been in the mind of God throughout. It appears that during those ages which so troubled Hugh Miller, when animals were torturing each other with ferocious horns and agonizing stings, Omnipotence was quietly waiting for the ultimate emergence of man, with his still more widely diffused cruelty. Why the Creator should have preferred to reach his goal by a process, instead of going straight to it, these modern theologians do not tell us. Nor do they say much to allay our doubts as to the gloriousness of the consummation.

But can't we be *Christian* evolutionists, they say. Yes, no doubt it is possible to be a Christian evolutionist. Likewise, one can be a Christian thief, or a Christian adulterer, or a Christian liar! Christians can be inconsistent and illogical about many things, but that doesn't make them right.

We are thankful for the great numbers of godly theologians who are true to the Scriptures, as well as to the real facts of science, and who therefore are strong creationists. We are concerned and sad for those out-of-character theologues who are not.

GENETIC INHERITANCE AND THE SIN NATURE

In a recent *Impact* article, it was pointed out that God must have performed a miracle of creation at the time of the conception of Christ in Mary's womb. This article[1] apparently stirred more interest than almost any we have published, with pastors and teachers ordering thousands of copies for distribution in their churches. Many have written indicating that the article has been of real help to them in resolving the scientific difficulties associated with the doctrines of the virgin birth and the divine-human nature of Christ. The ideas expressed in the article were not original with me, of course, but I am grateful that they have been found helpful by so many.

On the other hand, there have been a number of readers who have taken exception to the article, and several have written lengthy expositions opposing it. Since the available time simply precludes my answering and analyzing each of these expositions individually, and since other readers may have some of the same questions, I have decided to give a partial reply in this column, dealing here with the main problems with which these writers were concerned.

Their primary concern was that such a miracle of creation would somehow dilute the doctrine of the true humanity of the Lord Jesus. These men felt that Jesus would have to have possessed Mary's genes in order to be

---

1. *Impact* No. 30, "Creation and the Virgin Birth," December, 1975; the reader should study that article and this column together.

really human. If His body had been specially created, then they could not understand how He could really have been "touched with the feeling of our infirmities" and "in all points tempted like as we are" (Hebrews 4:15).

I would suggest, however, that such doubts may be due to our limited confidence in God's ability to **create!** To say that God could not create a truly human body for the Lord Jesus is to deny His omnipotence. Was the body which He created for Adam not a human body? Adam had no genetic inheritance from either mother or father, but he was surely a man! Why could this not be as true of the second Adam as of the first Adam?

That God did indeed in some miraculous way form such a human body (**perfectly** human, in fact) is evident from the Scriptures. "Wherefore in all things it behoved Him to be **made like** unto His brethren, . . . " (Hebrews 2:17). He was "**made** of the seed of David according to the flesh" (Romans 1:3). " . . . a body hast thou **prepared** me" (Hebrews 10:5). He was "**made** in the likeness of men" (Philippians 2:7). "The Word was **made** flesh . . . " (John 1:14).

Note, however, that this flesh was not **sinful** flesh. Rather, He was "in the **likeness** of sinful flesh" (Romans 8:3). In every other way, it was real human flesh. Prior to the entrance of sin into the world and prior to the curse on the ground, Adam's divinely formed body needed food and rest, and this was true of the divinely-formed body of the second Adam as well. Furthermore, since all of the very elements of the earth later came under the curse (Genesis 3:17, Romans 8:22), that curse must have affected those atoms and molecules which were gradually added to Jesus' body as it grew from the embryonic state into maturity, as well as the food He ate and air He breathed. He was, indeed, "touched with the feeling of our infirmities."

It is certain, however, that these infirmities did not include sin—either acts of sin or a sin-nature. He "did no sin," He "knew no sin," and "in Him is no sin" (I Peter 2:22, II Corinthians 5:21; I John 3:5). Neither can we allow even the bare possibility that He **could** have sinned. Though He is true man, He also is very God, and He did not in any wise relinquish His deity when He became man. He is not part man and part God, or sometimes man and sometimes God. Once He became incarnate in human flesh, He became **eternally** the God-man—all man and all God! Since "God cannot be tempted with evil" (James 1:13), the temptation of Christ (though a real **testing,** in the sense that His impeccability had to be demonstrated to all creation as genuine) could not possibly have resulted in sin on His part. For if He **could** have sinned, then God **might** indeed have been defeated by Satan. But this is unthinkable to one who truly believes in God as the omnipotent Creator of all things.

It was absolutely essential, therefore, that His human body be free of an inherited sin-nature, and even from mental or physical defects resulting from inherited mutations. Biologically and genetically, there was no way this could be assured except by a miraculous conception, so accomplished that none of the sinful and defective attributes of **either** parent could be transmitted to Him.

The question is—how could this be done? All who believe in the virgin birth recognize that a miracle was required—but what kind of miracle? Could it be merely a providential statistical juggling of Mary's genes so that those which carried the "sin-factor," as well as specific physical and mental defective mutations were somehow screened out? Hardly, because **all** of Mary's genes (no less than those of Joseph) would have been carriers of sin. There is neither biological nor theological basis for thinking that sin affects only certain genes and chromosomes and not others.

No, a "Grade A" miracle[2] is absolutely required, a

---

[2]A "Grade A" miracle involves setting aside one or both of the two laws of thermodynamics, creating either matter or energy or a higher degree of order. A "Grade B" miracle involves a providential control of the various factors affecting a particular phenomenon, but operating within the framework of the two laws of thermodynamics. For a discussion of this subject, see *Biblical Cosmology and Modern Science,* Baker Book House, 1970, pp. 37-45.

miracle of creation. Some suggest that this miracle was performed on Mary herself so that all her genes were made immaculate. Others suggest that the miracle was performed only on the genes in the particular egg cell which the Holy Spirit "artificially inseminated" with an immaculate sperm cell of His own creating. Still others think that Mary's egg cell was somehow purified by the Holy Spirit of all inherent sin and defects and then, caused to grow by a process of parthenogenesis.

Actually, any or all of these amount to the same thing as direct creation! The body formed in Mary's womb either must have been specially created or else all of the genes in Mary's egg must have been specially re-created, one or the other. In either case, there could have been no direct transmission of physical, mental or spiritual characteristics (all of which, in every man and woman, are contaminated by sin) from Joseph or Mary or David or Adam. To say otherwise is to imply that the Lord Jesus Christ received a sin-nature by inheritance, and this would disqualify Him as Savior.

But this wonderful miracle of creation in no way detracts from His full humanity. He experienced the same complete human life experienced by every other person, from the moment of conception to the moment of death— **except for sin!** Furthermore, He still occupies His human body, now resurrected and glorified. He is "holy, harmless, undefiled, separate from sinners, and made higher than the heavens." "Wherefore He is able also to save them to the uttermost that come unto God by Him" (Hebrews 7:25, 26).

CREATION IN THE CHRISTIAN SCHOOL

Although a considerable part of ICR's activity is aimed at the restoration of creationism in the nation's public schools and state universities, we realize this is difficult to accomplish and is a long-range goal rather than one quickly attainable. Though nothing is impossible with God, and it is our obligation to do all we can in this area for the honor of the Creator and for the sake of the millions of young people involved, it does seem realistic to anticipate that evolutionism will continue to dominate the secular scientific and educational establishments for many years to come.

In the meantime, many private Christian schools have been raised up, and new ones are being started every week. This is also a difficult undertaking—financially, academically and spiritually—but one which is tremendously needed and is being greatly used today. I would strongly advise parents to send their own children to Christian schools if at all possible, even while they continue to do all they can to restore sound morality and educational practices to the public schools of their communities.

In the public schools, for example, we urge that creationism be taught as an alternative to evolutionism, not on a religious basis but strictly on a scientific basis. This is a reasonable approach in a tax-supported institution, and the only one which is feasible in our present society.

In a private Christian school, however, this "neutral" approach is neither necessary nor desirable. Although students in such schools should be taught **about** evolution, the curriculum should stress throughout that creation is the only Biblical position and the only realistic scientific position as well. As a matter of fact, one major reason for the establishment of a Christian school in the first place is so that the educational process can be centered in the truth of God as Creator and Redeemer of all things. As Dr. Paul Kienel, Executive Director of the Western Association of Christian Schools, says: "Christian school students are **exposed** to the philosophy of evolution and they are **taught** the Biblical account of creation or the **creationist view.**" *(America Needs Bible Centered Families and Schools,* 1976, p. 103. Emphasis is his).

One of the problems Christian schools have faced, however, is the difficulty of obtaining the right kind of teachers and textbooks. Most Christian teachers have received their training either in secular colleges or in Christian colleges whose curriculum and emphasis is oriented to public school teaching. Many Christian colleges have, in fact, compromised their position on evolution to an alarming degree (See "Evolution in Christian Colleges," *Acts and Facts,* December 1974) and a "neo-evangelical" attitude naturally is transmitted to many of their graduates. However, there is an increasing number of education degree programs in Christian colleges which are strongly creationist and Bible-centered and oriented especially to preparing teachers for Christian schools (Christian Heritage College, of course is one of these). Administrators should be sure that all their faculty members are solidly committed to Biblical inerrancy, especially to strict creationism.

As far as textbooks are concerned, in most fields only evolutionary and humanistic textbooks have been available. This tragic lack is gradually being remedied. Some textbooks are now available which are either positively creationist or which present both evolution and creation (in order to be usable in public schools also). These include:

1. Biology, *Biology—a Search for Order in Complexity* (Zondervan, 1975) Teacher's Guide and Lab Manuals available.

2. Physical Science. *Physical Science for Christian Schools* (Bob Jones University Press, 1975), Teacher's Guide also available.

3. World History. *Streams of Civilization* (Creation-Life, 1976) Teacher's Guide and Home Study guide also available.

4. Teacher's Manual on Creationism. *Scientific Creationism,* (Creation-Life, 1974).

5. Student Unit Workbook on Creationism. *Origins: Two Models* (Creation-Life, 1976). Teacher's Guides available, one for public schools and one for Christian schools; overhead transparency set also available).

Other textbooks are in process of preparation. Although most Christian schools are anxious to use such textbooks as soon as available, we have found that a significant number seem to prefer to continue with the same old secular textbooks. Various reasons for this anomalous attitude are given (cost, work required by teachers to make changes, supposed lower quality or less up-to-date pedagogical approach of the Christian books, etc.) but none of these (even if they were valid) are significant compared to the overriding importance of the students having textbooks which provide them with a proper foundation of truth and purpose in their studies. Christian schools which fall into the snare of merely giving a secular education (public school curriculum, faculty with secular education, evolutionary textbooks, etc.) in a Christian environment will soon find the results are not worth the cost.

We urge Christian school teachers and administrators everywhere, as well as sponsoring churches and parents, to be sure to maintain and strengthen the creationist, Bible-centered, Christ-centered character of every aspect of their schools.

TEACHING CREATION IN THE CHURCHES

I believe true Christian pastors and teachers in churches everywhere should preach and teach frequently the doctrine of creation—not merely by incidental references in messages on other topics, but systematically and fully expounding this great truth, as revealed both in Scripture and in God's world. There are many reasons for emphasizing creation, but I would call attention especially to three urgent commands of Scripture to this effect.

1. *Guard the Faith!* These are days in which many in Christendom, even professing Christians, are departing from the Christian faith, which was "once for all delivered unto the saints" (Jude 3). Some have departed in the direction of cultisms and occultism (I Timothy 4:1), others in the direction of liberalism, humanism, and general ungodliness. (II Timothy 3:1-7). These trends will eventually become so widespread that the Lord Jesus had to ask the rhetorical question—"When the Son of Man cometh, shall He find the faith on the earth?" (Luke 18:8).

Now if one studies carefully the history of such apostasies, in all ages, he will find they always begin with the undermining of this doctrine of special creation. There is always an evolutionary cosmogony of some sort opposing the true Genesis record of the Creator and His creation attractively presented by the currently dominant philosophies in the name of "science" (this was as true with the ancient pagan philosophies as with the modern Darwinian philosophies; the Genesis record is the *only* cosmogony which begins with the transcendent God creating the very universe itself). This recurring tension between revelation and philosophy is inevitably followed by those men in the Christian world who seek to compromise. Compromise on special creation, however, is soon followed by a compromise on special inspiration and then a compromise on special incarnation, and so on; eventually this road of compromise ends in a precipice.

It is urgent, therefore, that each generation of pastors and teachers carefully transmit the full Christian faith to the next generation (II Timothy 2:2), especially its foundational doctrine of creation. The apostle Paul commanded, "Keep (literally *guard*) that which is committed to thy trust, avoiding profane and vain babblings (that is, ungodly and empty philosophies) and oppositions of science falsely so called" (I Timothy 6:20). The command to *avoid* such things does not mean to hide from them, but rather to keep the Christian faith utterly free from their contaminating influence! This can best be done by an informed and regular emphasis on Biblical creationism from both pulpit and classroom.

2. *Give the Answer!* In our day and age, when practically everyone has been indoctrinated in evolutionary philosophy most of his life, the Christian worker quickly finds that some application or other of this philosophy is the greatest obstacle to winning people to an intelligent and lasting conversion to Biblical Christianity. Most people realize that, if the first chapter of the Bible is unreliable or vague, there is no reason to take the rest of the Bible very seriously.

The command of the Apostle Peter is clear. "Be ready always to give an answer (literally, an *apologetic*—a systematic, logical, scientific defense) to every man that asketh you, a reason of the hope that is in you" (I Peter 3:15). Whatever problem an unbeliever may have with respect to the Christian faith, there *is* an answer! The Christian has not been asked to follow cunningly-devised fables. He must be saved by faith, of course, but that faith is a *reasonable* faith, founded on facts. It is not a credulous faith, like that of the evolutionist.

The Christian witness will not be ready always to give the answer, of course, unless he or she knows the answers. And they won't know them unless someone either teaches them or sees that they get them. This is the Scriptural function of the pastor and teacher (Ephesians 4:11-14).

3. *Preach the Gospel!* This command is the Great Commission, given by Christ to the church and to every believer. The Commission incorporates also the obligation to teach *all* things (Matthew 28:20) that Christ had taught (which obviously includes special creation), but it is even more important to realize that the Gospel itself must include the doctrine of creation.

The word "gospel" means *good news,* and it refers specifically in the New Testament to the glad tidings of all that Jesus Christ has done for mankind. This necessarily includes the entire scope of His work—past, present and future, from the creation of all things (Colossians 1:16) to the reconciliation of all things (Colossians 1:20).

It is significant that the final reference to the Gospel in the Bible is found in Revelation 14:6,7, in a context just prior to His glorious Second Coming. There it is called the "everlasting gospel" (thus stressing that it will be the same then as it is now), and the essential injunction is that men should "worship Him that made heaven, and earth, and the sea, and the fountains of waters." The everlasting gospel thus always stresses recognition of God as Creator, as well as Savior (the reference to "the fountains of waters" is probably a reference even to His sovereign judgment on sin during the great Flood—note

Genesis 7:10, 11).

The command to "preach the gospel to every creature" (Mark 16:15) therefore includes not only the substitutionary atonement and bodily resurrection of Christ (I Corinthians 15:1-4), but also—as a necessary foundational preparation (especially in the last days when there would be widespread denial of creation)—the great truth that God in Christ is the supernatural and omnipotent Creator of all things.

"Thou art worthy, O Lord, to receive glory and honor and power: for thou hast created all things, and for thy pleasure they are and were created" (Revelation 4:11).

CREATION AND PUBLIC OPINION

One of the characteristics of these latter days has been the emergence of the public opinion poll as a strong policy-making tool. Television programming is largely dependent on the famous "Nielsen ratings" and politicians seem to base their campaigns and programs almost entirely on a wide assortment of popularity polls conducted, supposedly, by scientific statistical techniques of opinion sampling.

So far as we know, neither the Gallup poll nor the Harris poll nor any other "official" sampling agency has conducted a survey of public opinion on the issue of creation or evolution. Nevertheless, evidence is accumulating that such a poll would show that a large majority of American citizens would say—if they had the chance—that they favor including creation as an alternative scientific model of origins in the nation's public schools and colleges, rather than the present practice of teaching only evolution.

For example, in a semi-rural northern California school district, the Del Norte County District, the Citizens Committee for Scientific Creationism conducted a survey of 1346 homes in the county, showing that 89% favored the teaching of creation (see *Acts and Facts,* April, 1974). A few months later, a similar survey was carried out in the more cosmopolitan Cupertino school district, the largest in the state. This survey reached 2000 homes, and found that

84% favored teaching creation along with evolution. Both polls were conducted on a scientific statistical sampling basis (see *Acts and Facts,* July, 1974).

Members of the ICR Midwest Center, headquartered in Wheaton, Illinois, under its president, Paul MacKinney, have recently been conducting a random telephone survey on this question, asking people whether they favor the teaching of: (1) Creation and evolution both, as scientific models; (2) Creation only; (3) Evolution only. So far the survey has interviewed 526 people in five midwestern states, with the following results: favoring the teaching of both creation and evolution, 68%; wanting only creation taught; 15%; wanted only evolution taught, 6%; no opinion, 11%. Thus it is reasonable to conclude that at least 83% of the citizens in the midwest want creation taught in the schools at least as a valid alternative to evolution.

It is interesting that one-subsample of the above group was a random telephone survey of 56 dormitory students (mostly male) at the University of Illinois. This group showed 84% favoring the impartial teaching of both evolution and creation, 4% wanting only creation taught and 12% wanting only evolution taught. Even university students, exposed as they have been to nothing but evolutionary teaching, thus turned out to show 88% preferring to have creation added to their curriculum on at least an equal basis with evolution.

A similar random survey was conducted among dormitory students at the University of Kansas at Lawrence by the same student group that organized the recent creation-evolution debate there (see *Acts and Facts,* November, 1976). Of the 173 students polled, 87% thought creation should be taught at least equally with evolution, while only 13% thought the present practice of teaching only evolution should be retained.

Thus, whenever and wherever public opinion polls have been taken on this issue, it has been found that a large majority of people of all ages and backgrounds agree that the present system is wrong, and that scientific creationism should be taught in all public schools and colleges on at least an equal basis with evolution. This conclusion is the more remarkable because most of these people—like everyone else—had probably been themselves indoctrinated solely in evolutionary thinking by their own schools.

School administrators, textbook publishers, and others in a position to do something about this matter should take note of these facts. They should themselves assume the lead in re-introducing creationism into our public educational systems, rather than waiting until they are pressured to do so by concerned parents and citizens everywhere.

Readers of *Acts and Facts* are encouraged to organize similar public opinion polls in their own communities. Even if others cannot be enlisted in such an effort, any individual can easily make his own random telephone survey. He should phrase the question somewhat as follows: "I am helping conduct a random telephone survey. We are attempting to determine community opinion about how our public school system should handle the subject of origins. Please tell us which of the following three choices represents your opinion: (1) only the evolution model should be taught as the explanation of how things began; (2) only the creation model should be taught; (3) *both* the evolution model and the creation model should be taught as alternative explanations of origins."

Any person or group making such a survey should also send the results to the ICR Midwest Center, Box 75, Wheaton, Illinois, 60187, where Mrs. Paul MacKinney, Secretary of the Center, will be glad to keep the results tallied and analyzed on a nationwide basis. Such data should be helpful to any local group seeking to encourage their own school boards to pass creation-evolution equal time resolutions (see Impact Series 26, *Acts and Facts,* Vol. 4, No. 6).

THE FUTILE SEARCH FOR LIFE IN SPACE

Evolutionists have been eagerly awaiting the results of the landing of the Viking spacecraft on Mars, hoping to find some evidence of life there. In a recent symposium in *Science News* entitled "Life on Mars: What Could It Mean?" (Vol. 109, June 5 & 12, 1976, pp. 378-379), several scientists tell why they are so concerned. James Christian, of Santa Ana College, says "Biochemical evolution already implies that life is all over the universe. It seems to me . . . if the theories are correct, that any time we have a congenial environment and some of the right chemicals are there, including carbon, that given enough time, life will evolve."

Evolutionists reason that, since life has evolved on **this** planet, it must also have evolved elsewhere in the universe, wherever there is a planet with conditions comparable to those on Earth. However, there was no life on the Moon, and the evidence is all against any life on Venus or any of the other planets in the solar system. Mars is just about the evolutionist's last chance of finding support for his ideas of universal biochemical evolution, except for the rather forlorn hope of receiving some kind of intergalactic radio message from some unknown intelligence out there in space.

Astronomer Carl Sagan, who has been speculating about extraterrestrial life for many years, is hopeful that Martian life will convince people once and for all that life has evolved:

> If it turns out that there is life there as well, then, I would say, it would convince large numbers of people that the origins of life exist.

But suppose that the Martian landing does **not** produce evidence of life. Even the most convinced evolutionists agree that the odds against it are very high. Since finding life on Mars would be strong evidence **for** evolution, would failure to find life on Mars be strong evidence **against** evolution? Not at all! Says Viking Project Biologist Gerald Soffen:

> If we don't find life, it doesn't prove anything

other than that it's difficult to find life on Mars.
That's all. *(Ibid.)*

Whatever of real scientific value may be learned from
the Martian landing remains to be seen, but it is disturbing
that the main purpose of this immensely costly tax-
supported project is to prove evolution, with no consideration for the possibility of disproving it! Since evolution is
not true, however, the entire venture (except for certain
spin-off values) is redundant.

I am writing these words prior to the actual landing
but, by the time you read them, it should be apparent
once again that there is no evidence of biological life on
Mars or anywhere else except on earth. I have been maintaining for many years—as have most other creationists—
that all such searches for extraterrestrial life are bound to
turn out negatively. (See, for example, *That You Might
Believe,* 1946, pp. 123-124; *The Bible Has the Answer,*
1976, pp. 76-78; *Scientific Creationism,* 1974, p. 30; *The
Troubled Waters of Evolution,* 1974, pp. 168-171, etc.)

One does not have to be a prophet to make such predictions, of course. The simplest living organism is so complex that it could never evolve by chance processes anywhere in the universe in astronomic time (see *Scientific
Creationism,* pp. 59-69). Wherever life exists, it must have
been **created** by God! Refusal to believe in God as Creator
is the **only** reason for believing that life has evolved from
non-life on the Earth or anywhere else.

The only real question then is: **where** has God created
life? The answer must be based on the revealed truth
that God has created the earth uniquely for man (Psalm
115:16; Acts 17:20), and that all other forms of biological
life were created to be under man's dominion (Genesis
1:28).

It is on the Earth alone that God, Himself, became man
(John 1:14), where He died for the sins of every man
(Hebrews 2:9), from which He arose and ascended into
heaven (Ephesians 4:8-10), and to which He will return
(Acts 1:11). It is on this earth—not somewhere else in the

universe—that He will live and reign in the ages to come (Revelation 21:1-3). The **Earth**—not Mars or Alpha Centauri or Orion—is the center of God's interest in this universe. It is **man on Earth** who is the object of God's creative and redemptive work, a fact proved beyond question when He became man on Earth Himself!

CREATION IN THE NEWS

The creation-evolution issue has been in the news intermittently during the past decade, but the pace seems to be accelerating rapidly. The concern of parental and church groups in many school districts across the nation has developed to the point that large numbers of schools and school boards are now directly confronting the decision whether to include creation as an alternative to evolution in their curricula.

As a consequence, many newspapers and even national magazines have been publishing articles and editorials on the issue, in each case followed by numerous "letters-to-the-editor" on both sides of the question. Many readers of *Acts and Facts* have been sending us copies of these publications, with the request that either I or another ICR staff member write replies to them, particularly if they oppose creation teaching.

We are not able to do this, of course, simply because the increasing number of such articles makes it humanly impossible for our own limited staff to keep up with them. The best we can do is to provide the facts and basic literature which people can use as appropriate in the battle for creationism in their own localities.

As a matter of fact, local school administrators, news editors, and others will pay much more attention to good articles or letters written by their own constituents than to any communication from us here in San Diego. I would strongly urge you (or some sympathetic leader whom you can reach in your own community) to write articles or letters or take such other action as may be helpful in the specific circumstances in your area, using ICR books and other materials for reference resources as needed, and to write with grace and good humor, rather than with anger or sarcasm.

The following suggestions may be helpful in drafting such an article or letter.

1. Stress that creation is at least as *scientific* as evolution and evolution requires as much faith as creation (since evolutionists commonly oppose the teaching of creation on the basis that it is a religious theory, while evolution supposedly is scientific).

2. Point out that today there are thousands of qualified scientists, in addition to thousands of professionals in other disciplines, who are creationists (since opponents usually give the impression that creationists are only a peculiar fringe group).

3. Show that, whenever unbiased statistics have been collected (whether from housewives, college students, or other groups), a large majority—always over 80%, usually over 90%—favors the teaching of creation in public schools, while less than 10% thinks the present practice of teaching only evolution is right (since evolutionists frequently claim that creation is of concern only to a tiny group of fundamentalists).

4. Stress that creationists are not proposing to teach the "creation story of Genesis" in the schools, but only to show that the facts of science can be explained in terms of the scientific model of creation (without reference to Genesis) as well as they can by the evolution model (since evolutionists frequently raise the "Bible in public schools" spectre when discussing this issue).

5. Assure everyone that we are not trying to outlaw the teaching of evolution in the schools, nor opening the door to a wide range of ethnic "cosmogonies," but only to teach the *two* models of origins (there are only two—evolution and special creation—the so-called cosmogonies of different religions are all merely special cases of one or the other), whereas the present practice of indoctrinating young people only in the evolutionary philosophy is contrary to the Constitution, to civil rights, to freedom

of inquiry, and to true science and education.

This is such a reasonable and fair request that it is amazing that so many scientists, teachers, and other people of influence (even clergymen!) seem to oppose it so emotionally. Surely, as we make the facts better known, this anomalous opposition will change to surprised awareness and finally support for the revolutionary idea that perhaps the Creator could really have *created* things, after all!

THE BASIS OF TRUE EDUCATION

In this "back-to-school" issue of *Acts & Facts,* the theme of education is paramount. The humanists whose philosophies have controlled our educational systems for so long are going all-out to keep creationist evidences and arguments out of the public schools and, wherever they can, are trying hard either to capture or to close the Christian schools. On the other hand, there is no question that the vast majority of American citizens favor the retention of our present system of pluralistic education (both public and freely independent private schools) and that they favor a fair presentation of both alternatives (creation/evolution—theism/humanism) in the public schools.

While it is true that our national Constitution (supplemented by court decisions) precludes public school indoctrination in any particular sectarian religion, it most certainly does not preclude the teaching of creationism as an alternative to evolutionism or theism as an alternative to humanism in the public schools when these are taught objectively and scientifically, rather than dogmatically and Biblically.

If evolutionary humanists desire that their beliefs be taught exclusively, they should establish private schools for that specific purpose. Similarly, Christians have every right under the Constitution (as well as under God) to organize and operate schools and colleges where Biblical creationism and Christian theism can be taught fully and authoritatively to their children, without interference by the humanists who control the political and educational bureaucracies. In the public schools, supported as they are by all taxpayers, it is right and proper that *both* basic world-views be taught, as nearly equally and objectively as possible. This is one of the major goals of the modern creationist movement.

Concurrently with the goal of fairness in public education, however, there is also the even more urgent need to establish and maintain true Christian schools at every level, in which the full Biblical doctrine of education can be implemented in accordance with God's commands. Such schools are not antipathetic to our national Constitution or to the American way of life in any sense, but stress patriotism and the American heritage as well as a fully Biblical world-view in general. They can and should, of course, be solidly creationist, rather than using the "two-model approach" of teaching both creation and evolution on an equal-time basis, as should be done in the public schools.

In this connection, I have just completed what I hope may be a definitive work on the Biblical doctrine of education. Lest anyone misunderstand, this book *(Education for the Real World)* is not meant as a guide for educational philosophy in public schools, but only for Christian schools. Even in this domain, it will probably be controversial, but the intent at least is to expound and apply the scriptural criteria in all aspects of true education as defined in the Word of God. I hope that Christians will find it an informative and effective guide for this purpose.

AN INACCURATE CRITIQUE OF CREATIONISM

A noteworth example of academic arrogance is the recent book by Dorothy Nelkin entitled *Science Textbook Controversies and the Politics of Equal Time* (1977, 174 pp.). Published by the prestigious M.I.T. Press, this book attempts to analyze the creationist movement as a sociological phenomenon. Ms. Nelkin, an Associate Professor at Cornell, writes in the style of an objective scientist, but comes to the sophomoric conclusion that creationists are merely afraid of the sociological impact of science.

I do not want to deal with Ms. Nelkin's simplistic assessment of creationism, however, but only to call attention to the excessive number of factual mistakes with which the book abounds.

The following comprises a small sampling of such errors.

1. *Nelkin.* "According to creation theory, biological life began during a primeval period only five to six thousand years ago." (p. 61). *Fact.* Most creationists believe the creation was between 6000 and 10,000 years ago.

2. *Nelkin.* "Creationists believe that all subsequent variation has occurred within the genetic limits built into each species by the Creator." (p. 62). *Fact.* All creationist scientists stress that the created *kind* is significantly broader than the biologist's "species."

3. *Nelkin.* Table 5 (p. 63) showing a comparison between the evolution and creation models is attributed to an article "Creation vs. Evolution" by Henry Morris in *American Biology Teacher,* March 1973. *Fact.* The cited article was by Duane Gish, contained no such table or comparison, and had a different title.

4. *Nelkin.* "The American Scientific Affiliation— Formed mostly by Lutherans." (p. 65). *Fact.* The ASA was formed at the instigation of Dr. Will Houghton, president of Moody Bible Institute, a Baptist, and has never had more than a small percentage of Lutherans in its membership.

5. *Nelkin.* "(The founders of the Creation Research Society) had been members of the ASA, but left the organization when it refused to take a political position on the teaching of evolution." (p. 66). *Fact.* Only a part of the founding members of CRS had been ASA members, none left it when they formed CRS, and CRS has never taken a political position on anything.

6. *Nelkin.* "With the formation of other creationist organizations in California, CRS moved to Lansing, Michigan, where a branch had developed in the early 1960s." (p. 66). *Fact.* The CRS headquarters have been in Ann

Arbor, Michigan, ever since it was founded. It has never had branches in California or Lansing.

7. *Nelkin.* "Active Michigan members included a retired chemist from Dow Chemical, several science instructors from Concordia Lutheran College, and a professor of science education at Michigan State University." (p. 67). *Fact.* These particular members were then-active Director of Research at Dow Chemical, the President and the Professor of Natural Sciences at Concordia and a Professor of Natural Science at Michigan State.

8. *Nelkin.* "CRS supports a stable of speakers" (p. 67). *Fact.* CRS has never had a list of speakers nor sponsored any speakers.

9. *Nelkin.* "CRS soon split into several groups. In 1970, in a struggle over leadership, several members broke away to form Creation Science Research Center" (p. 67). *Fact.* There has never been a split in CRS nor was there a struggle for leadership, nor did any members break away to form the CSRC. After forming the CSRC, I continued to serve for several more years as CRS President, and am still on its Board of Directors. Initially formed as the research division of Christian Heritage College, the CSRC did later (1972) separate from the College, at which time our College research division was renamed the Institute for Creation Research.

10. *Nelkin.* "ICR . . . claims to leave promotional activities to other organizations." (p. 69). *Fact.* One of ICR's main functions has always been that of promoting creationism in the scientific and educational worlds.

11. *Nelkin.* "John Morris . . . is also full-time public relations director for the Institute." (p. 69). *Fact.* The ICR has never had a public relations director.

12. *Nelkin.* "Other Bible schools, such as Bob Jones University in Arkansas." (p. 70). *Fact.* Bob Jones University is in South Carolina.

13. *Nelkin.* "Henry Morris, Director of the ICR . . . served at one time as a professor of hydraulic engineering and chairman of the department of civil engineering at Virginia Polytechnic Institute (1957-1960)." (p. 71). *Fact.*

The dates were 1957-70, thirteen years, not three years.

14. *Nelkin.* "During his college training at Minnesota, he accepted evolution theory" (p. 71). *Fact.* This training and acceptance were at Rice; before my later graduate training at Minnesota, I had already published one book on scientific creationism.

15. *Nelkin.* "Collegial pressures eventually forced him out of the secular university setting" (p. 72). *Fact.* My decision to leave the secular university setting was not forced, although there had indeed been a number of unsuccessful attempts by V.P.I. evolutionists to accomplish this. My department had one of the largest enrollments and largest sponsored research programs of any in the university or of any civil engineering department in the country at that time and this was recognized by university administrators, who left me a standing invitation to return to the faculty. The decision to leave in 1970 was solely for the purpose of forming Christian Heritage College and its center for creation studies.

16. *Nelkin.* "In January 1973, Henry Morris . . . wrote to the director of the BSCS and challenged him to a public debate on the scientific aspects of the creation/evolution controversy . . . . The outcome, essentially, would be determined by audience applause." (p. 134). *Fact.* This challenge was issued to William B. Mayer because he had, in his BSCS magazine, devoted an entire issue to an attack on the creationists. Dr. Mayer and others (including Ms. Nelkin, in a *Scientific American* article) have ridiculed my supposed proposal that the outcome be determined by audience applause. The fact is that no such proposal was made and both Mayer and Ms. Nelkin know this. The actual proposal was simply that Mayer himself should select the method by which the debate winner, if any, should be decided.

The danger of such a careless book, of course, is that its purported scientific objectivity, its patronizing attempt to "understand" the feelings of those concerned about anti-Christian textbooks, and its publication by such a prestigious academic institution as M.I.T., will cause many good people to take its superficial analyses and conclusions seriously.

Chapter 7

Impact
Series
1976-1977

Each month *Acts and Facts* includes an "Impact" article which is generally, although not always, directed toward some scientific aspect of the question of origins. While Impact articles are generally technical in nature, each author attempts to render his Impact article comprehensible to the layman as well as the scientist. Copies of Impact articles are available in quantity from ICR, 2716 Madison Avenue, San Diego, California 92116, at 25 for $1.00. Single copies are free.

The first three Impact articles contained in this chapter are Impact Series Nos. 31, 33, and 37 on the Origin of Life written by Dr. Duane Gish. These appeared in the January, March, and July issues, respectively, of 1976. Other Impact articles appear in the order published.

Any references will appear at the end of each article.

Dr. Duane T. Gish is Associate Director of the Institute for Creation Research, in direct charge of all research and writing activities. Dr. Gish has degrees from both U.C.L.A. and the University of California at Berkeley (Ph.D., Biochemistry), as well as 18 years experience in biochemical and biomedical research at Berkeley, Cornell University, and the Upjohn Company.

No. 31, January, 1976

ORIGIN OF LIFE: CRITIQUE OF EARLY STAGE CHEMICAL EVOLUTION THEORIES*

Duane T. Gish, Ph.D.

According to a mechanistic, naturalistic view of the universe, and thus of origins, the whole of reality is evolution—a single process of self-transformation. Everything in the universe, according to this view, has evolved from a primordial chaotic or random state of matter. This evolutionary continuum thus requires that life arose on this planet (or on some planet, at least) from inanimate matter via chemical and physical processes still operating today. It is generally believed that these processes acted for many tens of millions of years, most likely hundreds of millions of years, before true cellular life was brought into being.

The first thing that may be said about theories on the origin of life is that none satisfy the criteria of a scientific theory. There were no human observers of the origin of life, and it is impossible to reenact the process. If such a process did occur, it could have left no fossil record or history. There is no way to observe or test any postulated evolutionary origin of life. All such theories are mere postulates, all related laboratory experiments are mere

*An elaboration of this material in much greater detail may be found in Dr. Gish's monograph, "Speculations and Experiments Related to Theories on the Origin of Life." Creation-Life Publishers, 1972.

exercises in organic chemistry. This has been acknowledged even by a number of prominent evolutionists. Thus, Bernal, in a discussion of a paper by Mora, states " . . . Dr. Mora has shown that the principles of experimental science do not apply to discussions on the origin of life, and indeed cannot apply to any problem of origin."[1]

The immensity of the problem is rarely appreciated by laymen, and is generally ignored by evolutionary scientists, themselves. The simplest form of life imaginable would require hundreds of different kinds of molecules, perhaps thousands, most of them large and very complex. With respect to this point, Van Rensselaer Potter states, "It is possible to hazard a guess that the number is not less than 1,000, but whether it is 3,000 or 10,000 or greater is anyone's guess."[2] This statement not only acknowledges the immensity of the problem, but also is a tacit admission of how little is really known or knowable about the problem.

In addition to these many molecules, which would include the large and complex protein, DNA and RNA molecules, each with up to several hundred subunits arranged in a precise sequence, the origin of life would require many complex and dynamically functional structures, such as membranes, ribosomes, mitochondria (or energy-producing complexes of some kind), etc. Furthermore, life requires marvelous coordination in time and space, with many regulatory mechanisms. To believe that all of this came about by mere chemical and physical processes, does indeed constitute an immense exercise of faith.

In spite of the highly speculative nature of all origin of life theories, and the utter hopelessness of ever testing, let alone establishing, any comprehensive origin of life theory, a not insignificant proportion of our nation's scientific resources is being devoted to exploring these speculations. Much of the rationale for the design and objectives of our space program is related to this purpose. Thus, a recent publication of the National Aeronautics and Space Administration states "Recognizing that many scientific secrets still lie hidden throughout the solar system, NASA has a program of solar system exploration aimed at answering the following questions: (1) How did our solar system form and evolve? (2) How did life originate and evolve? (3) What are the processes that shape our terrestrial environment?"[3] Instructional material for high schools published by NASA include sections on chemical evolution. [4,5]

Many laboratories, supported by government and university funds, are devoted to pursuing origin of life theories. Laboratory exercises and the speculations that have inspired them have resulted in a large number of publications and national and international symposia. The latter have generated a number of symposia proceedings.[6-10] Beginning with the pioneer but classic work of Oparin,[11] a number of books have been written on the origin of life, a few of which are listed.[12-17] The book by Miller and Orgel[17] is recommended because it is especially well-written and because of the greater candidness of the authors in discussing the problems encountered in this field. Also available are a number of reviews[18-22] and critical and theoretical discussions.[23-25] Creation scientists, in addition to many articles published in the *Creation Research Society Quarterly* and elsewhere, have published a number of critical works.[26-28]

Primitive Earth Scenario

Origin of life theories require a primitive earth model that includes conditions that would tolerate postulated chemical reactions which are believed to have been involved in processes leading to the origin of life. It is the general consensus of geologists that the oceans would have formed rapidly, and thus early in the earth's history, and it has been generally assumed that the pH and temperature of the ocean would always have been approximately the same as at the present time. Evolution of life theorists are forced to postulate, however, that the primitive earth atmosphere was very different from the present atmosphere.

The present atmosphere consists of about 78% nitrogen, 21% oxygen, and 1% of other gases, including argon, carbon dioxide, and water vapor.

Present Atmosphere

Carbon dioxide CO_2
Nitrogen N_2
Oxygen O_2
Water H_2O

Postulated Primitive Atmosphere

Methane CH_4, Carbon Monoxide CO,
Carbon dioxide CO_2
Ammonia NH_3, Nitrogen N_2
Hydrogen H_2
Water H_2O

If the primitive earth atmosphere contained a significant quantity of oxygen, however, an evolutionary origin of life would have been thermodynamically impossible, since all substances would have been oxidized to carbon dioxide, water, nitrogen, and other oxidized products, leaving no organic chemical compounds to serve as precursors for biochemical evolution. Evolutionists are thus forced to assume, *a priori,* that the primitive earth atmosphere contained no oxygen, but rather contained hydrogen, and that carbon existed mainly in the form of methane and/or carbon monoxide.

Even some evolutionists have found difficulties with these assumptions, however. Brinkman has maintained, for example, that a high rate of photolysis of atmospheric water vapor by ultraviolet light would have generated a significant quantity of oxygen very early in the earth's history,[29] and Davidson has stated his conviction that there is no evidence that the atmosphere ever differed greatly from that of the present.[30] If this is so, then a naturalistic origin of life could be eliminated without further discussion.

At the very least, the assumption of a methane-ammonia atmosphere, which has served as the basis for most origin of life experiments, including many of those currently being performed, appears to be untenable on the basis of known facts. Abelson has pointed out that there is no geochemical evidence that the atmosphere ever contained methane, and that the rapid photolysis of ammonia to nitrogen and hydrogen by ultraviolet light would have reduced it to a negligible concentration.[31] Others have also concluded that atmospheric ammonia would have been far less than that employed in origin of life experiments.[32,33]

Abelson postulates a reducing atmosphere (i.e., devoid of free oxygen) in which carbon was mainly in the form of carbon monoxide, nitrogen existed as free nitrogen, and in which free hydrogen existed instead of free oxygen. One can arrive at such a conclusion only by employing a series of highly speculative assumptions, however. A reducing atmosphere is required for an evolutionary origin of life, so it is simply assumed by evolutionists to have existed.

There would have been much more energy available than required for these syntheses, most of it in the form of radiant energy from the sun, with minor amounts from electrical discharges, thermal sources, and radioactivity.[23]

Synthesis of Relatively Simple
Organic Chemical Compounds

The metabolism of even the simplest form of life imaginable would have required a wide variety of metabolites for its energy sources and other needs. Furthermore, vast quantities of amino acids, the building blocks or subunits of proteins; purines, and pyrimidines, constituents of DNA and RNA; and sugars, constituents of complex carbohydrates and of DNA and RNA, would have been required. Even if the dubious assumption is made that a primitive ocean system would have contained only 10% as much water as the present ocean, that would still amount to about 35 million cubic miles of water. Efficient methods of producing these compounds would have had to exist, then, since many billions of tons of each would have been required to give a significant concentration in such a vast body of water.

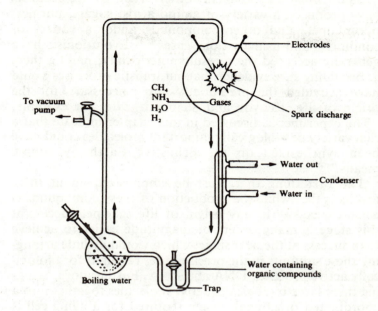

Figure 1. *The Miller "origin of life" apparatus.*

In 1953 Stanley Miller announced the first successful synthesis of amino acids and of a few other simple organic chemical compounds under assumed primitive earth conditions.[34] Miller circulated a mixture of methane, ammonia, hydrogen, and water vapor through an apparatus containing an electrical discharge chamber. Products of the reaction were collected in a cold trap. After circulating the gases for about a week, Miller analyzed the aqueous solution in the trap. He found that it contained glycine and alanine, the two simplest amino acids, plus small amounts of two other amino acids, glutamic acid and aspartic acid. In addition to these amino acids, which are constituents of proteins, several other non-protein amino acids, as well as a number of amines and acids were found.

Since Miller's experiment, other origin of life chemists have produced a variety of amino acids, sugars, purines, pyrimidines, and other compounds under a variety of conditions and using various gases.[9-17] Evolutionists have generally accepted these results uncritically, hailing them as providing sure evidence that naturalistic processes would have provided the prebiotic "soup" necessary for the origin of life. Kenyon and Steinman state, for example, "The experiments discussed in this chapter indicate that a rich variety of biologically important molecules could have been synthesized on the primitive Earth by simple means."[35]

The first thing that must be emphasized about these results is that while the production of these compounds is a vital necessity in any origin of life scheme, success at this stage is many orders of magnitude easier to achieve than success at the next stage, which would include arranging these subunits in the precise order required for biologically active proteins, DNA and RNA. Furthermore, bringing these large biologically active molecules together into a coordinated functional system required for a living cell is again many orders of magnitude more difficult and less likely. In other words, even if these results are accepted uncritically, they are trivial in view of the immensity of the overall problem.

Secondly, the success that was achieved in these experiments, limited as this actually may have been, was due to special conditions imposed by the research scientists, conditions that would not have existed on the primitive earth. In all origin of life experiments in which significant quantities of amino acids and other products have been produced, a trap or some means was used to isolate the product from the energy source used for the synthesis. In Miller's experiment,[34] for example, products produced in the sparking chamber were swept into a trap which isolated the non-volatile products. The gases continued to sweep through the sparking chamber, any minute quantity of non-volatile products being immediately trapped out and isolated so that they were no longer exposed to the energy source. Without this feature, no detectable quantity of product would ever have been produced.

Any energy source, in the above case the heat and radiant energy produced by the electrical discharge, is far more efficient in the destruction of the products than in their production, the quantum yield of destruction being many times the quantum yield in the synthetic step.[36,37] Furthermore, the amount of radiation available from the sun at the wave lengths at which these gases absorb (below 1500 angstroms), and thus available for synthesis, is less than one-thousandth of the light (up to 3500 angstroms) absorbed by the products, and thus available for destruction. The overall result is that destruction is 10,000 to 100,000 times more effective than production.

The time required for any products produced in the atmosphere to reach the ocean would have been several years.[36,37] During that time these products would be subject to the destructive effects of ultraviolet light, electrical discharges, and cosmic rays. Unfortunately, there were no organic chemists on the primitive earth to trap out products. Practically none of the products therefore would reach the surface of the earth in significant quantity.

Even the ocean would provide no haven of safety, for rates of destruction there would far exceed the rates at which these compounds could have become involved in further syntheses.[37,38] With reference to rates of destruction in the ocean, Miller and Orgel state: "The rates of depurination of DNA, of hydrolysis of peptide and polynucleotide polymers, and of decomposition of sugars, are so large that it seems impossible that such compounds could have accumulated in aqueous solution and have been used in the first organism, unless the temperature was low."[39] Later on, these same investigators state that because of the instability of organic compounds, there is a compelling argument that life could not have arisen in the ocean unless the temperature was below 25°C. They state that a temperature of 0°C would have helped greatly and that -21° would have been even better (at this temperature the ocean would have been frozen solid).

Thus, even if these compounds could have survived transit from the atmosphere to the ocean, which is contraindicated by all available evidence, these prominent origin of life chemists assert that these compounds could not have survived there unless the temperature of the ocean was about 0°C or lower. Could the ocean have been that cold four billion years ago on a ball that is supposed to have been cooling from a molten state for four and a half billion years to reach its present state, which still retains a large molten core? If the temperature were low enough to prevent the more facile destructive reactions, how could further reactions leading toward the origin of life have occurred? When origin of life theorists finally face up to the real facts, they are forced to make assumptions that are increasingly untenable.

The accumulation of significant quantities of even these simple organic chemical compounds seems definitely to be precluded, then, by the fact that their rates of destruction in the atmosphere and in the ocean would have far exceeded the rates at which they could have accumulated by synthesis. Hulett, in his excellent paper, after carefully and thoroughly considering all facets of the problem says, "It is in fact hard to reconcile the thermodynamics and kinetic characteristics of these compounds with the postulated pathways for chemical evolution in the primitive environment."[40] He still believes, nevertheless, that life must have evolved at least once, because life does, in fact, exist.

Hull, in his research, calculates that vanishingly small quantities of these relatively simple chemical compounds could have accumulated in the primitive ocean. His calculations showed, for example, that the simplest amino acid, glycine, would have had a concentration as low as 10^{-24} molar, which is negligible, and that glucose, a six-carbon sugar, more complex than glycine and thus harder to form but more easily destroyed, would have had a concentration of 10^{-134} molar, which means that the chances of finding a single molecule in the entire ocean would have been essentially nil. Hull concluded that: "The physical chemist, guided by the proved principles of chemical thermodynamics and kinetics, cannot offer any encouragement to the biochemist, who needs an ocean full of organic compounds to form even lifeless coacervates.''[37]

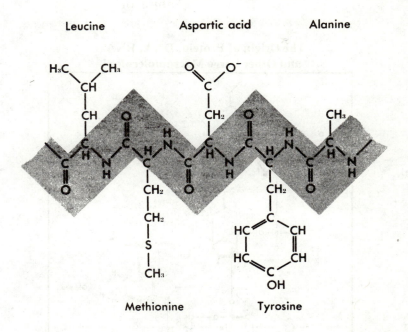

Figure 2. *A short section of a protein.*

There are yet a number of other serious problems. Amino acids react with sugars with mutual destruction of each, yet each would have been needed for the origin of life—amino acids to form proteins and sugars as consti-tuents of DNA and RNA. Phosphoric acid is a constituent of DNA and RNA as well as a constituent in other im-portant compounds. All of the phosphoric acid in the primitive ocean, however, would have been precipitated as the insoluble calcium salt.

It does indeed appear that even at the level of simple organic chemical compounds, there would have been chemical, thermodynamic, and kinetic barriers to processes required for the origin of life. In fact, if origin of life theorists carefully considered proven scientific principles, there would be no origin of life theorists.

The Origin of Protein, DNA, RNA and Other Large Macromolecules

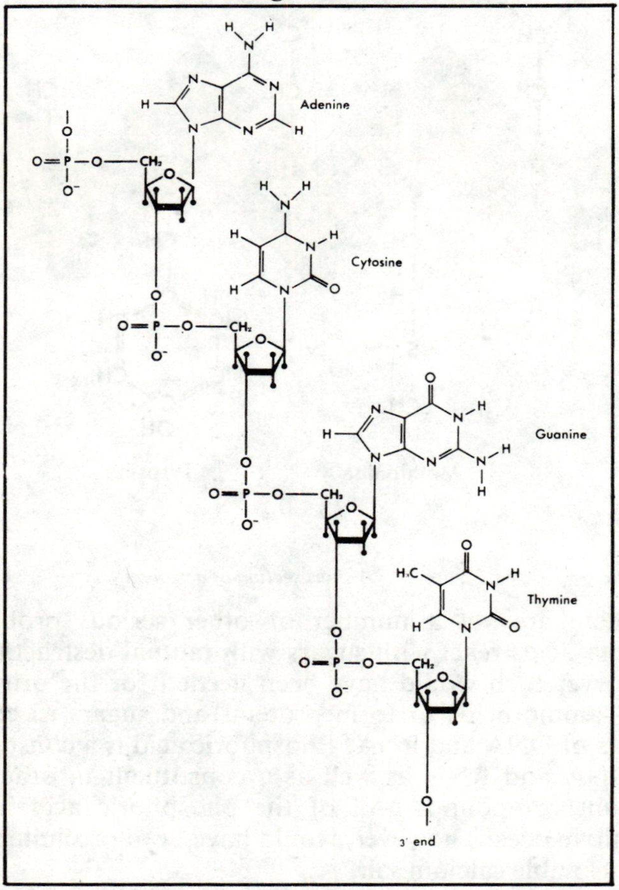

Figure 3. *A short section of a DNA molecule.*

The origin of a significant quantity of the large, complex macromolecules—proteins, DNA, RNA, and complex carbohydrates—is a problem that dwarfs all earlier problems, as impossible as their solution may seem. Huge quantities, billions of tons, of each of these molecules that eventually became involved in living systems, would have had to have been produced. These molecules generally have from more than one hundred to several hundred subunits arranged in precise sequence in the case of proteins, and up to several thousand precisely ordered subunits constituting the links in the chain. The subunits, or links, in proteins consist of amino acids. Of the hundreds of amino acids that are chemically possible, only 20 are found in proteins. The subunits of DNA, which make up the genetic material or genes, and of RNA, material used by the cell to translate the genetic messages contained in the genes into the specific structure of proteins and other structures found in living things, consist of four different kinds of nucleotides, units which include a sugar, phosphoric acid, and one of four purines or pyrimidines.

Thermodynamic Barrier to Polymerization

The first problem involved in the origin of these large complex molecules is the fact that there is a thermodynamic barrier to their spontaneous synthesis by chemical and physical processes. The formation of the chemical bonds between amino acids to form proteins; or between sugars, phosphoric acid, and the purines and pyrimidines to form nucleotides; and between the nucleotides to form DNA and RNA, requires an input of energy. Rupture of any of these bonds, on the other hand, releases energy. What happens naturally and spontaneously, therefore, is not the formation of these compounds, but their destruction. Automobiles do not spontaneously run uphill, they spontaneously run downhill. To drive an automobile uphill requires the expenditure of energy, and specific means must be used to utilize that energy, namely a complex engine and drive train. As long as this mechanism is operating, the automobile can be driven uphill, but if the motor stalls, or the automobile runs out of gas, it promptly runs back down to the bottom of the hill. So it would have been with these complex molecules.

Only what could have happened naturally and spontaneously would have happened on the primordial earth. Proteins and DNA and RNA do not form naturally and spontaneously, but if they do exist, they spontaneously disintegrate. How then could they ever have formed on the hypothetical primitive earth by natural processes? What mechanism or machinery could have existed on the primordial earth to force the synthesis of these molecules, to force chemical processes to run uphill against all the natural forces that would tend to make them run downhill? On the face of it, this problem defies explanation. Although a variety of attempts have been made to solve the problem, no plausible explanation has yet appeared.

This discussion will continue in the next article in this series on the origin of life which will appear in a future issue (No. 33).

REFERENCES

1. J.D. Bernal, in *The Origins of Prebiological Systems and of Their Molecular Matrices,* Ed. S. W. Fox, Academic Press, New York, 1965, p. 52.
2. Van Rennselaer Potter, "Bioethics," in *Perspectives in Biology and Medicine,* Autumn 1970, p. 139.
3. W.R. Corliss, *The Viking Mission to Mars,* National Aeronautics and Space Administration, Washington, D.C., 1974, p. 2.
4. F.S. Ruth, Ed., *Space Resources for Teachers: Biology,* National Aeronautics and Space Administration, Washington, D.C., 1969.
5. R.M. Lawrence, Ed., *Space Resources for Teachers: Chemistry,* National Aeronautics and Space Administration, Washington, D.C., 1971.
6. S.W. Fox, Ed., *The Origins of Prebiological Systems and of Their Molecular Matrices,* Academic Press, New York, 1965.
7. L. Margulis, Ed. *Origins of Life I,* Gordon and Breach, New York, 1970.
8. L. Margulis, Ed. *Origins of Life II,* Gordon and Breach, New York, 1971.
9. A.P. Kimball and J. Oro, Eds., *Prebiotic and Biochemical Evolution,* North-Holland, Amsterdam, 1971.
10. L. Margulis, Ed., *Origins of Life: Chemistry and Radioastronomy,* Springer, New York, 1973.
11. A.I. Oparin, *The Origin of Life on the Earth,* Academic Press, New York, 1957.

12. J. Keosian, *The Origin of Life,* Reinhold Pub. Co., New York, 1964.
13. J.D. Bernal, *The Origin of Life,* World Pub. Co., Cleveland, 1967.
14. M. Calvin, *Chemical Evolution,* Oxford U. Press, New York, 1969.
15. D.H. Kenyon and G. Steinman, *Biochemical Predestination,* McGraw-Hill, New York, 1969.
16. S.W. Fox and K. Dose, *Molecular Evolution and the Origin of Life,* Freeman Pub. Co., San Francisco, 1972.
17. S.L. Miller and L.E. Orgel, *The Origins of Life on the Earth,* Prentice-Hall, Englewood Cliffs, New Jersey, 1973.
18. N.H. Horowitz, F.D. Drake, S.L. Miller, L.E. Orgel, and C. Sagan, "The Origins of Life" in *Biology and the Future of Man,* Ed. P. Handler, Oxford U. Press, New York, 1970.
19. R.M. Lemmon, "Chemical Evolution," *Chemical Reviews,* Vol. 70, pp. 95-109 (1970).
20. C. Ponnamperuna, "Primordial Organic Chemistry and the Origin of Life," *Quarterly Review of Biology,* Vol. 4, pp. 77-106 (1971).
21. E. Stephen-Sherwood and J. Oro, "Recent Syntheses of Biorganic Molecules," *Space Life Sciences,* Vol. 4, pp. 5-31 (1973).
22. N.H. Horowitz and J.S. Hubbard, "The Origin of Life," *Annual Review of Genetics,* Vol. 8, pp. 393-408 (1974).
23. H.R. Hulett, "Limitations on Prebiological Synthesis," *Journal of Theoretical Biology,* Vol. 24, pp. 56-72 (1969).
24. M. Eigen, "Self Organization of Matter and the Evolution of Biological Macromolecules," *Naturwissenschaften,* Vol. 58, pp. 465-523.
25. S. Black, "A Theory on the Origin of Life," *Advances in Enzymology,* Vol. 40, pp. 193-234 (1973).
26. A.E. Wilder-Smith, *The Creation of Life,* Harold Shaw Publishers, Wheaton, Il. 1970.
27. D.T. Gish, *Speculations and Experiments Related to Theories on the Origin of Life: A Critique,* Institute for Creation Research, San Diego, 1972.
28. D. England, *A Christian View of Origins,* Baker Book House, Grand Rapids, Michigan, 1972.
29. R.T. Brinkman, "Dissociation of Water Vapor and Evolution of Oxygen in the Terrestrial Atmosphere," *Journal of Geophysical Research,* Vol. 74, p. 5355 (1969).
30. C.F. Davidson, "Geochemical Aspects of Atmospheric Evolution," *Proceedings National Academy of Science,* Vol. 53, p. 1194 (1965).
31. P.H. Abelson, "Chemical Events on the Primitive Earth," *Proceedings National Academy of Science,* Vol. 55, pp. 1365-1372 (1966).
32. J.P. Ferris and D.E. Nicodem, "Ammonia Photolysis and the Role of Ammonia in Chemical Evolution," *Nature,* Vol. 238, pp. 268-269 (1972).
33. J.L. Bada and S.L. Miller, "Ammonium Ion Concentration in the Primitive Ocean," *Science,* Vol. 159, pp. 423-425 (1968).
34. S.L. Miller, "A Production of Amino Acids under Possible Primitive Earth Conditions," *Science,* Vol. 117, pp. 528-529 (1953).
35. Reference 15, p. 158.
36. Reference 23, p. 60.
37. D.E. Hull, "Thermodynamics and Kinetics of Spontaneous Generation," *Nature,* Vol. 186, pp. 693-695 (1960).
38. Reference 23, p. 61.
39. Reference 17, p. 126.
40. Reference 23, p. 70.

No. 33, March, 1976
ORIGIN OF LIFE: THE FOX THERMAL MODEL
OF THE ORIGIN OF LIFE
Duane T. Gish, Ph.D.

In the first article (*Impact* No. 31, "The Origin of Life—
A Critique of Early Stage Chemical Evolution Theories,"
January, 1976) of this series on origin of life theories,
following the discussion of problems involved in a naturalistic origin of relatively simple organic compounds, the
problem of the origin of large molecules ("macromolecules"), such as the proteins, DNA, and RNA, was introduced. It was pointed out that one of the insuperable
barriers to the accumulation of significant quantities of
these very complex molecules (even assuming that the
ocean was populated with huge quantities of the necessary
chemicals) was the fact that energy is required to form the
chemical bonds between the units in these long-chain compounds.

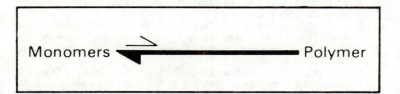

Figure 1.

As a consequence, there is, practically speaking, no tendency for these compounds to form, but, on the other
hand, they very readily tend to fall apart or disintegrate.
What happens naturally and spontaneously, then, is that
proteins break up into their constituent amino acids, and
DNA and RNA tend to break up into fragments, and
eventually into their constituent groups—a sugar, phosphoric acid, and purines and pyrimidines. If proteins,
DNA, RNA, and other complex macromolecules arose on
the hypothetical primitive earth by naturalistic processes,
some mechanism would have had to exist to drive this

process in the direction opposite to that which it tends to go. This mechanism would have had to be very efficient, since many billions of tons each of many different kinds of proteins, DNA, and RNA would have to be produced to provide enough of these vital compounds for the origin of life in an ocean containing somewhere between 35 and 350 million cubic miles of water.

Fox's Thermal Model

The suggestion that has gained more attention than all others is the idea of Sidney Fox. Fox has published papers on various aspects of his thermal theory in numerous scientific journals and in many books, a few of which are listed in the bibliography of this paper.[1-5] An outline of Fox's theory can be found in practically every modern high school and college text on biology, evolution, and related subjects. Recently a review volume was published in honor of his 60th birthday.[6] And yet if anything in science is certain, it can be said that however life arose on this planet, it did not arise according to the scheme suggested by Fox. One could not be judged to be too unkind or critical if he were to label Fox's suggestion as pseudoscience.

Fox uses intense heat as the driving mechanism in his model. In the laboratory demonstration of Fox's origin of life scheme, a particular mixture of pure, dry amino acids are heated at about 175°C (water boils at 100°C) for a limited time (usually about six hours). Intense heating is then ceased, and the product is stirred with hot water, and insoluble material is removed by filtration. When the aqueous solution cools, a product precipitates in the form of microscopic globules, which Fox calls proteinoid microspheres. Analysis of this material shows that it consists of polymers, or chains, of amino acids, although of shorter lengths than are usually found in proteins. Some of these globules resemble coccoid bacteria, and others bulge and superficially appear to be budding similar to certain microorganisms.

Fox claims that his proteinoid microspheres constitute protocells (that is, they are almost, but not quite, true cells), and were a vital link between the primordial chemical environment and true living cells. He claims that the amino acids in these polymers are not randomly arranged as would be expected, but that a few highly homogenous (having identical chemical structure) protein-like molecules are obtained with their amino acids arranged in a precisely ordered sequence. He further claims that these compounds possess detectable catalytic or enzyme-like properties. Finally, Fox claims that these microspheres multiply by division somewhat in the manner of true cells.

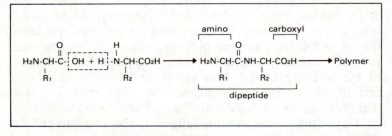

Figure 2.   *The above reaction represents the formation of dipeptide, which contains only two amino acids. The average protein contains several hundred amino acid residues. To form such a protein, the above reaction would be repeated many times as the amino acids are added successively to the end of the chain.*

When asked where on the primordial earth a locale could be found where amino acids might have been heated at about 175°C, Fox suggests that such a locale would have been found on the edges of volcanoes. When it was pointed out that heating at that high a temperature (not much reaction occurs at temperatures much below 175°C) would cause complete destruction of the products if heating continues much beyond six hours, Fox suggests that rain might occur just at the right time to wash away the products.

Fox's scheme would require such a unique series of

events and conditions, the probability of which would be so vanishingly small that it could be equated to zero. These are the following:

1. Heating at a high temperature for a limited amount of time.

Fox's suggestion that the combination of the edges of volcanoes with rain at just the right time would suffice to produce billions of tons of these polymers has been severely criticized even by numerous evolutionists.[7] Miller and Orgel point out that when lava solidifies, the surface of the lava is hardly warmer than air temperature. In discussing this feature of Fox's model they say, "Another way of examining this problem is by asking whether there are places on the earth today with appropriate temperatures where we could drop, say, 10 grams of a mixture of amino acids, and obtain a significant yield of polypeptides . . . . We cannot think of a single such place."[8] Even if there were such places, they would be so limited in extent, and the timing of the rain would be so restrictive (not much less nor much more than six hours from the time heating begins), that the rate of production would be very much less than the rate of destruction by hydrolysis and other degradative reactions once the products were washed into the ocean or other bodies of water.

2. Fox's reaction mixture consists solely (as far as organic material is concerned) of pure amino acids.

Where on earth could a mixture of pure amino acids be found? Only in the laboratory of a twentieth-century scientist! According to the chemical evolutionary scheme to which Fox and every other origin of life theorist subscribes, however, a great variety of organic chemical compounds, numbering in the thousands and most likely many tens of thousands, would have been produced on the primordial earth. The probability of a mixture of pure amino acids accumulating anywhere, assuming that they were being produced, would be absolute zero. Any amino acids produced would be admixed with sugars, aldehydes, ketones, carboxylic acids, amines, purines, pyrimidines, and other organic chemicals. Heating amino acids at almost any temperature with a mixture of such chemicals would be certain to result in complete destruction of the amino acids. Beyond question, no polypeptides or proteinoids would be produced. This factor alone completely eliminates Fox's scheme from any rational discussion.

3. A totally improbable ratio of amino acids is required.

If random proportions of amino acids are heated, no product is obtained. A very high proportion of one of the acidic amino acids, aspartic and glutamic acids, or of the basic amino acid, lysine, is required. Generally, about one part of one of the acidic amino acids, or one part of lysine, a basic amino acid, is heated with two parts of all the remaining amino acids combined. Under no naturally occurring conditions would any such ratio of amino acids ever exist. In all origin of life laboratory experiments, the amino acids produced in highest ratios are glycine and alanine, the simplest in structure and therefore the most stable of all the amino acids. Aspartic and glutamic acids are generally produced, but in small proportions. Detectable quantities of lysine are rarely, if ever, produced. Again, Fox's scheme is completely out of touch with reality.

4. Serine and threonine are mainly destroyed.

Two of the most commonly occurring amino acids in proteins consist of serine and threonine. Yet they undergo severe destruction during the heating process required in Fox's scheme. The resultant product thus contains only minor amounts of serine and threonine in contrast to naturally occurring proteins.

5. The claim that the products consist of a few relatively homogeneous polypeptides ("Proteinoids") with amino acids arranged in a highly ordered sequence is patently absurd.

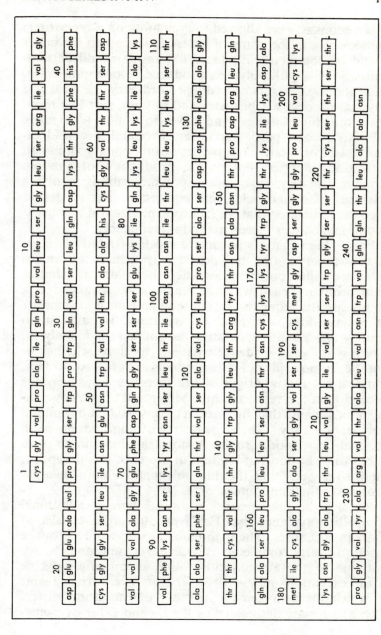

Figure 3.   The amino acid sequence of the protein chymotrypsinogen.

If a monkey were allowed to type away on a typewriter, the sequence in the string of letters produced on the paper would be completely random. The result would be nonsense. So it is with polymers produced from amino acids, nucleotides, or sugars according to ordinary chemical and physical processes. Chemistry and physics, just like monkeys, are dumb things, and have no ability to arrange subunits in any particular order. Probability considerations based on relative reactivities of functional groups and activation energies *require* the production of random structures or sequences in any polymerizations involving mixtures of amino acids, nucleotides, or sugars. It has been demonstrated that, in fact, polymerization of sugars[9] and of nucleotides[10] leads to random sequences.

Fox's claim that his product consists of relatively large quantities of a few polypeptides (polymers of amino acids are called polypeptides when the chains are shorter than proteins), each with the amino acids arranged in a highly specific sequence, rather than an enormous number of polypeptides with random structures, is based upon entirely inadequate separation techniques and analyses. There is no valid evidence whatever to show whether or not the amino acids in Fox's products are ordered. In fact, some of his fellow origin of life theorists accuse Fox of deception in this respect. Thus, Miller and Orgel, concerning Fox's claim that his product consists of nonrandom polypeptides, say "Thus, the degree of nonrandomness in thermal polypeptides so far demonstrated is minute compared with the non-randomness in proteins. It is deceptive, then, to suggest that thermal polypeptides are similar to proteins in their nonrandomness."[11]

Beyond the above considerations, there is additional compelling evidence that Fox's product must consist of random structures. The high temperature required for the reaction nearly completely racemizes the amino acids. All but one of the amino acids found in proteins (glycine is the exception) may exist in at least two forms, forms in which the arrangement in space of the atoms differ. These forms are designated as the D- and L-forms (sometimes called "right-" and "left-handed"). They bear the same relationship to each other that a right hand bears to a left hand; each is a mirror-image of the other but not superimposable. Chemically and physically they exhibit identical properties except that solutions of the two forms rotate plane-polarized light in opposite directions. Biologically the difference is enormous, however. All naturally occurring proteins contain exclusively the L-, or "left-handed," form. The replacement of a single amino acid in a protein with its D-form completely destroys all biological activity.

Racemization is the process which converts D-amino acids to a mixture of the D- and L-forms, or L-amino acids to a mixture of the D- and L-forms. When an amino acid is completely racemized, it consists of equal quantities of the D- and L-forms. All amino acids tend to racemize under natural conditions, the rate of racemization depending on the particular amino acid and environmental conditions. The brutal treatment of heating amino acids several hours at 175°C, as mentioned above, extensively racemizes the amino acids, changing the amino acids from L-forms to a mixture of L- and D-forms.

Since the D- and L-forms of amino acids have identical chemical properties, the probability of the D-form being incorporated at any point in the chain is equal to the probability of the incorporation of the L-form. There would be no way then, chemically, of specifying which form would be incorporated at any particular point. The sequence of the first two amino acids in the chain might thus be L-L, D-D, D-L, or L-D. Each would have equal probability. The sequence of the first three amino acids, whatever the particular amino acids, might be L-L-L, L-L-D, L-D-L, L-D-D, D-D-D, D-D-L, D-L-D, or D-L-L. Thus, it can be seen that even if the sequence of the first three amino acids were the same (such as, for example, arginine-valine-threonine), eight different structures can be obtained, differences which would exert enormous influence biologically. In fact, based on known biochemistry, only the L-L-L form could have had any potential significance.

It is thus impossible for Fox's product to consist of specific structures. A particular sequence of ten amino acids but consisting of mixtures of the D- and L-forms would yield a thousand different structures (2^{10}) and a particular sequence of 100 amino acids existing in D- and L-forms would yield 10 billion times 10 billion times 10 billion different structures (2^{100}, or approximately 10^{30}). It is apparent that Fox's claim for a high degree of homogeneity, or non-randomness, in his product is indeed absurd.

6. Catalytic, or enzymic, properties claimed for the product are barely detectable and unrelated to present enzymes.

The catalytic properties of enzymes found in present-day organisms are due to the precise sequence of the L-amino acids in these proteins. Fox's product consists of random sequences of these amino acids. Any enhancement of the catalytic activity of the free amino acids themselves by this polymerization would be no more than that conveyed by the incorporation of these amino acids into random polymers or nonspecific chemical structures. Furthermore, these polymers consist of mixtures of D- and L-amino acids. As mentioned earlier, the substitution of only one L-amino acid by its D-form in an enzyme (which may consist of several hundred amino acids) completely demolishes, for all practical purposes, its biological, that is, its catalytic, ability (residual activity, if any, is reduced below a detectable quantity). Further discussion of this point may be found in the monograph by Gish on the origin of life.[12] It is probable that if Fox had swept up the dust on the floor of the university administration building and thrown it into his test mixture, it would have had as much activity as his protenoid.

7. The proteinoid microspheres are unstable and are easily destroyed.

Fox claims a rather high degree of stability for his proteinoid microspheres, yet he, himself, reveals that microspheres contained in aqueous suspension between microscope slides can be easily redissolved by merely warming the slides.[13] Stable, indeed! Furthermore, dilution of an aqueous suspension by adding water also dissolves the microspheres.

8. Division of the microspheres is due to simple physicochemical phenomena and have no relation to cell division by living organisms.

Cell division in even the simplest organisms requires an incredibly complex process and machinery, involving duplication of each unit of the cell with extremely high fidelity. On the other hand, the division reported for Fox's microspheres is a simple physicochemical phenomenon, like the separation of a soap bubble into two bubbles. It has no greater significance. As material precipitates from solution in the form of globules, and as the quantity that has collected in any particular globule exceeds a certain amount, physicochemical forces may cause the globule to split into two globules. No reproduction, no replication of any kind, however, takes place. The material in the first globule would be randomly distributed between the two product globules.

This discussion of the Fox scheme for the origin of life, even though incomplete, has been relatively extensive. This is believed desirable, however, because of the tremendous promotion (and naive acceptance) of Fox's theories in high school and college texts and in scientific circles as well. Fox's success confirms the bias and unscientific attitudes that dominate the educational and scientific establishments in relation to the question of origins. Anything that incorporates evolutionary philosophy is acceptable, no matter how unscientific.

Other Models

Other suggestions have been offered (good but concise

reviews of these may be found in the paper by Horowitz and Hubbard [7b] and the book by Miller and Orgel [7a]). Those that involve reactions in aqueous solution (and thus in the oceans, lakes, and all other aqueous environments) can be effectively eliminated because the high energy reagents required to provide the energy to form the chemical bonds between the amino acids, nucleotides, etc., would be rapidly destroyed by water. These reagents are effective in laboratory syntheses because the reagents are prepared in non-aqueous solvents under anhydrous conditions, and the reactions in which these reagents are used are generally carried out under similar conditions. There is no possibility that these reagents could form on the primitive earth, however.

Other suggestions utilizing elevated temperatures in a dry environment, in addition to the suggestion of Fox, have been offered.[14] Orgel and his collaborators have published a series of papers, for example, on the thermal synthesis in a dry environment of nucleotides and of polymers of nucleotides,[15] but Orgel, himself, admits that these experiments have no relevance to the origin of life. After discussing the possibilities of such reactions occurring under primitive earth conditions, Miller and Orgel state, "However, we doubt that very extensive polymerization of nucleotides could have occurred in this way, or that *'biological' polymerization could have taken place except in an aqueous environment.*"[16]

Miller and Orgel have thus stated their conviction that polymerizations that gave rise to proteins, DNA, RNA, and other biological molecules (" 'biological' polymerizations") must have occurred in an aqueous environment. But as stated above, this would have been impossible because the high energy compounds needed to drive these polymerization reactions could not have formed or existed in an aqueous environment.

In the concluding paragraph to their chapter on polymerizations, Miller and Orgel state, "This chapter has probably been confusing to the reader. We believe this is because of the very limited progress that has been made in the study of prebiotic condensation reactions."[17] This lack of success has resulted from the extreme difficulties in attempting to imagine how such processes could have occurred under natural conditions. Some might suppose, on the other hand, that limited progress has been made mainly because comparatively little research has yet been done on the origin of life. In that limited amount of research, however, enough work has been done to test all principles involved. Further work will not alter the principles of thermodynamics, chemical kinetics, or other basic principles involved. These stand as barriers to a naturalistic origin of biologically active molecules.

This series on origin-of-life theories will be concluded in a future issue (No. 37).

REFERENCES

1. S.W. Fox, Ed., *The Origins of Prebiological Systems and of Their Molecular Matrices,* Academic Press, New York, 1965.
2. S.W. Fox and K. Dose, *Molecular Evolution and the Origin of Life,* Freeman Pub. Co., San Francisco, 1972.
3. S.W. Fox, "Self-ordered Polymers and Propagative Cell-Like Systems," *Naturwissenschaften,* Vol. 56, pp. 1-9 (1969), in English.
4. S.W. Fox, K. Harada, G. Krampitz, and G. Mueller, "Chemical Origins of Cells," *Chemical and Engineering News,* June 22, 1970, pp. 80-94.
5. S.W. Fox, "The Protein Theory of the Origin of Life," *American Biology Teacher,* Vol. 36, pp. 161-172 (1974).
6. D.L. Rohlfind and A.I. Oparin, Eds., *Molecular Evolution: Prebiological and Biological,* Plenum Press, New York, 1972.
7. a) S.L. Miller and L.E. Orgel, *The Origins of Life on the Earth,* Prentice-Hall, Englewood Cliffs, N.J., 1973, p. 145;
   b) N.H. Horowitz and J.S. Hubbard, "The Origin of Life," *Annual Review of Genetics,* Vol. 8, p. 399 (1974);
   c) C. Sagan, in Reference 1, p. 374;
   d) J.R. Vallentyne, in Reference 1, p. 379.
8. Reference 7a, p. 145.
9. P.T. Mora, in Reference 1, p. 287.
10. G. Schramm, in Reference 1, p. 299.
11. Reference 7a, footnote on p. 144.
12. D.T. Gish, *Speculations and Experiments Related to Theories on the Origin of Life,* Creation-Life Publishers, San Diego, 1972.
13. S.W. Fox, "A Theory of Macromolecular and Cellular Origins," *Nature,* Vol. 205, p. 336 (1965).
14. See for example Reference 7a, pp. 141-148, and Reference 7b, pp. 399-400.
15. For a brief review of this work, see Reference 7b, p. 400.
16. Reference 7a, p. 142.
17. Reference 7a, p. 148.

No. 37, July, 1976
THE ORIGIN OF LIFE:
THEORIES ON THE ORIGIN OF BIOLOGICAL ORDER
Duane T. Gish, Ph.D.

This is the concluding article in this series on origin of life theories. Earlier articles in the series may be found in Impact No. 31, January, 1976, and Impact No. 33, March, 1976.

The second article of this series included a discussion of Fox's scheme, or thermal model, for overcoming the thermodynamic barrier to the formation of proteins (amino acid polymers), and a discussion of other polymerization schemes. It was pointed out that Fox's thermal model involves a series of conditions and events, most of which would have had such a vanishingly low order of probability on any plausible primitive earth, that the overall probability of protenoid microspheres arising through natural processes would have been nil. It was further pointed out that, in any case, the polymers produced by such a postulated process would have consisted of randomly arranged amino acids with no significant biological activity and thus Fox's model has no relevance to the origin of living systems.

The problem of overcoming the thermodynamic barrier in the polymerization of amino acids and nucleotides, as insolvable as this appears to be, is dwarfed by a vastly greater problem—the origin of the highly ordered, highly specific sequences in proteins, DNA, and RNA which endow these molecules with their marvelous biological activities. Proteins generally have from about a hundred up to several hundred amino acids arranged in a precise order or sequence. Twenty different kinds of amino acids are found in proteins, so it may be said that the protein "language" has twenty letters. Just as the letters of the alphabet must be arranged in a precise sequence to write this sentence, or any sentence, so the amino acids must be arranged in a precise sequence for a protein to possess biological activity.

Human growth hormone has 188 amino acids arranged in a unique and precise sequence. Ribonuclease, an enzyme that catalyzes the hydrolysis of ribonucleic acids (RNA), has 124 amino acids arranged in its own unique sequence. Bovine glutamate dehydrogenase, another enzyme, has six identical chains of 506 amino acids each. The alpha chain of human hemoglobin, the red blood protein, has 141 amino acids, and the beta chain has 146 amino acids. Hemoglobin is a complex which includes four protein molecules, two each of the alpha and beta proteins, plus iron, plus a complex chemical called heme.

The particular amino acid sequence of each of these protein molecules is responsible for their unique biological activity. Furthermore, a change of a single amino acid generally destroys or severely diminishes this activity. For example, some individuals inherit a defective gene which causes the amino acid valine to be substituted for glutamic acid at position 6 in the beta chain of their hemoglobin. The other 286 amino acids (the remaining 145 in the beta chain and the 141 in the alpha chain) remain unchanged— only one out of 287 amino acids is affected. The defect, however, causes sickle cell anemia, a disease that is invariably fatal.

The genetic messages are encoded in the genes, which are composed of DNA, via the specific sequence of the nucleotides. There are four different nucleotides, but each "letter" of the genetic "language" consists of a set of three of the four nucleotides. Sixty-four such sets (4^3) can be derived from these four nucleotides, and thus the genetic "language" has an alphabet of 64 "letters." Genes generally have from a hundred or so of these sets up to several thousand of the sets. This would require the precise ordering of three times that many nucleotides, since there are three in each set. The various kinds of RNA would have equal complexity.

As mentioned earlier in the section of the last article in this series, in which Fox's scheme was being discussed, when amino acids and nucleotides are combined, or polymerized, by chemical methods, the amino acids in polypeptides (proteins) and the nucleotides in polynucleotides (DNA and RNA) so derived are arranged in disordered, or random sequences, just as a string of letters typed by a monkey would be randomly arranged. For biologically active molecules to have arisen on the earth by naturalistic processes, there would have had to be some machinery or mechanism in existence to cause ordering of the subunits in a precise or nearly precise fashion.

The ordering mechanism would have had to be highly efficient, since the precise structures required for biological activity impose the severest restraints on the structures of these molecules, just as writing this sentence correctly allows one way, and one way only, for the letters composing it to be arranged. No such ordering mechanism has yet been suggested, nor could any exist under natural conditions. Once ordered sequences, such as enzymes, DNA and RNA, as well as complex energy-coupling and energy-generating systems existed, one might imagine how these ordered sequences could have been duplicated, but that would never explain the origin of these ordered sequences in the first place.

Some have imagined that random processes, given the four or five billion years postulated by evolutionists for the age of the earth, could have generated certain ordered sequences by pure chance. The time required for a single protein molecule to arise by pure chance, however, would exceed billions of times five billion years, the assumed age of the earth.

For example, only seventeen different amino acids (one of each) can be arranged in over 355 trillion (17 factorial) different ways. Put another way, 17 people could line up over 355 trillion different ways (if you don't believe it, get 16 friends together and try it!). Furthermore, if one were to arrange a sequence of 17 amino acids, and could choose from 20 (the number of different amino acids found in proteins) instead of 17, and were allowed to repeat amino acids (as would have been the case in the origin of proteins), about ten sextillion sequences could be obtained (20^{17}, or 10^{22})!

Immense as these numbers are, it could be argued that their origin even by completely random processes would have a finite probability in five billion years. But 17 is far too short for biological activity. Proteins, DNA, and RNA usually contain hundreds of subunits. A sequence of 100 might be more realistic. One hundred amino acids of 20 different kinds could be arranged in 20^{100}, or 10^{130} different ways. What would be the probability of one unique sequence of 100 amino acids, composed of 20 different amino acids, arising by chance in five billion years?

Let it be illustrated in the following fashion. The number of different ways the letters in a sentence containing 100 letters of 20 different kinds could be arranged would be equal to the number of different protein molecules just mentioned (10^{130}). A monkey typing 100 letters every second for five billion years would not have the remotest chance of typing a particular sentence of 100 letters even once without spelling errors.

In fact, if one billion (10^9) planets the size of the earth were covered eyeball-to-eyeball and elbow-to-elbow with monkeys, and each monkey was seated at a typewriter (requiring about 10 square feet for each monkey, of the approximately 10^{16} square feet available on each of the 10^9 planets), and each monkey typed a string of 100 letters every second for five billion years (about 10^{17} seconds) the chances are overwhelming that not one of these monkeys would have typed the sentence correctly! Only 10^{41} tries could be made by all these monkeys in that five billion years ($10^9 \times 10^{16} \times 10^{17} \div 10 = 10^{41}$). There would not be the slightest chance that a single one of the 10^{24} monkeys (a trillion trillion monkeys) would have typed a preselected sentence of 100 letters (such as "The subject of this *Impact* article is the naturalistic origin of life on the earth under assumed primordial conditions") without a spelling error, even once.

The number of tries possible (10^{41}) is such a minute fraction of the total number of possibilities (10^{130}), that the probability that one of the monkeys would have typed the correct sentence is less than the impossibility threshold.

The degree of difference between these two numbers is enormous, and may be illustrated by that fact that 10^{41} times a trillion (10^{12}) is still only 10^{53}, and 10^{53} times a trillion is only 10^{65}, 10^{65} times a trillion is only 10^{77}, etc. In fact, 10^{41} would have to be multiplied by a trillion more than seven times to equal 10^{130}. Even after 10^{41} tries had been made, there would still be much, much more than 10^{129} arrangements that hadn't yet been tried (10^{41} is such an insignificantly small number compared to 10^{130} that 10^{130}-10^{41} is about equal to 10^{130} minus zero!).

Considering an enzyme, then, of 100 amino acids, there would be no possibility whatever that a single molecule could ever have arisen by pure chance on the earth in five billion years. But if by some miracle it did happen once, only a single molecule would have been produced, yet billions of tons of each of many different protein, DNA, and RNA molecules would have to be produced. The probability of this happening, of course, is absolutely nil. It must be concluded, therefore, that a naturalistic origin of the many biologically active molecules required for the most primitive organism imaginable would have been impossible.

Origin of Stable, Complex, Biologically Active Systems

The problem of explaining the manner in which the above macromolecules became associated into systems that would have had even the most rudimentary ability to function as metabolically active systems capable of assuring their own maintenance, reproduction, and diversification is tremendously more complex and difficult than any attempts to explain the origin of the macromolecules themselves. Green and Goldberger have stated, " . . . the macromolecule-to-cell transition is a jump of fantastic dimensions, which lies beyond the range of testable hypothesis. In this area all is conjecture. The available facts do not provide a basis for postulating that cells arose on this planet."[1] Kerkut, in his little book exposing the fallacies and weaknesses in the evidence usually used to support evolution (although he, himself, is not a creationist) said, "It is therefore a matter of faith on the part of the biologist that biogenesis did occur and he can choose whatever method of biogenesis happens to suit him personally; the evidence for what did happen is not available."[2]

Nevertheless, there are those who persist in attempts to provide a rational explanation for bridging the vast chasm separating a loose mixture of molecules and a living system. The extent of this chasm is enormous when we view the two extremes—an ocean containing a random mixture of macromolecules—proteins, nucleic acids, carbohydrates and other molecules essential for life, in contrast to an isolated, highly complex, intricately integrated, enormously efficient, self-maintaining and self-replicating system represented by the simplest living thing.

Assuming that there was, at one time, an ocean full of these marvelous macromolecules that somehow had become endowed with at least some measure of "biological" activity, one must explain, first of all, how these macromolecules disassociated themselves from this dilute milieu and became integrated into some crude, but functional and stable system.

We can say immediately that under no naturally occurring conditions could complex systems spontaneously arise from a random mixture of macromolecules. There is absolutely no tendency for disordered systems to spontaneously self-organize themselves into more ordered states. On the contrary, all systems naturally tend to become less and less orderly. The more probable state of matter is always a random state. Evolution of life theories thus contradict natural laws. Nevertheless, evolutionists persist in speculating that life arose spontaneously.

Oparin's Coacervate Theory

Because of limitation of space, only one theory, that of A.I. Oparin, the Russian biochemist and pioneer in origin of life theories, will be discussed. Most of the basic objections to his theory are applicable to Fox's microspheres and all similar suggestions. Oparin has proposed that coacervates may have been the intermediates between loose molecules and living systems (a review of Oparin's proposals may be found in Kenyon and Steinman[3]). Coacervates are colloidal particles which form when macromolecules associate with one another and precipitate out of solution in the form of tiny droplets. Complex coacervates are those that form between two different types of macromolecules. For instance, such a coacervate will form between a histone, which is a basic protein, and a nucleic acid, which is acidic. Another example is the coacervate that will form from a complex of gelatin (basic, and thus positively charged) and negatively charged gum arabic.

Oparin, and others, have claimed that complex coacervates possess properties that may have enabled them to form protocells. It was shown that certain coacervates absorbed enzymes from the surrounding medium and that these enzymes were able to function inside the coacervate.[4,5] It should be understood, however, that the association of macromolecules to form coacervates, and the absorption of molecules from the surrounding medium, is due to simple chemical and physical phenomena, and is thus not selective, self-organizing, or stable. Basic histones and nucleic acids form coacervates simply because one is basic, thus positively charged, and one is acidic, and thus negatively charged. There is a simple electrostatic attraction between the two. Basic histones, of course, would attract *any* acidic, or negatively charged, particles, and nucleic acids would attract *any* basic, or positively charged, particles. This attraction would not be selective, and if a chaotic mixture prevailed in the medium, the coacervates would be a chaotic mixture.

Enzyme activity is only useful when it is coordinated with other enzyme activities. We have already given reasons why it would have been impossible for any one particular macromolecule, such as a protein enzyme, to have been formed in any significant amount. But suppose that it did just happen that a few enzyme molecules were absorbed into a coacervate. The action of this enzyme would have been meaningless and useless unless some other enzyme was also present which produced the substrate for the first enzyme, and unless there was another enzyme that could utilize its product. In other words, it would be useless for a coacervate to convert glucose-1-phosphate into glucose-6-phosphate unless it also possessed a source of glucose-1-phosphate and unless it could further utilize the glucose-6-phosphate once it was produced. A factory that has no source of raw materials, or which has no market for its product must shut down in a short time. Living systems are extremely complex, having hundreds of series of metabolic pathways perfectly coordinated and controlled. Substrates are passed along these pathways as each enzyme performs its highly specialized chemical task, and coordination in space and time is such that each enzyme is provided with a controlled amount of substrate, and the successive enzyme is there to receive the substrate and in turn to perform its task. Each chemical task performed is useful and purposeful because it is coordinated in a marvelous way with all the other activities of the cell.

Without this coordination, enzyme activity would not only be useless, it would be destructive. Let us assume, for example, that a proteolytic enzyme (this is an enzyme which catalyzes the hydrolysis, or breakdown, of proteins) somehow did arise in the "primordial soup" and this enzyme was absorbed into a coacervate or one of Fox's proteinoid microspheres. The results would be totally disastrous, for the enzyme would "chew up" all the protein in sight, and that would be the end of the coacervate or microsphere! Similarly, a deaminase would indiscriminately deaminate all amines, a decarboxylase would decarboxylate all carboxylic acids, a DNAse would break down all DNA, and an RNAse would break down all RNA. Uncontrolled, uncoordinated enzymatic activity would be totally destructive.

Such control and coordination in a coacervate, microsphere, or other hypothetical system would have been nonexistent. The complex metabolic pathways and control systems found in living things owe their existence to the highly complex structures found only within living things, such as chloroplasts, mitochondria, Golgi bodies, microsomes, and other structures found within the cell. Some of these are enclosed within membranes, and the cell, itself, is of course, enclosed within a very complex, dynamically functioning multi-layered membrane. Control and coordination, absolutely essential to any living thing or to any metabolically active system, could only exist through the agency of complex structures similar to those mentioned above, but they, in turn, can only be produced by complex, metabolically active systems. One could not arise or exist in the absence of the other. They must have coexisted from the beginning, rendering evolutionary schemes impossible.

Another very serious objection to the idea of Oparin's coacervates is their inherent instability. They form only under special conditions, and readily dissolve with dilution, shift in pH, warming, pressure, etc. This instability has been cited by Fox[6], by Young[7], and by Kenyon and Steinman.[8] Instability is a most fundamental objection to any type of system that can be proposed to bridge the gap between molecules and living cells. All of these proposed models, whether they be Oparin's coacervates, Fox's microspheres, or any other model, suffer this basic and fatal weakness. One of the reasons living cells are stable and can persist is that they have membranes that protect the system within the membrane and hold it together. The membrane of a living cell is very complex in structure and marvelous in its function. A coacervate or a protein microsphere may have a pseudomembrane, or a concentration or orientation of material at the point of contact with the surrounding medium that gives it the appearance of having a membrane. There are no chemical bonds linking the macromolecules in this pseudomembrane, however, and it is easily broken up, and the contents of the coacervate or microsphere are then released into the medium.

Since these coacervates have this inherent instability, no coacervate could have existed for a length of time that would have had any significance whatsoever to the origin of life. Even if we could imagine a primitive "soup" concentrated sufficiently in macromolecules to allow coacervates to form, their existence would have been brief. Any organization that may have formed in these coacervates by any imaginable process would then have been irretrievably lost as the contents of the coacervate spilled out into the medium.

Theories that attempt to account for the origin of stable metabolic systems from loose macromolecules thus suffer from a number of fatal weaknesses. First is the requirement that the necessary macromolecules be produced in sufficiently vast amounts to saturate the primeval seas to the point where complex coacervates or protenoid microspheres would precipitate out of solution. Secondly, such globular products are inherently unstable and would easily be dissolved or disintegrated, spilling their contents out into the medium. Geological ages, however, would have been required for a loose system to evolve into a stable, living cell, assuming such a process were possible at all. As we have seen above, however, there is no tendency at all for complex systems to form spontaneously from simple systems. There is a general natural tendency, on the other hand, for organized systems to spontaneously disintegrate to a disordered state. Thirdly, even if it were imagined that a coacervate of some kind could accrete or inherently possess some catalytic ability, this catalytic ability would have been purposeless, and thus useless, and actually destructive.

The Origin of the First Completely Independent, Stable, Self-reproducing Unit—The First Living Cell

The simplest form of life known to science contains hundreds of different kinds of enzymes, thousands of different kinds of RNA and DNA molecules, and thousands of other kinds of complex molecules. As mentioned above, it is enclosed within a very complex membrane and contains a large number of structures, many of which are enclosed within their own membrane. The thousands of chemical reactions which occur in this cell are strictly coordinated with one another in time and space in a harmonious system, all working together towards the self-maintenance and eventual reproduction of this living cell. Every detail of its structure and function reveals purposefulness; its incredible complexity and marvelous capabilities reveal a master plan.

It seems futile enough to attempt to imagine how this amazingly complex system could have come into existence in the first place in view of the vast amount of contradictory evidence. Its continued existence from the very start, however, would have required mechanisms especially designed for self-maintenance and self-reproduction. There are numerous injurious processes which would prove fatal for the cell if repair mechanisms did not exist. These injurious processes include dimerization of the thymine units in DNA, deamination of cytosine, adenine, and guanine in DNA and RNA, deamidation of glutamine and asparagine in proteins, and the production of toxic peroxides, just to cite a few. The cell is endowed with complex, defense mechanisms, in each case involving an enzyme or a series of enzymes. Since these defense mechanisms are absolutely necessary for the survival of the cell, they would have had to exist from the very beginning. Life could not have waited until such mechanisms evolved, for life would be impossible in their absence.

The ultimate fate of a cell or any living thing is death and destruction. No dynamically functioning unit therefore can survive as a species without self-reproduction. The ability to reproduce, however, would have had to exist from the very beginning in any system, no matter how simple or complex, that could have given rise eventually to a living thing. Yet the ability to reproduce requires such a complex mechanism that the machinery required for this process would have been the *last* thing that could possibly have evolved. This dilemma has no solution and thus poses the final insuperable barrier to the origin of life by a naturalistic process.

We conclude that a materialistic, mechanistic, evolutionary origin of life is directly contradicted by known natural laws and processes. The origin of life could only have occurred through the acts of an omniscient Creator independent of and external to the natural universe. "In the beginning God created" is still the most up-to-date statement we can make concerning the origin of life.

REFERENCES

1. D.E. Green and R.F. Goldberger, *Molecular Insights into the Living Process,* Academic Press, New York, 1967, p. 407.
2. G.A. Kerkut, *Implications of Evolution,* Pergamon Press, New York, 1960, p. 150.
3. D.H. Kenyon and G. Steinman, *Biochemical Predestination,* McGraw-Hill Book Co., New York, 1969, p. 245.
4. A.I. Oparin, *The Origin of Life on the Earth,* Academic Press, New York, 1957, p. 428.
5. A.I. Oparin in *The Origins of Prebiological Systems and of Their Molecular Matrices,* S.W. Fox, Ed., Academic Press, New York, 1965, p. 331.
6. S.W. Fox in Reference 5, p. 345.
7. R.S. Young in Reference 5, p. 348.
8. Reference 3, p. 250.

No. 32, February, 1976
CONTINENTAL DRIFT, PLATE TECTONICS, AND THE BIBLE
Stuart E. Nevins, M.S.

Twenty years ago geologists were certain that the data correlated perfectly with the then-reigning model of stationary continents. The handful of geologists who promoted the notion of continental drift were accused of indulging in pseudo-scientific fancy. Today, the opinion is reversed. The theory of moving continents is now the ruling paradigm and those who question it are often referred to as stubborn or ignorant. This "revolution" in our concept of the earth's character is a striking commentary on the human nature of scientists and on the flexibility that scientists allow in use of the geological data.

Plate Tectonics

The popular theory of drifting continents and oceans is called "plate tectonics."[1] (*Tectonics* is the field of geology which studies the processes which deform the earth's crust.) The general tenets of the popular theory may be stated as follows. The outer lithospheric shell of the earth consists of a mosaic of rigid plates, each in motion relative to adjacent plates. Deformation occurs at the margins of plates by three basic types of motion: horizontal extension, horizontal slipping, and horizontal compression. Sea-floor spreading occurs where two plates are diverging horizontally (e.g., the Mid-Atlantic Ridge and East Pacific Rise) with new material from the earth's mantle being added between them to form a new oceanic crust. Transform faulting occurs where one plate is slipping horizontally past another (e.g., the San Andreas fault of California and the Anatolian fault of northern Turkey). Subduction occurs where two plates are converging with one plate underthrusting the other producing what is supposed to be compressional deformation (e.g., the Peru-Chile Trench and associated Andes Mountains of South America). In conformity with evolutionary-uniformitarian assumption, popular plate tectonic theory supposes that plates move very slowly—about 2 to 18 centimeters per year. At this rate it would take 100 million years to form an ocean basin or mountain range.

Fitting of Continents

The idea that the continents can be fitted together like a jigsaw puzzle to form a single super continent is an old one. Especially interesting is how the eastern "bulge" of South America can fit into the southwestern "concavity" of Africa. Recent investigators have used computers to fit the continents. The "Bullard fit"[2] gives one of the best reconstructions of how Africa, South America, Europe, and North America may have once touched. There are, however, areas of overlap of continents and one large area which must be omitted from consideration (Central

America). There are a number of ways to fit Africa, India, Australia, and Antarctica (only one can be correct!). Reconstructions have been shown to be geometrically feasible which are preposterous to continental drift (e.g., rotation of eastern Australia fits nicely into eastern North America).[3]

Those who appreciate the overall fit of continents call the evidence "compelling," while others who note gaps, overlaps, or emissions remain skeptical. It is difficult to place probability on the accuracy of reconstructions and one's final judgment is largely subjective.

Sea-Floor Spreading

Evidence suggesting sea-floor spreading is claimed by many geologists to be the most compelling argument for plate tectonics. In the ocean basins along mid-ocean ridges or rises (and in some shallow seas) plates are thought to be diverging slowly and continuously at a rate of several centimeters yearly. Molten material from the earth's mantle is injected continuously between the plates and cools to form new crust. The youngest crust is claimed to be at the crest of the ocean rise or ridge with older crust farther from the crest. At the time of cooling, the rock acquires magnetism from the earth's magnetic field. Since the magnetic field of earth is supposed by many geologists to have reversed numerous times, during some epochs cooling oceanic crust should be reversely magnetized. If sea-floor spreading is continuous, the ocean floor should possess a magnetic "tape recording" of reversals. A "zebra stripe" pattern of linear magnetic anomalies parallel in the ocean ridge crest has been noted in some areas and potassium-argon dating has been alleged to show older rocks farther from the ridge crest.

There are some major problems with this classic and "most persuasive" evidence of sea-floor spreading. First, the magnetic bands may not form by reversals of the earth's magnetic field. Asymmetry of magnetic stripes, not symmetry, is the normal occurrence.[4] It has been argued that the linear patterns can be caused by several complex interacting factors (differences in magnetic susceptibility, magnetic reversals, oriented tectonic stresses).[5]

Second, it is doubtful that the magnetic anomalies have been successfully dated. Wesson[6] says that potassium-argon dating when correctly interpreted shows no evidence of increasing age with distance from the ridge system. The greater argon content (giving older apparent age) of ocean basalt on the flanks of the ocean ridges can be explained easily by the greater depth and pressure at the time of solidification incorporating original magmatic argon.[7]

Subduction

Corollary to the idea of plate accretion by sea-floor spreading is the notion of plate destruction by subduction. (If sea-floor spreading occurs without plate destruction, the quantity of crust will increase and the *volume* of the earth must increase!). Subduction theory supposes that converging plates are destroyed below ocean trenches. The island arc or coastal mountain range associated with ocean trench subduction zones is claimed to form by compression as one plate is underthrusting another. The plate that is "subducted" below the trench is thought to be remelted at a depth of up to 700 kilometers. Gravity data indicate low density material of crustal character on the landward side below trenches. (Also, deep and high intensity earthquakes (i.e., earthquakes in Alaska, Peru, Nicaragua, etc.) are assumed to indicate break-up of the underthrust plate.

Two major difficulties are encountered by models supposing subduction to explain the modern tectonic phenomena in ocean trenches. First, if subduction theory is correct, there should be compressed, deformed, and thrust faulted sediment on the floors of trenches. Studies of the Peru-Chile Trench and the eastern Aleutian Trench[8], however, show soft flat lying sediment without compression structures. Second, seismic first-motion data indicate that modern earthquakes occurring approximately under trenches and island arcs are often *tensional,* but only rarely compressional.[9]

The Mysterious Cause of Drift

What is the driving force for continental drift and plate tectonics? How is a plate ten thousand kilometers long, several thousand kilometers wide, and one hundred kilometers thick, kept in constant but almost imperceptibly slow movement during millions of years? Will slow and continous application of stress on a plate 100 kilometers thick cause it to be torn asunder? How can a plate be broken and then rammed slowly into the earth's mantle to a depth of 700 kilometers? Here are some of the most baffling problems for plate tectonics.

Evolutionary-uniformitarian explanations for plate motion range from very doubtful to impossible. A popular idea is that rising convection currents in the earth's mantle exert lateral forces on plates moving them slowly and continuously. The best theory of the viscosity of the earth's mantle, however, shows that large-scale convection systems are impossible.[10] Three other theories are sometimes mentioned: (1) plates slide by gravity from the elevated mid-ocean ridge to the depressed trench, (2) plates are "pulled" into the mantle below trenches by chemical phase changes during melting, (3) plates are "pushed" apart along mid-ocean ridges by slow injection of magma into vertical cracks. Each of these mechanisms (alone or together) cannot overcome the viscous drag at the base of the plate, and cannot explain how the difference in elevation developed or how the plate boundary originally formed. The absence of sufficient mechanism for plate motion, the uncertainty regarding the existence of seafloor spreading, and the doubts about subduction cause us to question the popular geologic synthesis known as "plate tectonics."

Continental Drift and the Bible

The Bible framework for earth history makes no statement about continental splitting, so it is unnecessary and unwise to take a "biblical" position on the question. When

God created the land and sea, the waters were "gathered together unto one place" (Genesis 1:9), which may imply one large ocean and one large land mass. The scripture which says "the earth was divided" in the days of Peleg (Genesis 10:25) is generally thought to refer to the Tower of Babel division (Genesis 11:1-9) and some suppose this included continental separation. To believe, however, that the continents moved thousands of miles during the Tower of Babel incident without causing another global flood requires a miracle. Similarly, it is doubtful whether the long day of Joshua can be explained naturalistically by plate tectonics.

If continental separation did occur, the only place within the Bible framework where it could fit would be during Noah's Flood. The cause of Noah's Flood is described in tectonic terms: "all the fountains of the great deep broken up" (Genesis 7:11). The Hebrew word for "broken up" is *baga* and is used in other Old Testament passages (Zechariah 14:4; Numbers 16:31) to refer to the geologic phenomena of faulting. The mechanism for retreat of the Flood waters is also associated with tectonics. Psalm 104:6,7 describes the abating of the waters which stood above the mountains; the eighth verse properly translated says, "The mountains rose up; the valleys sank down." It is interesting to note that the "mountains of Ararat" (Genesis 8:4), the resting place of the Ark after the 150th day of the Flood, are in a tectonically active region at the junction of three lithospheric plates.[11]

If continental separation occurred during Noah's Flood, a host of problems in the tectonic dilemma can be solved. Rapid mid-ocean rifting can explain the large quantity of volcanic rocks on the sea floor. The presence of low density crustal rock down to a depth of 700 kilometers within the mantle below trenches can be attributed to rapid underthrusting. The cause for the ancient breaking up of continents can be explained easily by the enormous catastrophic forces of Noah's Flood which broke the lithosphere into moving plates which for a short time overcame the viscous drag of the earth's mantle. The amazing similarity of sedimentary Flood layers in the northeastern United States to those of Britain (i.e., Carboniferous coal strata and Devonian red sandstones) and the absence of these in the North Atlantic ocean basin suggests that continental separation occurred toward the end of the Flood.

Conclusion

The idea that sea-floor plates form slowly and continuously at a rate of a few centimeters each year as the ocean crust is being rift apart, is not supported by geologic data. The concept of destruction of sea-floor plates over millions of years by slow underthrusting below ocean trenches is also doubtful. Furthermore, the cause for the alleged gradual and uninterrupted motion of plates is an unsolved mystery. Despite these failures in the modern theory of "plate tectonics," the notion that the earth's surface has been deformed at the margins of moving plate-like slabs appears to be a valid one. The facts indicate that the separation of the continents, rifting of the ocean floor, and underthrusting of ocean trenches, were accomplished by rapid processes, not occurring today, initiated by a catastrophic mechanism. Noah's Flood, as described in the Bible, was certainly associated with tectonic processes and provides the time in the Biblical framework of earth history when continental separation may have occurred.

REFERENCES

1. For summaries of the literature see J.F. Dewey, Plate tectonics: *Sci. Amer.,* v. 226, 1972, p. 56-68 and W. Sullivan, *Continents in motion, the new earth debate:* New York, McGraw-Hill, 1974, 399 p. For collections of important, somewhat technical papers affirming plate tectonics, see: *Continents adrift, readings from Scientific American:* San Francisco, W.H. Freeman & Co., 1973, 172 p. and Allan Cox, ed., *Plate tectonics and geomagnetic reversals:* San Francisco, W.H. Freeman and Co., 1973, 702 p. For a technical critique of plate tectonics see C.F. Kahle, ed., *Plate Tectonics—assessments and reassessments:* Tulsa, Amer. Assoc. Pet. Geol., Memoir 23, 1974, 514 p.
2. E.C. Bullard, J.E. Everett and A.G. Smith, Fit continents around Atlantic, in P.M.S. Blackett *et. al.,* eds., A symposium on continental drift: *Roy. Soc. London, Phil. Trans.,* ser. A, V. 258, 1965, p. 41-75.

3. A.H. Voisey, Some comments on the hypothesis of continental drift, in *Continental drift, a symposium:* Hobart, Univ. Tasmania, 1958, p. 162-171.
4. A.A. Meyerhoff and H.A. Meyerhoff, "The new global tectonics": age of linear magnetic anomalies of ocean basis: *American Assoc. Pet. Geol. Bulletin,* v 56, 1972, p. 337-359.
5. *Ibid.,* p. 354-355.
6. P.S. Wesson, Objections to continental drift and plate tectonics: *J. Geol.,* v. 80, 1972, p. 191.
7. C.S. Noble and J.J. Naughton, Deep-ocean basalts: inert gas content and uncertainties in age dating: *Science,* v. 162, 1968, p. 265-267. G.B. Dalrymple and J.G. Moore, Argon-40: excess in submarine pillow basalts from Kilauea Volcano, Hawaii: *Science,* v. 161, 1968, p. 1132-1135.
8. D.W. Scholl, *et. al.,* Peru-Chile Trench sediments and sea-floor spreading: *Geol. Soc. Amer. Bull.,* v. 83, 1972, p. 3613-3626.
9. W.F. Tanner, Deep-sea trenches and the compression assumption: *Amer. Assoc. Pet. Geol. Bull.,* v. 57, 1973, p. 2195-2206.
10. For a review of arguments against convection currents see P.S. Wesson, *loc. cit.,* p. 187.
11. J.F. Dewey, *et. al., Plate tectonics and the evolution of the alpine system:* Geol. Soc. Amer. Bull., v. 84, 1973, p. 3139.

No. 34, April, 1976

CREATION AND THE CROSS

Henry M. Morris, Ph.D.

The two greatest events in all history are the creation of the world and the redemption of the world. Each of these events involved a great divine Week of work and a Day of rest. Creation Week accomplished the work of man's formation; the week that is called Holy Week or Passion Week (perhaps a better term would be Redemption Week) accomplished the work of man's salvation.

Creation Week, which culminated in a perfect world (Genesis 1:31), was followed by man's fall and God's Curse on the world (Genesis 3:17). Passion Week, which culminated in the death and burial of the maker of that perfect world, is followed by man's restoration and the ultimate removal of God's Curse from the world (Revelation 22:3). A Tree (Genesis 3:6) was the vehicle of man's temptation and sin; another Tree (I Peter 2:24) was the vehicle of man's forgiveness and deliverance.

The Two Weeks

It is fascinating to compare the events of the seven days

of Creation Week and Redemption Week, respectively. The chronology of the events of Redemption Week has been the subject of much disagreement among scholars, and it is not possible to be certain on a number of the details. The discussion below is not meant to be dogmatic, but only to offer a possible additional dimension to their understanding and harmony. The traditional view that Friday was the day of the crucifixion is further strengthened by the correlations suggested in this study.

First Day. The first day of creation involved the very creation of the universe itself (Genesis 1:1). An entire cosmos responded to the creative fiat of the Maker of heaven and earth. Initially this Space-Mass-Time (i.e., heaven, earth, beginning) continuum was created in the form of basic elements only, with no structure and no occupant (Genesis 1:2), a static suspension in a pervasive, watery matrix (II Peter 3:5). When God's Spirit began to *move,* however, the gravitational and electromagnetic force systems for the cosmos were energized. The waters and their suspensions coalesced into a great spherical planet and, at the center of the electromagnetic spectrum of forces, visible light was generated (Genesis 1:3).

In a beautiful analogy, on the first day of Passion Week, the Creator King of the universe entered His chosen capital city (Zechariah 9:9, 10; Matthew 21:1-9) to begin His work of redemption, as He had long ago entered His universe to begin His work of creation. Even the very elements He had created (Luke 19:39, 40) would have acknowledged His authority, though the human leaders of His people would not.

Second Day. Having created and activated the earth, God next provided for it a marvelous atmosphere and hydrosphere in which, later, would live the birds and fishes. No other planet, of course, is equipped with air and water in such abundance, and this is strong evidence that the earth was uniquely planned for man and animal life. The hydrosphere was further divided into waters below and waters above "the firmament." The waters above the firmament (the Hebrew word for firmament means, literally "stretched-out space") probably comprised a vast blanket of transparent water vapor, maintaining a perfect climate worldwide, with ideal conditions for longevity.

Paralleling the primeval provision of life-sustaining air and water, on the second day of Redemption Week, He entered again into the city (having spent the night in Bethany) and taught in the temple. As He approached the city, He cursed the barren fig tree (Mark 11:12-14) and then, in the temple, overthrew the tables of the money changers (Mark 11:15-19). This seems to have been the second time in two days that He had turned out the money changers (the parallel accounts in Matthew and Luke indicate that He also did this on the first day). Both actions—the cursing of the fig tree and the cleansing of the temple—symbolize the purging of that which is barren or corrupt in the Creator's kingdom. He had created a world prepared for life (air for the breath of life and water as the matrix of life), but mankind, even the very teachers of His chosen people, had made it unfruitful and impure. As physical life must first have a world of pure air and water, so the preparations for a world of true spiritual life require the purifying breath of the Spirit and the cleansing water of the Word, preparing for the true fruit of the Spirit and the true temple of God's presence, in the age to come.

Third Day. The next day, the sight of the withered fig tree led to an instructive lesson on faith in God, the Lord Jesus assuring the disciples that real faith could move mountains into the sea (Mark 11:29-24). In parallel, on the third day of creation, God had literally called mountains up out of the sea (Genesis 1:9, 10).

It was also on this day that the Lord had the most abrasive of all His confrontations with the Pharisees and Sadducees. He spoke many things against them and they were actively conspiring to destroy Him. It is appropriate that His challenges to them on this day began with two parables dealing with a vineyard (Matthew 21:28-32 and Matthew 21:33-43; see also Mark 12:1-11 and Luke 20:9-18), in which He reminded them that they had been called to be in charge of God's vineyard on the earth, and had failed.

Like the fig tree, there was no fruit for God from their service, and therefore, they would soon be removed from their stewardship.

Likewise, the entire earth was on the third day of Creation Week prepared as a beautiful garden, with an abundance of fruit to nourish every living creature (Genesis 1:11, 12) and it had been placed in man's care (Genesis 1:28-30; 2:15). But mankind in general, and the chosen people in particular, had failed in their mission. Before the earth could be redeemed and made a beautiful garden again (Revelation 22:2), it must be purged and the faithless keepers of the vineyard replaced.

This third day of Passion Week was climaxed with the great Sermon on the Mount of Olives in which the Lord promised His disciples that, though Jerusalem must first be destroyed, He would come again, in power and great glory, to establish His kingdom in a new Jerusalem (Matthew 24 and 25; Mark 13; Luke 21). It was appropriate that He should then spend the night following that third day, with the handful of disciples who were still faithful to Him, on the Mount of Olives (Luke 21:37), for the Mount would call to memory that far-off third day of Creation Week when He had drawn all the mountains out of the sea. Also, the Garden of Gethsemane on its slopes, with its little grove of vines and fruit trees, would bring to mind the beautiful Garden of Eden and the verdant world He had planted everywhere on the dry land on that same third day. Because of what He was now about to accomplish at Jerusalem (Luke 9:31), the ground would one day be cleansed of its Curse, and all would be made new again (Revelation 21:5).

Fourth Day. On the fourth day of Creation Week, the Lord Jesus had formed the sun and the moon and all the stars of heaven. There had been "light" on the first three days, but now there were actual *lights!* Not only would the earth and its verdure be a source of beauty and sustenance to man, but even the very heavens would bring joy and inspiration to him. Furthermore, they would guide his way and keep his time.

But instead of the stars of heaven turning man's thoughts and affections toward His Creator, they had been corrupted and identified with a host of false gods and goddesses. Furthermore, instead of creating a sense of awe and reverence for the majesty of the One who could fill all heavens, they had bolstered man's belief that the earth is insignificant and meaningless in such a vast, evolving cosmos. Perhaps thoughts such as these troubled the mind of the Lord that night as He lay on the mountain gazing at the lights He had long ago made for the darkness.

When morning came, He returned to Jerusalem, where many were waiting to hear Him. He taught in the temple (Luke 21:37, 38), but the synoptic gospels do not record His teachings. This lack, however is possibly supplied in the apparently parenthetical record of His temple teachings as given only in the fourth gospel (John 12:20-50) because there the Lord twice compared Himself to the Light He had made: "I am come a light into the world, that whosoever believeth in me should not abide in darkness." "Yet a little while is the light with you. Walk while ye have the light, lest darkness come upon you; for he that walketh in darkness knoweth not whither he goeth" (John 12:46, 35). He who was the true Light must become darkness, in order that, in the new world, there would never be night again (Revelation 22:5).

Fifth Day. There is little information given in the gospels about the fifth day of Redemption Week. When there were yet "two days until the Passover" (Mark 14:1), right after the bitter confrontation with the scribes and chief priests on the Third Day, the latter began actively seeking a means to trap and execute Jesus, though they feared to do it on the day on which the Passover Feast was to be observed (Mark 14:2). It was either on the Fourth Day or possibly on this Fifth Day, which was the feast day, that Judas went to them with his offer to betray Jesus. He had apparently been seriously thinking about this action ever since the night when the Lord had rebuked him for his cupidity. This had been in the home in Bethany, on the night of the Sabbath, just before the day when Christ entered Jerusalem riding on the ass (John 12:1-8). This seems to have been the same supper described in Matthew 26:6-13 and Mark 14:3-9, even though in these it is inserted parenthetically after the sermon on the Mount of Olives, probably in order to stress the direct causal relation of this supper to Judas' decision to betray his Master (Matthew 26:14-16; Mark 14:10-11).

On this day of the Passover, the Lord Jesus instructed two of His disciples to make preparations for their own observance of the feast that night (Mark 14:12-17). So far as the record goes; this is all that we know of His words during that day, though there is no doubt that He was teaching in the temple on this day as well (Luke 21:37, 38). Perhaps this strange silence in the record for this Fifth Day is for the purpose of emphasizing the greater importance of these preparations for the Passover. The fact that John indicates the preparation day to have been the following day (John 19:14) is probably best understood in terms of the fact that, at that time, the Galileans are known to have observed the Passover on one day and the Judeans on the following day.

Multitudes of sacrificial lambs and other animals had been slain and their blood spilled through the centuries, but this would be the last such acceptable sacrifice. On the morrow, the Lamb of God would take away the sins of the world (John 1:29). He would offer one sacrifice for sins forever (Hebrews 10:12). With the blood of His cross, He would become the great Peace Maker, reconciling all things unto the Maker of those things (Colossians 1:16, 20).

As the Lord thought about the shedding of the blood of that last Passover lamb on that Fifth Day of Holy Week, He must also have thought of the Fifth Day of Creation Week, when He had first created animal life. "God created every living creature (Hebrew *nephesh)* that moveth" (Genesis 1:21). This had been His second great act of creation, when He created the entity of conscious animal life (the first had been the creation of the physical elements, recorded in Genesis 1:1). In these living animals, the "life" of the flesh was in their blood, and it was the blood which would later be accepted as an atonement for sin (Leviticus 17:11). Note that the words "creature," "soul," and "life" all are translations of the same Hebrew word *nephesh*. Surely the shedding of the innocent blood of the lamb that day would recall the far-off day when the "life" in that blood had been created. And because He, the Lamb of God, was about to become our Passover (I Corinthians 5:7), death itself would soon be swallowed up in victory and life (I Corinthians 15:54).

Sixth Day. On the Sixth Day, man had been created in the image and likeness of God, the very climax and goal of God's great work of creation (Genesis 1:26, 27). But on *this* Sixth Day, God, made in the likeness of man, finished the even greater work of redemption.

Under the great Curse, the whole creation had long been groaning and travailing in pain (Romans 8:22). But now the Creater, Himself, had been made the Curse (Galatians 3:13; Isaiah 52:14), and it seemed as though the Creation also must die. Though He had made heaven and earth on the First Day, now He had been lifted up from the earth (John 3:14) and the heavens were silent (Matthew 27:46). Though He had made the waters on the Second Day, He who was the very Water of Life (John 4:14), was dying of thirst (John 19:28).

On the Third Day He had made the dry land, but now the "earth did quake and the rocks rent" (Matthew 27:51) because the Rock of salvation had been smitten (Exodus 17:6). He had also covered the earth with trees and vines on that third day, but now the True Vine (John 15:1) had been plucked up and the Green Tree (Luke 23:31) cut down. He had made the sun on the Fourth Day, but now the sun was darkened (Luke 23:45) and the Light of the World (John 8:12) was burning out. On the Fifth Day He had created life, and He Himself *was* Life (John 11:25; 14:6), but now the life of His flesh, the precious blood, was being poured out on the ground beneath the cross, and He had been brought "into the dust of death" (Psalm 22:15). On the Sixth Day He had created man and given him life, but now man had despised the love of God and lifted up the Son of Man to death.

Seventh Day. But that is not the end of the story, and all was proceeding according to "the determinate counsel and foreknowledge of God" (Acts 2:23). "On the seventh day God ended His work which He had made" (Genesis 1:21). Furthermore, "everything that He had made "was very good" (Genesis 1:31). God's majestic work of Creation was complete and perfect in every detail.

And so is His work of salvation! This is especially emphasized in John's account: "After this, Jesus knowing that all things were now *accomplished,* that the Scripture might be *fulfilled,* saith, "I thirst . . . . When Jesus therefore had received the vinegar, He said, it is *finished;* and He bowed His head, and gave up the ghost" (John 19:28, 30) (the emphasized words are all the same word in the Greek original). Jesus had finished all the *things* He had to do, and then He finished the last of the prophetic *scriptures* that must be carried out. Then, and only then, was the work of redemption completed and the price of reconciliation fully paid, so that He could finally shout (Matthew 27:50) the great victory cry, *"It is finished."*

The record of Creation stresses repeatedly that the entire work of the creation and making of all things had been *finished* (Genesis 2:1-3). In like manner does John's record stress repeatedly the *finished* work of Christ on the cross.

Furthermore, as the finished creation was "very good," so is our finished salvation. The salvation which Christ thus provided on the cross is "so great" (Hebrews 2:3) and "eternal" (Hebrews 5:9), and the hope thereof is "good" (II Thessalonians 2:13).

Then, finally, having finished the work of redemption, Christ rested on the seventh day, His body sleeping in death in Joseph's tomb. He had died quickly, and the preparations for burial had been hurried (Luke 23:54-56), so that He could be buried before the Sabbath. As He had rested after finishing His work of Creation, so now He rested once again.

On the third day (that is the First Day of the new week), He would rise again, as He had said (Matthew

16:21, *et al*). His body had rested in the tomb all the
Sabbath Day, plus part of the previous and following days,
according to Hebrew idiomatic usage, "three days and
three nights" (Matthew 12:40) — but death could hold
Him no longer. He arose from the dead, and is now alive
forevermore (Revelation 1:8).

No. 35, May, 1976

THE PALUXY RIVER TRACKS

John D. Morris, B.S.*

It has been over a hundred years since the concept of
evolutionary uniformitarianism began to be taught as
scientific fact. With only a few isolated exceptions up until
the past decade, every scientific discussion, every academic
lecture, and every technical article that dealt with the past
was centered around the framework of evolutionary uniformitarianism.

In the last ten or fifteen years, however, many scientists
and laymen alike are waking up to the fact that much solid
scientific evidence exists that contradicts evolutionary
notions. One of the most shattering pieces of evidence
comes from the Paluxy River basin in central Texas, near
the town of Glen Rose, where fossilized tracks of man and
dinosaur appear together.

History Of The Find

The Paluxy River is a paradox in itself. At normal water
levels it sparkles calmly through the area and empties into
the nearby Brazos River. Often, for several months of the
year it is completely dry. At other times it changes into a
raging torrent. The river averages a drop of 17 feet per
mile and is the second swiftest river in Texas.

The local residents are very much aware of the power of
the Paluxy at flood stage. They say that during the worst

---

*ICR Field Scientist, currently on leave taking post-graduate studies in geo-
science.

floods the noise of the rushing water is drowned out by the frightening sound of boulders and rock shelves the size of automobiles grinding and breaking as they are swept downstream.

Man and dinosaur trails together. Dinosaur trail from right to left, man trail from bottom to top.

One of the worst floods of record ransacked the generally flat countryside in 1908 when the river rose 27 feet, and it was after this flood that prints began to be spotted. The erosion of a clay layer over a limestone shelf in one area revealed both human and dinosaur tracks, and the removal of an entire shelf in another area exposed others. After this it wasn't long before numerous similar tracks were discovered throughout the area.

Glen Rose is basically an agricultural community and few of the residents were aware of the meaning of the discovery. News of the prints eventually reached several universities and museums, and scientists were dispatched to study them. In 1938, a trail of brontosaurus tracks was removed from the river bottom under the supervision of the paleontologist, Roland T. Bird, and shipped to the American Museum of National History in New York, to be used in a display.[12]

Mr. Bird commented to one of the local discoverers that he must be mistaken about the man's tracks, because man had not yet evolved at the time of the dinosaurs. He claimed they must have been made by some sort of ape.

But even that possibility would not solve the problem for the evolutionists, for apes and dinosaurs living together would be almost as devastating to the geologic time table as man and dinosaur together.

The Geologic Time Frame

Almost everyone who has taken a course in geology has been required to memorize the geologic time chart. Specifics vary between individual charts, but all show a gradual evolution of life from the late pre-Cambrian period up to the present. The fossil record is sparse and highly speculative before the Cambrian which is thought to have witnessed the beginning of abundant marine invertebrate life about 500-600 million years ago. The Cretaceous period is known as the age of dinosaurs and is thought to have spanned about 70 million years, ending at the very latest about 65 million years ago. But man did not appear, according to evolutionists, until around four million years ago, at the earliest.

Thus, evolutionists face a dilemma. There is, at the very least, a 60-million-year gap between the age of the dinosaur and the advent of man, a gap during which there should be neither man nor dinosaur. But in Glen Rose, the fossils indicate that man and dinosaur lived not only at the same time but even at the same place! To make matters worse, the particular layer in which the footprints are found is known as the Glen Rose formation, designated lower Cretaceous, and supposedly was laid down early in the Cretaceous period, estimated about 120 million years ago.

Dinosaur trail in excavation area. This shelf was sandbagged, and several feet of overburden was removed to reveal several trails of both man and dinosaur.

Several uniformitarian scientists have been to Glen Rose to view the tracks. One made the following remarkable suggestion: "These man-like tracks couldn't be true man tracks, because man and dinosaur didn't live at the same time. Therefore, they must have been made by some undiscovered bipedal dinosaur with feet like human feet!" Another recognized that man must have made the tracks but explained the situation by an equally remarkable deduction: "This find doesn't disprove evolution; rather, it indicates that man appeared before dinosaurs became extinct and forces a revision of the geologic time scale."

But what a revision! Since evolutionists estimate about 600 million years for the evolution of all life, this revision would wipe out at least 20 percent of earth history! And if the time scale has been so wrong in the most recent age, how can we trust it in the dim past?

Two samples of carbonized plant remains found in these

strata provide the only real physical data for establishing a firm date according to uniformitarian assumptions. They were dated by the Carbon 14 dating method (which has been shown by creationist scientists to give ages higher than true ages). The calculated ages were 38,000 to 39,000 years before present even though they were found in strata thought to be 100,000,000 years old.[3]

The creationist does not face such a problem. This evidence harmonizes with a great deal of data indicating that the earth and all its strata are quite young and that all of the earth's inhabitants were created essentially at the same time. These footprints, (which everyone would agree were man's tracks if situated in strata designated as recent), imply the existence of man in the Cretaceous by all modes of logical thought, by the scientific method, and by open-minded analysis of raw data.[4]

Proper Identification

Seldom does one find a perfect footprint in the Glen Rose formation, a print that clearly shows all the features of a human foot. This is as it should be, of course, for a man walking in mud or wet sand without consciously trying to leave good tracks will slip, change stride, alter directions, stop or do other things that will mar his trail. Evolutionists have sometimes said that these markings are merely erosional features, or that they are not sufficiently detailed to be designated as man tracks. Such explanations, however, miss the mark.

Several tell-tale signs should be present if a marking is to be identified either as a man track or as a track of any sort of animal. Walking in mud not only produces an indentation where the foot sank down, but invariably also produces a "mud up-push", a place where the surrounding mud has been pushed up higher than it was before. Generally, this occurs around the outside of the foot, behind the heel, and adjacent to the big toe and ball of the foot— places where most of the weight of the body was borne by the mud itself. "Erosional processes" would obviously not leave a "mud up-push" or pressure ridges around an elongated marking—features which are common in the Glen Rose tracks.

Perhaps the most complete man track located in Paluxy in recent years. Notice distinct toe markings, pressure ridges between toes, "mud up-push" on side of big toe and above it, and arch. Print is 13 inches long.

Another feature is not so easy to discern, but again is consistent with simple logic. The weight of the man or animal making the track not only deforms the mud, but causes vertical displacement below the foot. As the mud is forced down into the subsurface, it becomes compacted, the amount of compaction decreasing with depth. If the mud has any layers of discoloration or special composition, these laminations will deform beneath the print. Unless the print were originally made on a steep slope, such that the striations become visible on the surface, the only way to see these deformed laminations is by removing the print and slicing it open in a laboratory. Even in the case of a smooth, homogenous material, the pressure will tend to cause a slight line of metamorphism or change in crystallization below the track.

These lines of stratification will bend downward to assume a contour essentially parallel to the contour of the foot. In the case of fossil footprints in limestone, we are dealing with rock material that once was a layer of sediments. There is no conceivable way to produce such striations artificially, but they may be present if the tracks are genuine. The absence of deformed laminations does not disprove genuineness, as may be demonstrated by observing a section through a plaster-of-paris mold in which a footprint had been made while the plaster was soft.

In times past, several prints were removed from the river and some of these have been sectioned in this manner. At the present time, it is illegal to remove any track from its original position and so this method of analysis is limited. Of those that have been sawed open, however (and despite some claims to the contrary), some indeed *have* shown the tell-tale laminations, including a "sabre-toothed tiger" track and at least one human track.

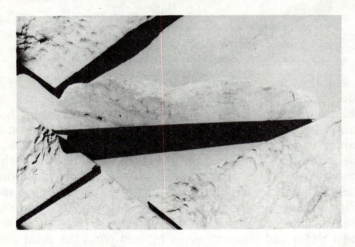

What has been designated as a sabre-toothed tiger print was removed from river and sectioned. Pressure striations are clearly seen following contour of print.

Photo: Burdick

To identify a tract *in situ* as a bona fide man track is not an easy task. Several criteria have been established to distinguish such a track from a freak rock formation and a man track from that of an animal. First of all, the track must be consistent with the general contour of the human foot. The ball of the foot is generally most easily preserved along with the arch and heel. Individual toe depressions are rare, but generally toe markings, made as the foot left the newly formed print, are preserved.

Quite commonly, as might be expected, the ball of the foot leaves the deepest impression, due to the fact that the entire weight of the body concentrates in this spot while walking, just before the opposite foot strikes the ground. At this point the hell is off the ground and mud is squeezed up between the toes, as they are pressed into the mud. Generally, these toe ridges were too fragile to be preserved,

Man tracks in obvious stride. Site of excavation by Films for Christ and later by ICR under direction of Mike Turnage.   *Photo: Turnage*

Even if a perfect human footprint were found, it would not be very convincing unless it were found as one of a series, a right-left-right-left trail of prints, all conformable to one another in size and shape. The prints should be separated by a relatively consistent length, representing the stride of the individual, and laterally by a few inches representing the natural straddle between the two feet. This trail should tend in one direction and each individual track should also be oriented in that same direction. The size of the tracks should be reasonable when compared to the length of the stride.

It is estimated that over a hundred such trails have been studied in the Paluxy River area. When an evolutionist claims that such tracks are simply erosional features (i.e., that erosion has consistently carved out man-like tracks in proper sequence) he must exercise the same blind faith and disregard for data that he uses when claiming that random mutations can produce complex ordered systems.

The great majority of these tracks are in the normal range of adult foot size today, from about shoe size 7 to 13. However, a number of prints of small children are found with the larger ones. Sometimes the prints appear to be made by a moccasin or wrapping covering the print. Unconfirmed reports persist of a nearby trail so detailed that the lacing on the moccasin was clearly visible. Most, however, are unshod.[5]

Prints of different sizes are often found together. Twelve feet to the lower left is trail of a man with 21½ inch feet. Between the trails is a dinosaur trail.

One aspect that has caused no little amount of speculation has been the presence of giant tracks, prints made by individuals with huge feet and huge strides. It may be that humans before the Flood were much larger on the average than today. This is consistent with the fossil record, which frequently exhibits animals larger than their modern-day counterparts. Scripture may provide an insight when it claims so matter of factly that "There were giants in the earth in those days" (Genesis 6:4). Quite a few of the tracks are in the 16-inch range, but several trails are of a man with a seven-foot stride and a foot of 21½ inches in length.[6] Whether or not there is any connection, has not yet been determined, but several years ago the skeleton of a woman seven feet tall was excavated from the Paluxy River Basin and exhibited in the Somervell County Museum in Glen Rose.

The Problem of Carved Tracks

Accusations have arisen from still another front. Skeptics have claimed that the prints are carvings, not real prints at all. Unfortunately, this charge has some basis; in fact, several enterprising Texans from Glen Rose did make their living during the Great Depression by digging out the best tracks and selling them. The going price ranged from $10 to $25, and the dinosaur tracks were much more in demand than the man tracks. Soon, however, the best tracks were gone and a few men began to carve new tracks (especially dinosaur tracks) out of any limestone block available. As near as researchers can determine, however, only a very few "man tracks" were carved, probably less than six, certainly less than ten. These were all giant tracks, ranging from 16 to 20 inches in length and showed all features of the foot. These counterfeit tracks do not, of course, disprove the genuine tracks. In fact, it could only have been the existence of genuine tracks that made the manufacture of counterfeits profitable.

One of the many hand carved *footprints found on a rock ledge with numerous* genuine *animal prints near Alex, Oklahoma. Note: unnatural contour, no "mud up-push", no arch. Prints were not in sequence.*

These carved tracks are all produced after carving the block of limestone out of the river first. No one would ever sit down and carve out a series of imperfect tracks in the river bottom and leave these simply to rile the evolutionists! And many of the tracks have been recently uncovered (by Taylor, Dougherty and others) by excavation of the banks of the river and even in construction sites nearby. There can be no doubt whatsoever that the human tracks *in situ* are true tracks and not carvings. One who would make such a charge is obviously grasping at straws. A number of individuals have gone to Glen Rose to see whether there are any human tracks there, and have been unable to find them, reporting then to outsiders that the whole story is fallacious. The problem was simply that they did not know where to look. Many, of course, were skeptical and tended to jump to negative conclusions too quickly. The fact is, however, that there really are many tracks there which, to all appearances, were made by real human beings who lived at the same time as the dinosaurs.

Formation Of The Tracks

Three geologic units bear on the existence of the tracks: (1) The Paluxy Formation, (2) The Glen Rose Formation, (3) The Twin Mountains Formation, which comprise the Trinity Group. The Twin Mountains Formation immediately underlies the track-containing Glen Rose Formation and is the oldest Cretaceous layer in Central Texas.

The Glen Rose Formation is described as "Limestone, alternating with units composed of variable amounts of clay, marl, and sand. Limestone, distinctly bedded, in part with variable amounts of clay, silt, and sand, soft to hard, in various shades of brownish yellow and grey. Gradational to Paluxy Formation above and Twin Mountain Formation below, bench-forming beds included in the Glen Rose Formation. Thickness 40-200 feet, thins northward."[7]

Physically, the Glen Rose Formation consists of shelves of limestone, generally 60 to 10 inches thick separated by layers of bluish clay, coarse conglomerate or limey marl, generally 12 to 18 inches thick, although dimensions at any one point vary widely. Tracks are found in several of the layers of limestone as they are exposed by river erosion. In fact, man tracks have even been found in layers *below* units containing dinosaur tracks! This interbedding seems to be cyclic in nature and has seemingly been repeated seven times within the Glen Rose Formation.

The evolutionary interpretation of the formation would include consistent transgression and regression of the sea, each stage laying down strata in the general sequence of subtidal, restricted, intertidal, supratidal, and marsh deposits. The fact that all of the deposits are from regressive phases is usually explained as simply due to the fact that the transgression phase was poorly developed. Fossils from land, margin, and sea areas are found throughout the formation and brand it as a lagoon or bay depositional system.[8]

But there are some major problems with this interpretation, not the least of which is that corresponding members of the cycles in the formation are uniform in composition and fossil content, even though a great length of time, on the order of several million years, is represented. To expect this lagoon to remain completely unchanged throughout seven major changes in sea level is unreasonable. Problems are compounded by the fact that most of the fossils clearly represent plants and animals buried alive, by massive inundations of water laden with the organisms.

The conclusive evidence of rapid formation, however, is the fact that tracks exist in the limestone. Forget for a moment that man, bear, sabre-toothed tiger, mammoth, and dinosaur tracks appear together, for just the fact that the tracks are preserved at all is incompatible with the uniformitarian model.

Consider how a track is made and then preserved. First, a layer of mud must be deposited. This mud must contain a stabilizer of some sort; in this case, lime, in order for it to begin to turn to stone. Once a print is made, it will not last for any length of time at all, particularly in a water environment, and so the mud must quickly harden to protect the print from erosion. But even a print in hardening rock will eventually disappear unless other preservative steps are taken. No doubt, soon after the print was made, a layer of clay, sand, and gravel washed in, filling the print with a different material, preserving its integrity and not allowing further erosion to take place. In places where the mud had not sufficiently hardened, the gravel matrix itself would have destroyed it. Once the print was preserved, nothing could alter it while the mud continued hardening into firm limestone.

These steps are somewhat speculative, but some similar process is necessary. At any rate, the process must be rapid. A print in mud will disappear within a few days. Any exposed print in hard rock will disappear in a few years. The hardening mud must be protected by an overlying layer, but the deposition of that layer must not destroy the print. There is no room here for millions or even hundreds of years. The process has to happen fast.

But the process is undoubtedly rare, as evidenced by the fact that fossil footprints are relatively rare on a worldwide scale.

Proper Interpretation

The evidence presented by the basal Cretaceous rocks in Central Texas is incompatible with uniformitarian geology. The addition of the fossil footprints is icing on the cake. However, catastrophists have not yet come up with a complete solution to the problem either. Although the basic framework is compatible with the evidence, the details are lacking.

The creation record in Genesis indicates that man and dinosaur did indeed live together. Man was created on the sixth day of creation week and dinosaurs probably on the fifth. A proper translation of Genesis 1:21 would read "and God created great dragons" or possibly "sea monsters." Dinosaurs evidently survived the Flood, either on board Noah's Ark or somehow surviving outside. Job, who lived soon after the Flood, was familiar with these creatures and detailed descriptions of two types of dinosaurs (translated "behemoth" and "leviathan") are given in Job 40:15-21 and 41:1-34.

The main problem of geologic interpretation for Biblical catastrophists stems from the fact that underlying the Paluxy River basin is nearly 8,500 feet of sedimentary rock. According to the catastrophic model, this must all have been laid down by the Flood of Noah's day. The problem is how could man and dinosaur witness such massive deposition at the beginning stages of the Flood and survive long enough to leave their prints so high up in the geologic column? Just to the east, the strata dip away and plunge into the Gulf Coast Basin, where similar sequences of strata are 50,000 feet thick in places. It seems unreasonable that man could have postponed annihilation for so long.

Some creationists have postulated that the print-bearing formations are post-Flood, most likely made during the

closing years of the Ice Age as huge volumes of melt
water once again deposited sediments. Certainly man was
in North America by the time of the Ice Age, for his
fossils are found in glacial deposits. And probably dinosaurs were here also, for pictographs of them have been
found etched into the wall of a canyon in Arizona, made
by some early tribe inhabiting the region.

But this cannot be. The strata in central Texas are
definitely of marine origin. The composition of the rocks
testifies to a mixing of fresh and salt water. The fossils
are also mixed land and marine organisms; even a thick
layer of fossil clams, all buried alive, has been found in
strata less than 100 feet above the track-bearing layers. To
the east the beds are conformable and thick, and are
undoubtedly ocean flood deposits.

To the southwest of Glen Rose lies a possible answer.
Almost in the very center of Texas a pre-Cambrian granite
has been forced to the surface. A nearly circular feature,
with a diameter of about 60 miles, the Llano Uplift,
forms a stratigraphic high.[9] This highly resistant basement
rock was evidently being uplifted at the beginning stages
of the Flood because it received only minimal amounts of
the earliest sediments and projected above the waters of the
Flood until the very late stages. The strata on all sides
not only dip away from this feature, due to a combination
of its uplift with sinking of the adjacent basins, but pinch
out or become thinner as they near it, indicating that the
uplift did not receive these sediments. The rock on either
side is totally different indicating that the uplift and its
northerly extension formed a temporary barrier that separated two bodies of Flood waters during the beginning
stages of the Deluge.

The conclusion seems justified that the Llano Uplift was
one of the last areas to be inundated by the Flood. Man
and some of the more mobile animals would surely have
sought the highest ground for safety, which, in this region,
would have been this great rock mass. Perhaps here the
men built rafts in a futile effort to save themselves,
although this is speculation, to be sure.

The rim of the Gulf Coast Basin swings northward with a circular arc from the Llano Uplift. Glen Rose is only about 25 miles from the high point of that rim, and only about 100 miles from the uplift itself. It is not at all inconceivable that a few hardy souls, both man and beast, could have survived for many days in the uplift area as the Flood waters relentlessly advanced. To surmise how they got to the Glen Rose area would not be best, but perhaps if tidal or tectonic activities caused a temporary lowering of the local water level, it is possible that by following the ridge or on rafts they made the journey, looking for safety.

Continuing Studies

The preceding synthesis should definitely not be considered yet as established fact. It is a workable solution that is harmonious with all geologic facts that have come to the author's attention. But a great deal more work needs to be done. The Institute for Creation Research has been actively interested in this fascinating and important area, as well as other sites of anomalous fossils, and has sponsored several field studies there. The author has spent three periods there under ICR sponsorship, and Houston biologist Mike Turnage has also led ICR teams there on two occasions. New tracks were identified each time, both man and dinosaur.

In August of 1975, Drs. Clifford Burdick and Harold Slusher revisited the area, studying a number of Dr. Dougherty's sites for ICR, as did Dr. Ed Blick and the author in October, 1975. Conditions were excellent and numerous new prints were discovered, including what seems to be the most precise print ever photographed *in situ*. Plans are being made to sponsor excavation work during July and August of 1976 in the most promising area, with the aid of Dr. C. N. Dougherty, local footprint investigator, and volunteer workers.[10]

So much evidence has come from Glen Rose indicating a vast discrepancy in the geologic time table that those who disagree with the conclusions must fit into one of two categories: (1) They have not sufficiently investigated the evidence, or (2) They have not studied it with an open mind. Once again, in the case of the Paluxy River Basin, where man tracks and dinosaur tracks are found in the same strata, strata clearly laid down by catastrophic methods, true science has been shown to harmonize much better with the predictions of the creation-catastrophe model, than those of the evolutionary-uniformitarian model.

REFERENCES

1. Roland T. Bird, "Thunder in His Footsteps," *Natural History* (May, 1939).
2. Clifford L. Burdick, "When Reptiles Ruled the Earth," *Signs of the Times* (May, 1955). [Dr. Burdick, a creationist geologist, has been doing research on these tracks since 1945 when they first came to the attention of a number of creationist scientists in the old Society for the Study of Creation, the Deluge and Related Sciences. Photographs taken by him were published in 1961 in *The Genesis Flood* by Dr. Henry Morris, who had been a member of that Society at the time and was teaching at Rice Institute in 1945 when Dr. Burdick, E. L. Beddoe, Ben F. Allen, and others began corresponding with him about them. These photographs in *The Genesis Flood* rekindled interest in the tracks, and led to the further research which has confirmed their authenticity.]
3. According to reports from dating laboratories employed by Stanley Taylor [producer of a motion picture documenting the tracks, "Footprints in Stone"] to determine radiocarbon dates on these samples.
4. A. Wilder Smith, *Man's Origin, Man's Destiny,* (Wheaton, Ill.: Harold Shaw Co., 1968), pp. 135-141, 293-299. [Dr. Smith, intrigued by the photographs in *The Genesis Flood,* later made a special trip to Glen Rose all the way from Germany, with Dr. Burdick in order to get further documentation and photographs for his own book.]
5. Stanley E. Taylor, "The Mystery Tracks in Dinosaur Valley," *Bible-Science Newsletter* (April 15, 1971). See also movie "Footprints in Stone," (Producer Stanley E. Taylor, Films for Christ, Elmwood, Ill.). [Taylor's excavations in connection with the production of this film uncovered many new tracks, both human and dinosaur. In recent years (1972-76) this film has been shown very widely, including showings in about 300 public high schools, and has been attracting much interest. Though some scientists viewing it have reacted angrily and incredulously, none have been able to refute its strong evidence.]
6. C. N. Dougherty, *Valley of the Giants,* 4th ed. (Published by the author: Glen Rose, 1967). [Dr. Dougherty is a local chiropractor in Glen Rose who has found many additional tracks in the area after Taylor had completed his own work there.]
7. The Geologic Atlas of Texas, Dallas Sheet (University of Texas at Austin, 1972).

8. J. Stewart Nagle, "Glen Rose Cycles and Facies, Paluxy River Valley, Somervell County, Texas," *"Bureau of Economic Geology, Geologic Circular 68-1* (University of Texas at Austin, 1968).
9. "Geologic Highway Map of Texas," *AAPG*.
10. Students or others willing to help in this work, and who can provide their own expenses, should contact the author in care of the Institute for Creation Research headquarters office, 2716 Madison Ave., San Diego, CA 92116.

No. 36, June, 1976

A TWO-MODEL APPROACH TO ORIGINS: A CURRICULUM IMPERATIVE

Richard Bliss*

Within the last decade, the whole concept of science and social science instruction has centered around the inquiry approach. Researchers have gathered data that show many satisfying spinoffs in reading, language arts, and logical thought within science and social studies. The inquiry approach centers around a presentation of data by the teacher, through reading and via experimentation. This data is then acted upon by the students from a logical framework. This, of course, means that the role of the professional teacher now takes the form of a person skilled in questioning techniques rather than a disseminator of all knowledge. Inquiry in its best context never reflects teacher bias, but rather is objective and develops logical thought and decision-making skills among students. The objectives of good instruction and inquiry will be centered around process skills, such as:

1. Observation (sight, hearing, smell, etc.)
2. Classification (placing information in categories)
3. Inferring (general assumptions about data)
4. Predicting (always done from considerable data)
5. Measuring (using standards for measurement)
6. Communicating (oral, written charts, graphs, etc.)
7. Interpreting Data (from all aspects of the investigation: classifying, communicating, inferring, etc.)
8. Making Operational Definitions (definitions that are clear and expressive of the process)

*Former Director of Science Education, Unified School District #1, Racine, Wisconsin. Currently ICR's Director of Curriculum Development.

9. Formulating Questions and Hypothesis (a sophisticated stage, including all he presently knows)
10. Experimentation (one of the best ways of making judgments relative to a problem; empirical knowledge)
11. Formulating Models (models are temporary structures that quickly change when new information becomes available)

These skills teach young people to make critical observations when dealing with data. Are the data complete? Are they significant to the problem? Teachers cannot justify instruction that does not develop these skills, as the ramifications have broad social, as well as scientific, implications. Young people are not just naturally operational to these skills; they must be taught. Instruction, then, must come from educators who are willing to coach the student in these skills without developing a dependence upon the teacher's bias.

Some considerations brought out by the National Education Association in the publication "The Spirit of Science," were values in affective domain. These values are what educators in private and public education, K-12, as well as college, should be most concerned about, for it reflects the final product of an education system. Reflecting on these values, they are reported as follows:

1. Respect for Logic
2. Search for Data and Its Meaning
3. Long for Knowledge and Understanding
4. Consideration of Consequences
5. Consideration of Premises
6. Demand for Verification
7. Question All Things

Values, to be sure, are not easy to evaluate or test in a paper and pencil way, but are, nevertheless, values that can become operational to young minds if they are trained through objective, unbiased inquiry. This will, in fact, develop the logical thought patterns, decision-making ability, and critical thinking that is so often missing among our high school and university graduates. We cannot escape the fact that this young person is going to be the decision-maker of the future, and we have the role of guiding him toward opportunities that will enable him to be a wise decision-maker. It is unconscionable for any educator to knowingly instill a dogmatic world view into his or her students and thus attempt to make them carbon copies, coached in their own bias. The data must be presented; the decision must be their own. What an empty mind it must be that can only regurgitate someone else's ideas.

Science should be a search for truth; however, too often we hear comments such as those stated to this writer by two of his graduate students. "I will decide what is good science for my class to consider and what is not;" "I don't care how many faults there are to evolution. I will insist that my students modify the evolution model. I will in no instance present creation as an alternative to evolution;" "Evolution is science, creation is religion, we cannot have religion in the classroom." All too often this is the rule when it comes to the manner in which teachers perceive their role in the instruction of origins in the classroom. Fortunately, this type of thinking does not prevail in the majority of cases.

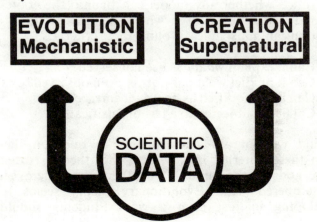

Those who have been exposed to a Two-Model Approach in college methods classes are less likely to take the view expressed above, for they cherish the freedom they had to examine all data and the freedom to come to their own conclusions. Those teachers who have been exposed to severe dogmatism in their high school or college training are not likely to have such an open mind on the subject, nor are they likely to tolerate others that oppose them.

A Two-Model Approach to Origins should not include sectarian religion for the public schools; the approach should base its emphasis on the interpretation of scientific data presently available. It is conceivable, even desirable, that sectarian schools will embellish the scientific limits of the model by making open reference to biblical history. A Two-Model Approach, in essence, is significant only when students have had an opportunity to hear, see, or read all pertinent data on topics relating to origins. When students have had an opportunity to make these observations and evaluate data from their level of understanding, then a teacher might ask them to determine which model they feel the data fits best. Educators must somehow recognize how crucial it is to train their students in objective inquiry and that non-testable dogma is, in fact, a religion of its ov . The tests that we must give to determine whether any model can fit into the context of a valid scientific theory, which neither evolution nor creation can, must at least follow these criteria:

1. Can it explain what has been observed?
2. Can it predict what has not yet been observed?
3. Can it be modified as new data emerge?
4. Can it be subjected to a test of falsification?

Should we not ask our students to question theories from these criteria? It is evident that theories often become gods in the minds of many, and as such, cannot be tampered with. Evolutionary theory seems to be developing in just such a way. Students should be cautioned to hold their theories with a light hand and thus spare themselves the agony of seeing these theories fall apart before their eyes. A current example of this lies within the evolution model.

For the past 100 years or more, Darwin's ideas have become a not-to-be-challenged byword of science. Interestingly enough, there are growing amounts of data and a significant number of scientists that are beginning to feel free about challenging these ideas. There are many that question interpretations as they review this emerging data. They are now ready to look at these data in a new light and from a competing model. Questions are arising as to whether the evolution model will be able to hold the attention of the thoughtful mind for the not-too-distant future. Evolutionary dogma is facing the most difficult challenge of its life. We must, as educators, allow our young people the option of this challenge and to present them with truly a better scientific view based upon inquiry. In this respect, they can observe data and its meaning without fear of demeaning reprisal. There is no question in my mind concerning teachers that are dedicated to a student product that is capable of making rational judgments on its own, for they will welcome this view; after all, isn't this what education is all about?

The following statements have been made by biology students after completing a unit on Origins from A Two-Model Approach (conducted in the Racine, Wisconsin Public School System):

> I was on the creationist side of our debate, but I am "in the middle of the road," so to speak. In the molecules, the lectures you gave, and in the debate, so many good arguments were given by both sides. I thought the debate was a very good way to teach and to make us want to dig up more information to prove our point. I thought it was a good way to make us think about both sides. I also thought both sides did very well in sup-

porting their model and I think it was one of the best things we have ever done to learn about subjects. Thank you for coming to our class and helping us research our sides and learn about both sides and for not letting your own personal views interfere on the subject. You gave us a chance to think for ourselves.

I think the best arguments for creation are the Laws of Thermodynamics, the complexity of natural laws and systems. Also there is the evidence of sediments and other rocks, fossilization, continental drift, volcanoes, pluviation, and mountain building. A good argument for creation is the explanation of many pieces of data such as different races, languages, and adaptation (which in no sense of the word is evolution). In fact, one could say that the earth and its interacting laws and systems and structures is the only needed evidence, since it would be impossible to argue that this huge universe of complexity could have come from complete and absolute randomness which came from an anti-everything VOID.''

I have learned very much from this debate. Both sides put up good arguments. I still haven't decided what I am, a creationist or evolutionist. The creationists put up a good argument about the missing links. It would be possible to say that one missing link is Bigfoot. There is only one problem—no evidence there is a Bigfoot. Another one is that Sidney Fox thought of a good theory that shows living things all started from one cell and that they could have started from what is supposedly the earth's first atmosphere.

I thought the best evolution argument was the way in which organisms evolve from simple to complex was stated. They used this argument to support the theory of all living things evolving from one cell. Mainly I was interested in the way autotrophic organisms stretch from little few-celled organisms to more complex organisms like trees, etc.

These unedited comments from biology students are typical responses made in biology classes that were given two models from which to choose. There can be no question in the minds of objective teachers that students will appreciate the opportunity to make their own decisions based upon logical thought processes, as opposed to dogmatic views that are fast being shown to be wrong. I could think of nothing more embarrassing than to have a student come back to me after he has taken my class to say: "You denied me the opportunity to make my own decision; you denied me the opportunity to see, in a fair context, what scientific data was available for me to study on this subject."

It has been said that "it is no mean pedagogical feat to teach a child the facts of science, but it is a pedagogical triumph to teach these facts in the context of scientific inquiry." All teachers can view the outcome of this student product with elation when the instructor realizes that he has taught the child to think and make his own decisions. True, these decisions may not be in keeping with the instructor's view, but nevertheless, the student will have been given the opportunity to make these decisions for himself.

The world is flat! Does this sound familiar? Well, for many years the historical view of the world was just so. Only the inquiring mind of man and the freedom to hear and collect all data allowed him to find that another model would fit the data better.

Consider the following general format in the context of a biology class studying the idea of origins:

First Phase: Discussion (Teacher directed)

1. Introduction by the teacher: motivational
2. Origins: where and how did it all begin: (a) very general: some ideas about the first cell; (b) some ideas about the Geologic Column; (c) some ideas about Flood Geology; (d) some ideas about time and earth history; (3) some ideas about genetics and natural selection; (f) other topics

Second Phase: Team Organization and Research (divide class into groups of 4 or 5)

1. Research topics in evolution and creation (teacher allows group to choose topics)
2. Materials: (a) *Origins: A Two-Model Approach* (general); (b) *Time and Earth History* (module); (c) Geology module (general); (c) Creation filmstrips on topic; (e) Evolution filmstrips on topic, etc.

Third Phase:

1. Teacher brings new ideas (factual data only) to students without biased comment
2. Students work in groups on research project
3. Students are encouraged to continue research after school

Fourth Phase:

1. Teacher introduces an evolution-slanted film to class for critical examination
2. Students work in groups

Fifth Phase:

1. Teacher introduces creation-slanted (design) film to class
2. Students work in groups

Sixth Phase:

Somewhere in this phase of the lesson, the students prepare to react on a discussion panel with another group

The foregoing can be modified to the teacher's needs, and certainly needs additions to complete the topics for a lesson plan; however, this general approach has been used in the Racine Unified District with very encouraging results.

Presently, the Institute for Creation Research is developing supportive materials that will enable the teacher to instill variety and excitement to a stimulating, interdisciplinary topic, and what is even more significant, this is being done in a way that will meet the very important skill and value objectives in inquiry-based instruction.

No. 38, August, 1976
UP WITH CATASTROPHISM!
Henry M. Morris, Ph.D.

The Uniformitarian Century

One of the surprising developments of the past decade has been the resurgence of catastrophism in geological interpretation. Although the great men who were the real founders of geology (Steno, Woodward, *et al*) were not only catastrophists but believed in the Noahic Flood as the most important geologic event in earth history, the principle of uniformitarianism has dominated geological thinking for the past 150 years. The Scottish agriculturalist, James Hutton, and then the British lawyer, Charles Lyell, persuaded their contemporaries to reject the Biblical chronology and its cataclysmic deluge in favor of very slow processes acting through aeons of time. In his widely used textbook, Zumberge stated as recently as 1963:

> Opposed to this line of thinking was Sir Charles Lyell (1797-1875), a contemporary of Cuvier, who held that earth changes were gradu-

al, taking place at the same uniform slowness that they are today. Lyell is thus credited with the propagation of the premise that more or less has guided geological thought ever since, namely, that the present is the key to the past. In essense, Lyell's doctrine of uniformitarianism stated that past geological processes operated in the same manner and at the same rate they do today.[1]

Nevertheless, the evidence for catastrophism was there in the rocks and it could not be ignored indefinitely. Uniformitarianism was proving sterile—present processes operating at present rates simply could **not** explain the great geological formations and structures in the earth's crust, not to mention its vast fossil graveyards. Zumberge noted:

> From a purely scientific point of view, it is unwise to accept uniformitarianism as unalterable dogma . . . . (One) should never close his mind to the possibility that conditions in past geological time were different than today . . . . [2]

A few geologists (Krynine, Bretz, Dachilee, *et al)* had even earlier begun to call attention to certain strong geologic evidences of more than normal catastrophism in the geologic column. Even Lyell, of course, had recognized the significance of local floods, volcanic eruptions, etc., but had included these in his overall uniformitarian framework. Such phenomena as the "scabland" areas of Washington and the earth's many meteoritic scars, however, had begun to convince some geologists that even "ordinary" catastrophes were not the whole story.

The New Catastrophism

The recent revival of catastrophism seems to have been associated with a number of brilliant papers by Stephen

Jay Gould, a geologist and historian of science with impeccable credentials. Gould first stressed the necessity to distinguish between uniformity of natural laws and uniformity of process rates.

> Uniformitarianism is a dual concept. Substantive uniformitarianism (a testable theory of geologic change postulating uniformity of rates of material conditions) is false and stifling to hypothesis formation. Methodological uniformitarianism (a procedural principle asserting spatial and temporal invariance of natural laws) belongs to the definition of science and is not unique to geology.

It is interesting to note that writers on Biblical catastrophism have always stressed that they are only rejecting the concept of uniform **rates,** not that of uniformity in natural laws. Gould was merely repeating what catastrophists had long emphasized.

More recently, Gould has recognized this fact, while also calling attention to the devious methods by which Lyell and others in the 19th century had persuaded their contemporaries to reject Biblical catastrophism in favor of uniformitarianism:

> Charles Lyell was a lawyer by profession, and his book is one of the most brilliant briefs ever published by an advocate . . . . Lyell relied upon true bits of cunning to establish his uniformitarian views as the only true geology. First, he set up a straw man to demolish . . . . In fact, the catastrophists were much more empirically minded than Lyell. The geologic record does seem to require catastrophes: rocks are fractured and contorted; whole faunas are wiped out. To circumvent this literal appearance, Lyell imposed his imagination upon the evidence. The geologic record, he argued, is extremely imperfect and we

must interpolate into it what we can reasonably
infer but cannot see. The catastrophists were
the hard-nosed empiricists of their day, not the
blinded theological apologists.[4]

Lest anyone misunderstand, it should be emphasized
that Gould is neither a creationist nor a Biblical catastrophist. In fact he and other modern geological quasi-
catastrophists are confident that their battle with the
Bible has been won and that they can now safely and
openly revert to catastrophism in their geological interpretations without the danger of appearing to support Biblical
supernaturalism. Gould had said, for example:

As a special term, methodological uniformitarianism was useful only when science was
debating the status of the supernatural in its
realm; for if God intervenes, then laws are not
invariant and induction becomes invalid . . . .
The term today is an anachronism . . . .

Similarly, another modern writer criticizing uniformitarianism explains why the principle is nevertheless useful
in argumentation.

Frequently the doctrine of uniformitarianism
is used fruitfully to explain the anti-catastrophist
viewpoint of history . . . .

The author of a recent book promoting geological catastrophism feels it necessary to hedge his conclusions with
the following caution:

It is both easy and tempting . . . to adopt a neo-
catastrophist attitude to the fossil record . . . .
This is a heady wine and has intoxicated paleontologists since the day when they could blame it
all on Noah's flood. In fact, books are still being
published by the lunatic fringe with the same

explanation. In case this book should be read by
some fundamentalist searching for straws to
prop up his prejudice, let me state categorically
that all my experience (such as it is) has led me to
an unqualified acceptance of evolution by natural selection as a sufficient explanation for what I
have seen in the fossil record. I find divine
creation, or several such creations, a completely
unnecessary hypothesis. Nevertheless this is not
to deny that there are some very curious features
about the fossil record.[7]

Another recent book[8] documents that the modern approach to geomorphology (which stresses erosion by hydraulic processes) was originally established by Woodward
and the other catastrophist founders of geology, and was
believed by them to be perfectly consistent with the Biblical
history of the earth under the divine Curse. This true
empirical approach to geology has been retarded by Hutton and other deists with their principle of uniformitarianism, and a steady-state earth. A reviewer of this book
makes the following interesting comment:

With the Mosaic chronology finally discredited
and denudation again theologically respectable
[that is, by Hutton's rationalizations], nineteenth
century British geologists could return to the
issue of fluvialism.[9]

Uniformitarian Catastrophism

Creationist writers have been saying for years[10] that
uniformitarianism was inadequate to explain any of the
important types of geologic formations. It is not only that
uniformitarianism does not explain everything—the fact is,
it explains nothing! More and more, it has become apparent that the present is **not** the key (not even **a** key) to
the past, as far as process rates are concerned.

This important fact, categorically denied for so long by

evolutionists and uniformitarians, is now being acknowledged more and more openly by both. Typical of this
modern trend is the important book by Derek Ager, *The
Nature of the Stratigraphical Record*, mentioned earlier.
Although Ager insists he is an evolutionist and uniformitarian, the theme of his book is that **every** type of geologic
formation and structure was formed by some kind of
catastrophe. He does not believe they were all formed by
the same catastrophe, of course, but by many different
catastrophes, separated from each other in a typical
uniformitarian framework of billions of years of time—a
sort of "uniformitarian catastrophism," in other words.

Dr. Ager discusses in detail all the various types of
geologic formations, even those traditionally believed to
have been formed very slowly, concluding that all must
have been formed rapidly.

> The hurricane, the flood, or the tsunami may do
> more in an hour or a day than the ordinary
> processes of nature have achieved in a thousand
> years.[11]

This assessment by Ager almost sounds Biblical—"one
day is with a catastrophe as a thousand years!" As a matter
of fact, the famous verse in II Peter 3:8, though commonly
misinterpreted to teach that the "days" of creation were
"thousands of years" long, really means exactly what
Ager implied. God is not limited to uniformitarian rates
to accomplish his work. He can do in one day what uniformitarian assumptions indicate would require a thousand
years. Ager continues:

> Given all the millennia we have to play with in
> the stratigraphical record, we can expect our
> periodic catastrophes to do all the work we want
> of them.[12]

The conclusion of Ager's book, after examining all the
evidence, is as follows:

In other words, the history of any one part of
the earth, like the life of a soldier, consists of
long periods of boredom and short periods of
terror.[13]

That is, everything we can actually **see** in the geologic
strata is the product of catastrophism. The intervening
periods, which supposedly totaled billions of years, presumably left no record in the rocks. Individual formations
were deposited rapidly; the "unconformities" between formations were periods of either erosion or inactivity.

One or Many?

The question remaining is whether these really do
represent a myriad of individual catastrophes or whether
they might possibly all be parts of the same catastrophe.
If it is true, as Ager and others are contending, that we
cannot really see the evidences of the ages between the
various catastrophes, then it is legitimate to ask how we
know such ages really occurred. There is nothing remaining
there to measure!

But I maintain that a far more accurate picture
of the stratigraphical record is of one long gap
with only very occasional sedimentation.[14]

How long does it take to form a gap?
The only real reason for imposing a billion-year time
frame on the catastrophes is the necessity to provide time
for evolution. As a matter of fact, the strata themselves
show evidence of being a complex of interconnected and
continuous regional catastrophes combining to comprise a
global cataclysm.
In the first place, the rocks of all "ages" **look** the same.
That is, there are rocks of all kinds, minerals of all kinds,
structures of all kinds, in rocks of all ages.
Secondly, every formation grades, somewhere, up into
another formation continuously without a time break.

This followed from the fact that there is no worldwide "unconformity." An unconformity is a supposed erosional surface between two adjacent rock formations, representing a time break of unknown duration between deposition periods. It was once believed that such unconformities were, indeed, worldwide:

> In the early history of stratigraphy, unconformities were overestimated in that they were believed to represent coeval diastrophism over areas of infinitely wide extent.[15]

It is now known, however, that all such unconformities are of very limited extent, and furthermore, that they have no particular time significance.

> Many unconformity-bounded units are considered to be chrono-stratigraphic units in spite of the fact that unconformity surfaces inevitably cut across isochronous horizons and hence cannot be true chrono-stratigraphic boundaries.[16]

From these facts, a simple syllogistic line of reasoning can proceed as follows: (1) since every formation was produced rapidly and catastrophically; and (2) since every such formation somewhere grades into another above it without an interruption in the deposition process; and (3) since the whole (of the geologic column) is the sum of its parts; therefore (4) the entire geologic column was formed continuously and rapidly, in a worldwide interconnected complex of catastrophes.

The Geological Quandary

The above discussion is very abbreviated and inadequate, but it does point up the dilemma confronting modern geologists. Having rejected the Biblical record of creation and the flood as the true key to earth history, geologists for a hundred years relied on uniformitarianism as their rule of interpretation. This system has proved utterly sterile, so that they are now being forced to rely increasingly on neo-catastrophism in their current thinking.

However, if all the geologic formations must be explained by catastrophic phenomena which are inaccessible to observation or measurement, and which are incommensurate with present processes, then historical geology is not science, but speculation.

> Of late there has been a serious rejuvenation of catastrophism in geologic thought. This defies logic; there is no science of singularities. If catastrophe is not a uniform process, there is no rational basis for understanding the past. For those who would return us to our Babylonian heritage of "science" by revelation and possibility, we must insist that the only justifiable key to the past is probability and the orderliness of natural process; if uniformity is not the key, there is no key in the rational sense, and we should pack up our boots and go home.[17]

This lament would, in fact, be realistic if we were limited to naturalistic and speculative catastrophism for our interpretations of earth history, for that would be even worse than uniformitarianism! There would remain no possibility at all of acquiring real knowledge about the origin and early history of the world.

But when all else fails, read the instructions! The rocks do bear witness everywhere to a worldwide hydraulic cataclysm. The causes, nature, duration and effects of that cataclysm are recorded accurately, by infallible divine inspiration, in the Holy Scriptures, and all the actual facts of geology can be correlated perfectly with that record. The founders of the science of geology believed that, and it is time for their latter-day intellectual children to return to the faith of their fathers.

REFERENCES

1. James H. Zumberge, *Elements of Geology* (New York, 2nd ed., John Wiley and Sons, 1963), p. 200. Zumberge and the writer were graduate students together at the University of Minnesota, in the period 1946-50, in its Department of Geology. He was more favorably inclined toward Biblical catastrophism than were others in the Geology Department and we had a number of good discussions and seemed to have much in common at that time.
2. Ibid., p. 201.
3. Stephen Jay Gould, "Is Uniformitarianism Necessary?" *American Journal of Science,* Vol. 263, March 1965, p. 223. This same point had been stressed earlier by the writer *(The Twilight of Evolution,* Philadelphia, Presbyterian and Reformed Publ. Co., 1963, pp. 59-64). Gould has been on the geology faculty at Columbia University and is currently Professor of Geology at Harvard.
4. Stephen Jay Gould, "Catastrophes and Steady-State Earth," *Natural History,* February 1975, pp. 16-17.
5. Stephen Jay Gould, "Is Uniformitarianism Necessary?" p. 227.
6. James W. Valentine, "The Present is the Key to the Present," *Journal of Geological Education,* Vol. XIV, April 1966, p. 60.
7. Derek V. Ager, *The Nature of the Stratigraphical Record* (New York, John Wiley and Sons, 1973), p. 19. Ager is Professor and Head of the Department of Geology and Oceanography at the University College of Swansea, England.
8. Gordon L. Davies, *The Earth in Decay—A History of British Geomorphology,* 1578-1878 (New York, American Elsevier, 1970), 370 pp.
9. R.H. Dott, Jr., *Review of "The Earth in Decay,"* Journal of Geology, Vol. 79, September 1971, p. 633.
10. See, for example, *The Genesis Flood,* by John C. Whitcomb and Henry M. Morris (Philadelphia, Presbyterian and Reformed, 1961), pp. 200-203, etc., as well as still earlier writings by George McCready Price, Harold W. Clark, and others.
11. D.V. Ager, op. cit. p. 49.
12. Ibid.
13. Ibid., p. 100
14. Ibid., p. 34.
15. K. Hong Chang, "Unconformity-Bounded Stratigraphic Units," *Bulletin, Geological Society of America,* Vol. 86, November 1975, p. 1545.
16. Ibid., p. 1544.
17. B.W. Brown, "Induction, Deduction, and Irrationality in Geologic Reasoning," *Geology,* Vol. 2, September 1974, p. 456.

No. 39, September, 1976

THE SPIRITUAL IMPACT OF CREATIONISM

Henry M. Morris, Ph.D.

"The heavens declare the glory of God" (Psalm 19:1). "For the invisible things of Him from the creation of the world are clearly seen, being understood by the things that are made, even His eternal power and Godhead, so that they are without excuse" (Romans 1:20). " . . . the living God, which made heaven, and earth, and the sea, and all things that are therein . . . left not Himself without witness, in that He did good, and gave us rain from heaven, and fruitful seasons, filling our hearts with food and gladness" (Acts 14:15-17).

These and many other Scriptures unite in testimony to the spiritual impact of creationism. That is, the structure and processes of the created cosmos, properly understood and explained, bear irrefutable witness to the glory and power of God, as well as His grace and goodness—even His very nature, His Godhead. This is as it should be, of course. There can be no conflict between the Creator and His creation and the proper study of the natural world must direct men to the true God.

Unfortunately, the **wrong** study of nature—"science falsely so called" (I Timothy 6:20)—has generated a serious dichotomy between cosmology and theology ("the study of the cosmos" and "the study of God"). The educational and scientific establishments today believe there are irreconcilable conflicts between science and Scripture, between God's world and God's Word. Unfortunately the same attitude prevails in the religious establishment. Consequently, even many who theoretically believe in its verbal inspiration and scientific accuracy in a practical sense tend to downgrade doctrine and objective truth—especially topics related to science and history—in favor of subjective evangelism and an introspective emphasis on the spiritual life.

The Great Commission, however, enjoins Christians not only to "preach the Gospel," but also to teach "all things whatsoever I have commanded you" (Matthew 28:20). In fact, the very emphasis of the "everlasting Gospel" is on the Creator of all things (Revelation 14:6,7). It is vital to preach the necessity of saving faith in Christ, who died for our sins, but it is essential to preach Christ **as He is,** not a Christ of one's subjective experience. The Lord Jesus

Christ was Creator and Sustainer of the universe (Colossians 1:16,17), before He became its Redeemer (Colossians 1:20,21), and He must be presented in His fullness. A religious experience based only on an emotional decision without roots in objective truth will "wither away" when "persecution ariseth because of the word" (Matthew 13:6, 20,21).

Because of the widespread belief that "science" has disproved Scripture, especially its accounts of Creation, the Flood and other great events of history, many Christians feel they should avoid such "controversial" questions in their witnessing. This tactic, of course, is tacit admission to the unbeliever that the Scriptures indeed are mistaken on these matters, and therefore not really reliable at all.

But this is all wrong. The Biblical records are completely true and there is no need for compromise or equivocation. Furthermore, instead of hindering the presentation of Christ to an unsaved person, or the spiritual growth of the Christian, the great truths of creationism, rightly expounded from both science and Scripture, will be found an invaluable foundation for true Christian faith and life.

The ICR Survey

In an attempt to evaluate this issue quantitatively, the Institute for Creation Research recently conducted a mail survey among the readers of its monthly publication *Acts and Facts,* asking them to respond to a brief questionnaire, "Spiritual Values in ICR Ministry." They were asked to indicate whether the science-Bible ministries of ICR (lectures, debates, books, radio broadcasts, literature, etc.) had been of definite spiritual help to them in any of the following ways: (1) "Instrumental in leading us to Christ;" (2) "Helpful in our personal spiritual growth as Christians;" (3) "Effective in helping us win others to Christ;" (4) "Other." Comments also were invited.

The readers of *Acts and Facts* come from a large range of denominational backgrounds. Most are either college graduates or college students, so that the educational level is probably somewhat higher than among people in general. A very large number are pastors or Christian leaders of one sort or another. Therefore, the results of the survey should be more meaningful than a typical man-in-the-street poll.

Over 2,800 questionnaires were filled out and returned, and they are still coming in! Almost half were accompanied by comments, some by long letters. The evangelistic effectiveness of the ICR ministry was clearly indicated by the fact that, to date, 80 people indicated it had been instrumental in leading them to Christ, while 850 said it had been effective in helping them win others to Christ.

As far as personal Christian life is concerned, 1,800 replies stated the ICR ministry had been helpful in their own spiritual growth. There were 325 who indicated it had helped them in various "Other" ways. Since normally only one questionnaire was returned for each family, all the above figures should be increased by some factor.

Perhaps of more interest than the numerical statistics are the comments. These were far too numerous to reproduce in a brief article, but typical comments appear below:

> *Genesis Flood* instrumental in leading me to Christ. Conference at Bibletown in 1974 was a great blessing.

> Although I am a Catholic, I commend you highly for the admirable defense of the Scriptures.

> Instrumental in our seeing the possibility of God and rethinking our naturalistic presuppositions.

> I was a hard-core skeptic.

> As a scientist I would not have understood the reality of God and Christ if it weren't for ICR.

> Your materials have helped me to gain assurance in the Word of God as authority for living a practical Christian life.

> The ICR ministry has helped increase my faith more than any other work.

As a science teacher, I am very grateful for the information, which has opened my eyes.

Your ministry had a lot to do with winning my wife to Christ.

Really exciting Praise the Lord for your work.

Before your information shattered my evolutionary beliefs, my chances of becoming a Christian were virtually nil.

The search for Noah's Ark played a part in my conversion from atheism to Christ.

Belief in evolution is the main factor that prevents many persons from becoming Christians.

Apologetics is a very vital part of evangelism, and a must for building up Christians in the Lord.

I was saved in a church I was visiting through the speaker's message on the Noahic flood.

I passed your materials on to my (unsaved) husband, who was first outraged by your "biased" opinions—now he loves you!

The Genesis Flood broke the barrier (veil)!

Your message is clear—a Christ-centered life means salvation! Your work in creationism is wonderful.

This literature has helped some of my students to accept creation and to believe in Christ!

To a Christian biologist—ICR is as vital as any other Gospel area, including Moody, Wycliffe, Billy Graham, etc.

I saw one science teacher come to Christ through this.

As a biological scientist (Ph.D.), I had almost overwhelming conflict with evolutionary "law" as taught in our universities. ICR has helped resolve this conflict.

I had been brainwashed by evolution while pursuing my biology degree, but have just finished reading *Scientific Creationism* and it was a real eye opener.

As a Director for Child Evangelism Fellowship, I have found many opportunities to use the knowledge with young people personally, as well as with teachers.

People are generally astounded when they find there is scientific evidence supporting creationism. They are quicker to find a personal Savior who has suddenly become tangible.

I enjoyed the Santa Ana seminar immensely and use the scientific knowledge of creation I acquired in my witnessing regularly.

Tremendous witnessing tool, especially to the college student.

Especially helpful in the academic community in witnessing to other professional educators.

I regard your ministry, along with the Christian school movement, as the most valuable spiritual ministry today!

The issue of origins is an exceptional tool in apologetics and evangelism. A very vital ministry.

A debate with Morris and Gish—was the most refreshing thing which ever happened in my scientific study. It helped me to worship God through what He has made.

My opportunities to witness for Christ in a public classroom setting has increased from practically nothing to a common occurrence.

Started out totally brainwashed in evolution . . . now use the material in my own teaching . . . virtually all in my classes have become creationists.

This has helped me to realize the truth of God's Word. I am soon to enter a Russian Orthodox monastery.

I doubted the Bible as being true until ICR. One year later I was born again!

One student was led to Christ by Morris' *Bible and Modern Science.*

Dennis was a boy in our youth group to whom my husband made available several of his ICR books and Impact Series. As a result of this . . . we have watched Dennis grow into an enlightened and bold witness . . . He has led friends to Christ.''

I am a science teacher and find everything you write helpful to me personally.

As an airline pilot, it has been used tremendously.

Dr. Morris' book *The Bible and Modern Science* was very instrumental in my conversion.

Accepted Christ as a result of your weekend seminar in Philadelphia.

Dr. Gish's book *Evolution the Fossils Say No* helped give a confused young man faith to trust Scripture.

His reading of Dr. Morris' books led him, occupied by geology, to Christ.

A friend of mine committed his life to Christ as a result of Dr. Morris' book *Scientific Creationism.*

The ICR is an answer to prayer.

I as a science teacher have seen that students must see Christ as Creator before they will ever see Him as a "Purpose Giver."

I was turned away from the Scriptures as a high school freshman when I was taught evolution.

The work of ICR is so essential that it would be a great loss if it would ever be curtailed.

Have seen many young believers greatly strengthened by use of your materials. One young man decided to go into the ministry.

Helped me to accept the Bible as the Word of God.

Words do not express the worth of *Acts and Facts* to our spiritual encouragement.

You are doing what organized religions have failed to do.

I have just completed a 13-week course using Dr. Morris' tapes, and it was a pleasure to see the growth in the lives of those participating.

I am 63 years of age. Thank God and you, I've had the privilege to live to see this *great, important* ministry, finally. (From a foreign missionary.)

This has given me a much stronger testimony to the saving power of Jesus Christ.

ICR—one of the all-time great events of Christian Bible history.

The Genesis Flood is the most exciting book (next to the Bible) I have ever read.

I have found that, after they digest scientific creationism, they are very open to witnessing.

My wife and I work with Campus Crusade for Christ, and are so grateful for your dedication to this ministry.

Reading the ICR publications has had a great deal to do with my being a convinced follower of Christ.

I have found it very helpful in my preaching and teaching ministry in the church.

This material has been invaluable in my teaching and preaching ministry.

Four years ago Dr. Gish and Dr. Morris were on the campus at Oklahoma University. I attended on a lark and was amazed . . . . God used that debate and subsequent material to change the direction and course of my entire life and ministry. (From a Methodist pastor.)

I personally have had my own Christian life deepened and strengthened through the various ministries of ICR.

Acts and Facts has enriched my life this year and added to my love for God's Word.

I really appreciate your weekly radio broadcast. I just wish it were longer.

I was a trained evolutionist, and I went to hear Dr. Morris fall on his face. He didn't—instead I fell to my knees.

The above comments are only a very small sampling of all the encouraging testimonies received. There can no longer be any doubt that a creationist ministry does have an exceedingly significant spiritual impact on the lives of thousands.

In contrast, there were 24 replies that were negative or critical in one way or another. Most of these were from non-Christians whose names were on the mailing list inadvertently (ICR only adds names to its mailing list by request, but occasionally people will sign requests for friends to whom they wish to send *Acts and Facts* without their friends' consent).

Some might feel that the poll was biased in that the questionnaire only went to people already interested in creationism. As a matter of fact, this makes it all the more significant. That is, these are the people best qualified, in terms of knowledge and experience, to make an intelligent appraisal of the spiritual impact of creationism. Those who have not "tried it" are hardly able to evaluate it!

Conclusions

It is now evident, both from Scripture and from experience, that scientific Biblical creationism can and should play a vital role in evangelism and in Christian faith and life, as well as in true science and education. It is especially important when dealing with those who have been educated in public schools and colleges in recent decades.

In no way does this conclusion minimize the importance of prayer and the Bible in witnessing, or of the need of faith and the work of the Holy Spirit in regeneration. It is not "either-or," but "both-and." It is a matter of being ready to "give an answer to every man" (I Peter 3:15), as need and opportunity arise, and as God has commanded.

No. 40, October, 1976
ENTROPY AND OPEN SYSTEMS
Henry M. Morris, Ph.D.

The most devastating and conclusive argument against evolution is the entropy principle. This principle—also known as the Second Law of Thermodynamics—implies that, in the present order of things, evolution in the "vertical" sense (that is, from one degree of order and complexity to a higher degree of order and complexity) is completely impossible.

The evolutionary model of origins and development requires some universal principle which *increases* order, causing random particles eventually to organize themselves into complex chemicals, non-living systems to become living cells, and populations of worms to evolve into human societies. However the only naturalistic scientific principle which is known to effect real changes in order is the Second Law, which describes a situation of universally deteriorating order.

CRITERIA	S Y S T E M	
	GROWING PLANT	BUILDING CONSTRUCTION
1. Open System	Seed	Materials
2. Available Energy	Sun	Sun
3. Directing Program	Genetic Code	Blueprint
4. Conversion Mechanism	Photosynthesis	Workmen

Figure 1. *Criteria for increasing order.*

This law states that all natural processes generate entropy, a measure of disorder."[1]

CRITERIA TO BE SATISFIED	S Y S T E M	
	FIRST LIVING MOLECULE	POPULATION OF COMPLEX ORGANISMS
Open System	Complex Inorganic Molecule	Population of Simple Organisms
Available Energy	Sun	Sun
Directing Program	None	None (Natural Selection?)
Conversion Mechanism	None	None (Mutations?)

Figure 2. *Absence of ordering criteria in evolution.*

Entropy, in short, is the measurement of molecular disorder. The law of the irreversible increase in entropy is a law of progressive disorganization, of the complete disappearance of the initial conditions.[2]

It can hardly be questioned that evolution is at least superficially contradicted by entropy. The obvious prediction from the evolution model of a universal principle that *increases* order is confronted by the scientific fact of a universal principle that *decreases* order. Nevertheless evolutionists retain faith that, somehow, evolution and entropy can co-exist, even though they don't know how.

In the complex course of its evolution, life exhibits a remarkable contrast to the tendency expressed in the Second Law of Thermodynamics. Where the Second Law expresses an irreversible progression toward increased entropy and disorder, life evolves continually higher levels of order. The still more remarkable fact is that this evolutionary drive to greater and greater order also is irreversible. Evolution does not go backward.[3]

Back of the spontaneous generation of life under other conditions than now obtain upon this planet, there occurred a spontaneous generation of elements of the kind that still goes on in the stars; and back of that I suppose a spontaneous generation of elementary particles under circumstances still to be fathomed, that ended in giving them the properties that alone make possible the universe we know.[4]

Life might be described as an unexpected force that somehow organizes inanimate matter into a living system that perceives, reacts to, and evolves to cope with changes to the physical environment that threatens to destroy its organization.[5]

When confronted directly with this problem (e.g., in creation/evolution debates), evolutionists often will completely ignore it. Some will honestly admit they do not know how to resolve the problem but will simply express confidence that there must be a way, since otherwise one would have to believe in supernatural creation. As Wald says:

> In this strange paper I have ventured to suggest that natural selection of a sort has extended even beyond the elements, to determine the properties of protons and electrons. Curious as that seems, it is a possibility worth weighing against the only alternative I can imagine, Eddington's suggestion that God is a mathematical physicist.[6]

Some evolutionists try to solve the problem by suggesting that the entropy law is only statistical and that exceptions can occur, which would allow occasional accidental increases in order. Whether this is so, however, is entirely a matter of faith. No one has ever *seen* such an exception— and science is based upon observation!

> There is thus no justification for the view, often glibly repeated, that the Second Law of Thermodynamics is only statistically true, in the sense that microscopic violations repeatedly occur, but never violations of any serious magnitude. On the contrary, no evidence has ever been presented that the Second Law breaks down under any circumstances . . . . [7]

By far the majority of evolutionists, however, attempt to deal with this Second Law argument by retreating to the "open system" refuge. They maintain that, since the Second Law applies only to isolated systems (from which external sources of information and order are excluded), the argument is irrelevant. The earth and its biosphere are open systems, with an ample supply of energy coming in from the sun to do the work of building up the complexity of these systems. Furthermore, they cite specific examples of systems in which the order increases,—such as the growth of a crystal out of solution, the growth of a seed or embryo into an adult plant or animal, or the growth of a small Stone Age population into a large complex technological culture—as proof that the Second Law does not inhibit the growth of more highly-ordered systems.

Arguments and examples such as these, however, are specious arguments. It is like arguing that, since NASA was able to put men on the moon, therefore it is reasonable to believe cows can jump over the moon! Creationists have for over a decade been emphasizing that the Second Law really applies only to *open* systems, since there is no such thing as a truly isolated system. The great French scientist and mathematician, Emil Borel, has proved this fact mathematically, as acknowledged by Layzer:

> Borel showed that no finite physical system can be considered closed.[8]

Creationists have long acknowledged—in fact *emphasized*—that order can and does increase in certain special types of open systems, but this is no proof that order increases in *every* open system! The statement that "the earth is an open system" is a vacuous statement containing no specific information, since all systems are open systems.

The Second Law of Thermodynamics could well be stated as follows: "In any ordered system, open or closed, there exists a *tendency* for that system to decay to a state of disorder, which tendency can only be suspended or reversed by an external source of ordering energy directed by an informational program and transformed through an ingestion-storage-converter mechanism into the specific work required to build up the complex structure of that system."

If either the information program or the converter mechanism is not available to that "open" system, it will *not* increase in order, no matter how much external energy surrounds it. The system will proceed to decay in accordance with the Second Law of Thermodynamics.

To cite special cases (such as the seed, for which the genetic code and the conversion mechanism of photosynthesis *are* available) is futile, as far as "evolution" is concerned, since there is neither a directing program not a conversion apparatus available to produce an imaginary evolutionary growth in complexity of the earth and its biosphere.

It is even more futile to refer to inorganic processes such as crystallization as evidence of evolution. Even Prigogine recognizes this:

> The point is that in a non-isolated system there exists a possibility for formation of ordered, low-entropy structures at sufficiently low temperatures. This ordering principle is responsible for the appearance of ordered structures such as crystals as well as for the phenomena of phase transitions.
>
> Unfortunately this principle cannot explain the formation of biological structures. The probability that at ordinary temperatures a macroscopic number of molecules is assembled to give rise to the highly-ordered structures and to the coordinated functions characterizing living organisms is vanishingly small. The idea of spontaneous genesis of life in its present form is therefore highly improbable, even on the scale of the billions of years during which prebiotic evolution occurred.[9]

Thus the highly specialized conditions that enable crystals to form and plants and animals to grow have nothing whatever to do with evolution. These special conditions themselves (that is, the marvelous process of photosynthesis, the complex information programs in the living cell, even the electrochemical properties of the molecules in the crystal, etc.) could never arise by chance—their own complexity could never have been produced within the constraints imposed by the Second Law. But without these, the crystal would not form, and the seed would never grow.

But what is the information code that tells primeval random particles how to organize themselves into stars and planets, and what is the conversion mechanism that transforms amoebas into men? These are questions that are not answered by a specious reference to the earth as an open system! And until they *are* answered, the Second Law makes evolution appear quite impossible.

> To their credit, there are a few evolutionists (though apparently very few) who recognize the critical nature of this problem and are trying to solve it. Prigogine has proposed an involved theory of "order through fluctuations" and "dissipative structures."[10]

But his examples are from inorganic systems and he acknowledges that there is a long way to go to explain how these become living systems by his theory.

> But let us have no illusions—our research would still leave us quite unable to grasp the extreme complexity of the simplest of organisms.[11]

Another recent writer who has partially recognized the seriousness of this problem is Charles J. Smith.

> The thermodynamicist immediately clarifies the latter question by pointing out that the Second Law classically refers to isolated systems which exchange neither energy nor matter with the environment; biological systems are open and exchange both energy and matter.—This explanation, however, is not completely satisfying, be-

cause it still leaves open the problem of how or
why the ordering process has arisen (an apparent
lowering of the entropy), and a number of scientists have wrestled with this issue. Bertalanffy
(1968) called the relation between irreversible
thermodynamics and information theory one of
the most fundamental unsolved problems in biology. I would go further and include the problem of meaning and value.[12]

Whether rank-and-file evolutionists know it or not, this
problem they have with entropy is thus *"one of the most
fundamental unsolved problems in biology."* It is more
than a problem in fact—it is a devastating denial of the
evolution model itself. It will continue to be so until
evolutionists can demonstrate that the vast imagined evolutionary continuum in space and time has both a program
to guide it and an energy converter to empower it. Otherwise, the Second Law precludes it.

It is conceivable, though extremely unlikely, that evolutionists may eventually formulate a plausible code and
mechanism to explain how both entropy and evolution
could co-exist. Even if they do, however, the evolution
model will still not be as good as the creation model. At
the most, such a suggestion would constitute a secondary
modification of the basic evolution model. The latter could
certainly never predict the Second Law.

The evolution model cannot yet even explain the Second
Law, but the creation model *predicts* it! The creationist
is not embarrassed or perplexed by entropy, since it is
exactly what he expects. The creation model postulates a
perfect creation of all things completed during the period
of special creation in the beginning. From this model,
the creationist naturally predicts limited horizontal changes
within the created entities (e.g., variations within biologic
kinds, enabling them to adapt to environmental changes).
If "vertical" changes occur, however, from one level of
order to another, they would have to go in the downward
direction, toward lower order. The Creator, both omni-

scient and omnipotent, made all things perfect in the beginning. No process of evolutionary change could improve them, but deteriorative changes could disorder them.

Not only does the creation model predict the entropy principle, but the entropy principle directly points to creation. That is, if all things are now running down to disorder, they must originally have been in a state of high order. Since there is no naturalistic process which could produce such an initial condition, its cause must have been supernatural. The only adequate cause of the initial order and complexity of the universe must have been an omniscient Programmer, and the cause of its boundless power an omnipotent Energizer. The Second Law of Thermodynamics, with its principle of increasing entropy, both repudiates the evolution model and strongly confirms the creation model.

REFERENCES

1. David Layzer, "The Arrow of Time," *Scientific American* (Vol. 223, December 1975), p. 56. Dr. Layzer is Professor of Astronomy at Harvard.
2. Ilya Prigogine, "Can Thermodynamics Explain Biological Order?" *Impact of Science on Society,* Vol. XXIII, No. 3., 1973) p. 162. Dr. Prigogine is Professor in the Faculty of Sciences at the University Libre de Belgique and is one of the world's leading thermodynamicists.
3. J.H. Rush, *The Dawn of Life* (New York, Signet 1962) p. 35.
4. George Wald, "Fitness in the Universe," *Origins of Life* (Vol. 5, 1974) p. 26.
5. Mars and Earth, National Aeronautics and Space Administration (Washington, U.S. Govt. Printing Office, NF-61, August 1975) p. 5.
6. George Wald, *op. cit.,* p. 26. Wald is a famous humanistic biologist at Harvard.
7. A.B. Pippard, *Elements of Chemical Thermodynamics for Advanced Students of Physics* (Cambridge, England, Cambridge University Press, 1966), p. 100. Pippard was Professor of Physics at Cambridge.
8. Layzer, *op. cit.,* p. 65.
9. Ilya Prigogine, Gregoire Nicolis & Agnes Babloyants, "Thermodynamics of Evolution." *Physics Today* (Vol. 25, November, 1972) p. 23.
10. *Ibid,* pp. 23-28.
11. Ilya Prigogine, "Can Thermodynamics Explain Biological Order?" p. 178.
12. Charles J. Smith, "Problems with Entropy in Biology," *Biosystems* (Vol. 1, 1975), p. 259.

No. 41, November, 1976
THE ORIGIN OF COAL
Stuart E. Nevins, M.S.*

Accumulated, compacted, and altered plants form a sedimentary rock called coal. It is not only a resource of great economic importance, but a rock of intense fascination to the student of earth history. Although coal forms less than one percent of the sedimentary rock record, it is of foremost importance to the Bible-believing geologist. Here is where he finds one of his strongest geological arguments for the reality of the great Noachian Flood.

Two theories have been proposed to explain the formation of coal. The popular theory held by many uniformitarian geologists is that the plants which compose the coal were accumulated in large freshwater swamps or peat bogs during many thousands of years. This first theory which supposes growth-in-place of vegetable material is called the *autochthonous* theory.

The second theory suggests that coal strata accumulated from plants which had been rapidly transported and deposited under flood conditions. This second theory which claims transportation of vegetable debris is called the *allochthonous* theory.

Fossils in Coal

The types of fossil plants found in coal do not clearly support the autochthonous theory. The fossil lycopod trees (e.g., *Lepidodendron* and *Sigillaria)* and giant ferns (especially *Psaronius*) common in Pennsylvanian coals may have had some ecological tolerance to swampy conditions, yet other Pennsylvanian coal plants (e.g., the conifer *Cordaites,* the giant scouring rush *Calamites,* the various

---

*Professor of Geology and Archaeology, Christian Heritage College, El Cajon, California

extinct seed ferns) by their basic construction must have preferred well-drained soils, not swamps. The anatomy of coal plants is considered by most investigators to indicate tropical or subtropical climate, a conclusion which can be used to argue against autochthonous theory, for modern swamps are most extensive and have the deepest accumulation of peat in the higher-latitude cooler climates. Because of the increased evaporative power of the sun, modern tropical and subtropical regions have the most meager peats.

It is not uncommon to find marine fossils such as fish, moluscs, and brachiopods in coal. Coal balls, which are rounded masses of matted and exceptionally well preserved plant and animal fossils (including marine creatures)[1] are found within coal strata and associated with coal strata. The small marine tubeworm *Spirorbis* is commonly attached to plants in Carboniferous coals of Europe and North America.[2] Since there is little anatomical evidence suggesting that coal plants were adapted to marine swamps, the occurrence of marine animals with nonmarine plants suggests mixing during transport, thus favoring the allochthonous model.

Among the most fascinating types of fossils associated with coal seams are upright tree trunks which often penetrate tens of feet perpendicular to stratification. These upright trees are frequently encountered in strata associated with coal, and on rare occasions are found in the coal. In each case the sediments must have amassed in a short time to cover the tree before it could rot and fall down.

One's first impression may be that these upright trees are in their original growth position, but several lines of evidence indicate otherwise. Some of the trees penetrate the strata diagonally, while others are found upside down. Sometimes an upright tree *appears* to be rooted in growth position in a stratum which is entirely penetrated by a second upright tree. The hollow trunks are commonly filled with sediment unlike the immediately surrounding rocks. Logic applied to the previous examples demonstrates transportation of the trunks.

Fossil Roots

The most important fossil relating to the controversy over the formation of coal is *Stigmaria,* a fossil root or rhizome. *Stigmaria* is frequently found in strata below coal seams and is commonly associated with upright trees. *Stigmaria* studied nearly 140 years ago by Charles Lyell and J. W. Dawson in the Carboniferous coal sequence of Nova Scotia was considered to provide unambiguous proof of growth-in-place. Many modern geologists still insist that *Stigmaria* represents an *in situ* root in the soil below the coal swamp. The Nova Scotia coal sequence was recently restudied by N. A. Rupke[3], who found four types of sedimentary evidence for the *allochthonous origin of Stigmaria.* The fossil is usually fragmental and is rarely attached to a trunk, it shows a preferred orientation of its long axis due to current action, it is filled with sediment unlike the immediately surrounding rock, and it is often found on multiple horizons in beds which are entirely penetrated by upright trees. Rupke's research brings serious doubt upon the popular autochthonous interpretation of other *Stigmaria*-bearing strata.

Cyclothems

Coal commonly occurs in a sequence of sedimentary strata called a *cyclothem.* An *idealized* Pennsylvanian *cyclothem* may have strata deposited in the following ascending order: sandstone, shale, limestone, underclay, coal, shale, limestone, shale. A *typical cyclothem* will normally be missing one or more of the component strata. In any one locality *cyclothems* commonly repeat tens of times with each cycle of deposition accumulated on a previous one. There are fifty successive cycles in Illinois and over a hundred in West Virginia.

Although the coal bed forming a portion of the typical *cyclothem* is usually quite thin (commonly an inch to a few tens of feet thick), the lateral extent of coal is often incredible. Modern stratigraphic research[*] has correlated the Broken Arrow coal (Oklahoma), Croweburg coal (Mis-

souri), Whitebrest coal (Iowa), Colchester No. 2 coal
(Illinois), Coal IIIa (Indiana), Schultztown coal (W. Kentucky), Princess No. 6 coal (E. Kentucky), and Lower
Kittanning coal (Ohio and Pennsylvania). These form a
single, vast seam of coal exceeding one hundred thousand
square miles in area in the central and eastern United
States. No modern swamp has an area remotely approaching the great Pennsylvanian coals.

If the autochthonous model for coal formation is correct, a very unusual set of circumstances must have prevailed. An entire region, often encompassing many tens of
thousands of square miles, would have to be raised simultaneously relative to sea level to permit swamp accumulation and then lowered to permit the ocean to flood the
area. If the coal forest was raised too far above sea level,
the swamp and its antiseptic water necessary for the accumulation of peat would have been drained. If during the
peat accumulation time the sea invaded the swamp, the
marine conditions would have killed the plants, and other
sediment instead of peat would have been deposited. According to the popular model, the formation of a thick bed
of coal, then, would indicate the maintenance of an incredible balance over many thousands of years between
the rate of peat accumulation and the rise of sea level.
Such a situation seems most improbable especially when
the *cyclothem* is known to recur a hundred times or more
in a vertical section. Could such cycles be better explained
by accumulation during successive advances and retreats
of flood waters?

Underclay

One of the most talked about portions of the *cyclothem* is the underclay. The non-bedded, plastic layer of
clay often underlies the coal stratum and is considered by
many geologists to be a fossil soil on which the swamp
existed. The presence of underclay, especially when it
posseses *Stigmaria*, is often claimed to be *prima facie*

evidence for the autochthonous origin of coal-forming plants.

Modern research, however, has cast some doubt on the fossil soil interpretation of underclays. No soil profile similar to modern soils is evident in underclays. Some of the minerals found in the underclay are not the type which would be expected in a soil. Instead underclays commonly show graded bedding (coarser grained material at the base) and evidence of clay flocculation. These are simple sedimentary features which would form in any water accumulated layer.

Many coal seams do not rest on underclays and little evidence of soil exists. In some cases coal strata rest on granite, schist, limestone, conglomerate or other rock unsuitable for soil. Underclay without a coal bed above is common as well as underclay resting on top of coal. The absence of recognizable soils below beds of coal shows the improbability of any type of luxuriant vegetation growing in place and argues for transportation of the coal-forming plants.

Texture of Coal

Investigation of the microscopic texture and structure of peat and coal contributes to the understanding of the origin of coal. A.D. Cohen[5] initiated a comparative structural study between modern autochthonous mangrove peats and a rare modern allochthonous beach peat from southern Florida. Most autochthonous peats had plant fragments showing random orientation with a dominant matrix to finer material, while the allochthonous peat showed current orientation of elongated axes of plant fragments generally parallel to the beach surface with a characteristic lack of the finer matrix. The poorly sorted plant debris in the autochthonous peats had a massive structure due to the intertwining mass of roots, while the allochthonous peat had characteristic microlamination due to the absence of intergrown roots.

Following this study Cohen remarked: "A peculiar

enigma which developed from study of the allochthonous peat was that vertical microtome sections of this material looked more like thin sections of Carboniferous coal than any of the autochthonous samples studied."[6] Cohen noted that the characteristics of his allochthonous peat (orientation of elongated fragments, sorted granular texture with general lack of finer matrix, microlamination with lack of matted root structure) *are also general characteristics of Carboniferous coals!*

Boulders in Coal

One of the most striking inorganic features of coal is the presence of boulders. These have been noted in coal beds all over the world for more than one hundred years. P. H. Price[7] conducted a study of boulders in the Sewell Coal of West Virginia. The average weight of 40 boulders collected was 12 pounds with the largest weighing 161 pounds. Many of the boulders were igneous and metamorphic rocks *unlike any rock outcrops in West Virginia.* Price suggested that the boulders may have been entwined in the roots of trees and transported from a distant area. Thus, the occurrence of boulders in coal favors the allochthonous model.

Coalification

The nature of the process of metamorphosis of peat to form coal has been disputed for many years. One theory suggests that *time* is the major factor in coalification. The theory, however, has become unpopular because it has been recognized that there is no systematic increase in the metamorphic rank of coal with increasing age. There are some blatant contradictions: lignites representing low metamorphic rank occur in some of the oldest coal-bearing strata while anthracites representing the highest metamorphic rank occur in some of the youngest strata.

A second theory supposes *pressure* to be the major factor in coal metamorphosis. The theory is refuted by numerous geological examples where metamorphic rank does not increase in highly deformed and folded strata. Furthermore, laboratory experiments demonstrate that increase of pressure can actually *retard* the chemical alteration of peat to coal.

A third theory (by far the most popular) suggests the *temperature* is the important factor in coal metamorphosis. Geological examples (igneous intrusions into coal seams and underground mine fires) demonstrate that elevated temperature can cause coalification. Laboratory experiments have also been quite successful. One experiment[8] produced a substance like anthracite in a few minutes by using a rapid heating process with much of the heat being generated by the cellulosic material being altered. Thus, the metamorphosis of coal does not require millions of years of applied pressure and heat, but can be produced by quick heating.

Conclusion

We see that many positive evidences have appeared which strongly support the allochthonous theory and the accumulation of many of the coal layers during the Noachian Flood. Upright fossil trees within coal seams suggest rapid accumulation of the vegetable debris. Marine animals and terrestrial (not swamp-dwelling) plants in coal imply transporation. The microstructure of many coal strata shows particle orientation, sorted texture, and microlamination indicting transportation (not growth-in-place) of plant material. Boulders present in coal demonstrate transportation processes. The absence of a soil below many coal strata argues for the drifting of coal-forming plants. Coal appears to form a regular and typical portion of the *cyclothem* being as clearly water-laid as the other rocks. Experiments in the alteration of vegetable material show that coal resembling anthracite does not require millions of years to form, but can be produced rapidly by a short heating process.

REFERENCES

1. S.H. Mamay and E.L. Yochelson, "Occurrence and Significance of Marine Animal Remains in American Coal Balls," U.S. Geological Survey Professional Paper 354-1, 1962, pp. 193-224.
2. H.G. Coffin, "A paleoecological Misinterpretation," *Creation Research Society Quarterly,* 1968, vol. 5, pp. 85-87.
3. N.A. Rupke, "Sedimentary Evidence for the Allochthonous Origin of Stigmaria, Carboniferous, Nova Scotia, *Geological Society of America Bulletin,* 1969, vol. 80, pp. 2109-2114.
4. C.R. Wright, "Environmental Mapping of the Beds of the Liverpool Cyclothem in the Illinois Basin and Equivalent Strata in the Northern Mid-Continent Region," unpublished Ph.D. thesis, 1965, Univ. of Illinois; R.M. Kosanke, "Palynological Studies of the Coals of the Princess Reserve District in Northeastern Kentucky," U.S. Geol. Survey Prof. Paper 839, 1973, 20 p.
5. A.D. Cohen, "An Allochthonous Peat Deposit from Southern Florida," *Geological Society of America Bulletin,* 1970, vol. 81, pp. 2477-2482.
6. Ibid., p. 2480.
7. P.H. Price, "Erratic Boulders in Sewell Coal of West Virginia," *Journal of Geology,* 1932, vol. 40, pp. 62-73.
8. G.R. Hill, *Chemical Technology,* May 1972, p. 296.

No. 42, December, 1976

CRACKS IN THE NEO-DARWINIAN JERICHO

(Part I)

Duane T. Gish, Ph.D.

The modern theory of evolution, commonly known, as the neo-Darwinian theory of evolution, and sometimes referred to as the synthetic theory, since it purports to be a synthesis of modern scientific knowledge rooted in classical Darwinism, has been set forth during the past few decades by leading evolutionary theorists, such as R.A. Fisher,[1] George Gaylord Simpson,[2,4] Theodosius Dobzhansky,[5,6] Ernst Mayr,[7] G. Ledyard Stebbins,[8] and Sir Julian Huxley.[9] This modified form of the Darwinian theory of evolution has never been unanimously accepted by evolutionists, but nevertheless has been so widely accepted that Mayr, with reference to the many symposia held to mark the one hundredth anniversary in 1959 of the publication of Darwin's *Origin of Species,* said " . . . we are almost startled at the complete unanimity in the interpretation of evolution presented by the participants.

Nothing could show more clearly how internally consistent and firmly established the synthetic theory is.''[10]

But even at that time there were some evolutionists who were beginning to express doubts concerning this formulation of evolution theory. A decade later, these incipient cracks have widened to the point that some, formerly strongly committed to this theory, are now expressing disillusionment.

Recently, for example, Pierre P. Grassé, one of the most distinguished of all French scientists, published a book, *L'Evolution du Vivant*,[11] which constituted a strong attack on all aspects of modern evolution theory. Dobzhansky, in his review of this book, states: "The book of Pierre P. Grasse is a frontal attack on all kinds of 'Darwinism'. Its purpose is 'to destroy the myth of evolution as a simple understood and explained phenomenon,' and to show that evolution is a mystery about which little is and perhaps can be, known. Now, one can disagree with Grassé, but not ignore him. He is the editor of the 28 volumes of 'Traite de Zoologie,' author of numerous original investigations, and ex-president of the Academie des Sciences. His knowledge of the living world is encyclopedic.''[12] The closing sentence of Grasse's book is most interesting (and disturbing to Dobzhansky). In that sentence Grassé says, "It is possible that in this domain biology, impotent, yields the floor to metaphysics."

Thus, this "most distinguished of all French zoologists" (not some obscure French scientist), vigorously attacks "all kinds of Darwinism," and states that in the domain of origins, the science of biology can supply no answers, and that it must therefore yield to metaphysics, or a supernatural explanation for the origin of living things.

The neo-Darwinian theory is based on two basic assumptions. These are that all heritable variations may be ascribed to random or chance mutations, and that there is natural selection for fitness. Furthermore, there has been a redefinition of fitness. Darwin envisioned a struggle for existence in which those that survived this struggle ("red in tooth and claw" according to Thomas Huxley) were deemed to be the fittest. Today, evolutionists, such as Lewontin, sternly admonish that the term "struggle for existence" must be banished from evolutionary literature,[13] and he, and others, are now defining fitness in terms of differential reproduction.[13,14]

That is, those that are the fittest, and thus selected in a Darwinian sense, are defined as those that reproduce in large numbers. In fact, Lewontin, flatly states that "Natural selection *is* differential reproduction."[13] This leaves unstated *why* some organisms reproduce in larger numbers than others, they just do.

The concept of natural selection, actually not original with Darwin, but nevertheless popularized by him in his 1859 publication, *The Origin of Species by Natural Selection or the Survival of Favored Races,* known since simply as *The Origin of Species,* has for over a century been held in almost religious reverence by Darwinists. It seemed to explain so much, and was in fact responsible for the rapid acceptance of evolution theory by the majority of scientists.

Creationists have long maintained that the Darwinian concept of natural selection (and now the neo-Darwinian concept) as a force which enables chance variations or mutations of the genetic material to produce an increase in complexity and to change one basic kind of organism into another, is not only a tautology (that is, a product of circular reasoning and vacuous in explanatory content), but that it is also incapable of either test or proof. The classical Darwinian concept of natural selection was tautological because those that survived were said to be fittest, while the fittest were defined as those that survived. In neo-Darwinian terms it is said that those that reproduce in larger numbers are the fittest, while the fittest are defined as those that reproduce in larger numbers.

That neo-Darwinism is a theory that is no more testable than is creation, and thus no more scientific, is being recognized. Paul Erhlich and L.C. Birch, biologists at Stanford University and Sydney University, respectively, state:

Our theory of evolution has become . . . one
which cannot be refuted by any possible observations. Every conceivable observation can be
fitted into it. It is thus "outside of empirical
science" but not necessarily false. No one can
think of ways in which to test it. Ideas, either
without basis or based on a few laboratory experiments carried out in extremely simplified
systems have attained currency far beyond their
validity. They have become part of an evolutionary dogma accepted by most of us as part of
our training.[15]

Even more recently, C. Leon Harris, has published an
article in which he states that the neo-Darwinian theory of
evolution is axiomatic (axioms are assumptions which can
be neither tested nor proved). In his conclusion to this
article Harris states:

I have suggested that the neo-Darwinian theory
of evolution rests on the axioms that all heritable variations in fitness result from chance mutations and that there is natural selection for fitness. There are several consequences for evolution and for biology in general.

First, the axiomatic nature of the neo-Darwinian
theory places the debate between evolutionists
and creationists in a new perspective. Evolutionists have often challenged creationists to
provide experimental proof that species have
been fashioned *de novo*. Creationists have often
demanded that evolutionists show how chance
mutations can lead to adaptability, or to explain
why natural selection has favored some species
but not others with special adaptations, or why
natural selection allows apparently detrimental
organs to persist. We may now recognize that
neither challenge is fair. If the neo-Darwinian

theory is axiomatic, it is not valid for creationists to demand proof of the axioms, and it is
not valid for evolutionists to dismiss special creation as unproved so long as it is stated as an
axiom.[16]

Harris, strongly committed to evolutionary theory and
philosophy, thus denies the usual claim of evolutionists
that creation is mere religious dogma while evolution is a
scientifically testable theory.

Some years ago the British geneticist and mathematician, R.A. Fisher, gave great comfort to neo-Darwinists
with his elegant mathematical treatment of evolution
theory and population genetics. While all this looked so
wonderfully scientific and convincing, Waddington, a well-
known British biologist and evolutionist, had this to say
about this mathematical treatment:

> The theory of neo-Darwinism is a theory of the
> evolution of the population in respect to leaving
> offspring and not in respect to anything else . . . .
> Everybody has it in the back of his mind that the
> animals that leave the largest number of off-
> spring are going to be those best adapted also
> for eating peculiar vegetation or something of
> this sort, but this is not explicit in the theory . . . .
> There you do come to what is, in effect, a va-
> cuous statement: Natural selection is that some
> things leave more offspring than others: and it is
> those that leave more offspring, and there is
> nothing more to it than that. The whole real guts
> of evolution—which is how do you come to have
> horses and tigers and things—is outside the
> mathematical theory.[17]

Thus, Waddington not only admits that the most highly
cherished concept of neo-Darwinism, natural selection, is
vacuous, but also that the attention and research of
evolutionists have all been focused on intrapopulational

studies. These are merely attempts, as Waddington points out, to explain why some tigers and horses become more numerous, but does not even attempt to explain how horses and tigers arose in the first place. The same objections to the neo-Darwinian theory of evolution have been eloquently expressed by Marjorie Grene, one of the world's leading philosophers of science.[18]

Grene was expressing her doubts even at the same time Mayr was declaring that unanimity among evolutionists in accepting the neo-Darwinian theory was so startling. Concerning the possibility of the evolution of the horse via random mutations and natural selection, she said (p. 50):

> In other words, if horses have evolved—and few are those who would like to deny it—and if an explanation of this transformation through random mutations alone is excessively unlikely—as indeed it seems to be, since the great majority of mutations so far observed are adverse or even lethal—then it must be the automatic selection in each generation, of very slightly advantageous variants that has built up the otherwise astonishing result. But how, one may ask, do we know this? If mutation alone cannot explain the evolutionary process—the origin of life, of sentient life, of intelligent life—why is natural selection— the elimination of the worst mutations, a negative and external agency—the only conceivable alternative?

Later (p. 52) she had this to say about the shift in populations of varieties of peppered moths in England from a population in which the light-colored variety was predominant to a population in which the dark-colored variety was predominant,

> . . . the recent work of H.B.D. Kettlewell on industrial melanism has certainly confirmed the hypothesis that natural selection takes place in

nature. This is the story of the black mutant of the common peppered moth which, as Kettlewell has shown with beautiful precision, increases in numbers in the vicinity of industrial centres and decreases, being more easily exposed to predators, in rural areas. Here, say the neo-Darwinians, is natural selection, that is, evolution, actually going on. But to this we may answer: selection, yes; the colour of moths or snails or mice is clearly controlled by visibility to predators; but "evolution"? Do these observations explain how in the first place there came to be any moths or snails or mice at all? By what right are we to extrapolate the pattern by which colour or other such superficial characters are governed to the origin of species, let alone of classes, orders, phyla of living organisms?

In the concluding portion of this two-part series, we will document challenges to the modern neo-Darwinian theory of evolution by mutations and natural selection from evolutionists during the past decade.

REFERENCES

1. R.A. Fisher, *The Genetical Theory of Natural Selection,* Clarendon Press, Oxford, 1930.
2. G.G. Simpson, *Tempo and Mode in Evolution,* Columbia University Press, New York, 1944.
3. G.G. Simpson, *The Meaning of Evolution,* Yale University Press, New Haven, 1949.
4. G.G. Simpson, *The Major Features of Evolution,* Columbia University Press, New York, 1953.
5. T. Dobzhansky, *Genetics and the Origin of Species,* 3rd Ed., Columbia University Press, New York, 1951.
6. T. Dobzhansky, *Mankind Evolving,* Yale University Press, New Haven, 1962.
7. E. Mayr, *Animal Species and Evolution,* Belknap Press of Harvard University Press, Cambridge, 1966.
8. G. Ledyard Stebbins, *Processes of Organic Evolution,* 2nd Ed., Prentice-Hall Inc., Englewood Cliffs, N.J. 1971.
9. J. Huxley, *Evolution, the Modern Synthesis,* Allen and Univin, London, 1942.

10. Ref. 7, p. 8.
11. P. Grassé, *L'Evolution du Vivant,* Editions Albin Michel, Paris, 1973.
12. T. Dobzhansky, "Darwinian or 'Oriented' Evolution," *Evolution,* Vol. 29, pp. 376-378 (1975).
13. R.C. Lewontin, "Selection in and of Populations," in *Ideas in Modern Biology,* Natural History Press, Garden City, N.Y., 1965, p. 304.
14. G.G. Simpson and W.S. Beck, *Life an Introduction to Biology,* 2nd Ed., Harcourt, Brace and World, Inc., New York, 1965, p. 438.
15. P. Ehrlich and L.C. Birch, "Evolutionary History and Population Biology," *Nature,* Vol. 214, p. 352 (1967).
16. C. Leon Harris, "An Axiomatic Interpretation of the Neo-Darwinian Theory of Evolution," *Perspectives in Biology and Medicine,* Winter 1975, p. 179-184.
17. Quoted by Tom Bethell, in "Darwin's Mistake," *Harper's Magazine,* February 1976, p. 75.
18. Marjorie Grene, "The Faith of Darwinism," *Encounter,* November 1959, pp. 48-56.

No. 43, January, 1977

CRACKS IN THE NEO-DARWINIAN JERICHO

(Part II)*

Duane T. Gish, Ph.D.

Ever since Darwin first put forth his theory, creation scientists have maintained that at best natural selection could only be a conservative force, weeding out the unfit, but would be powerless to generate increasing complexity and to originate something new or novel and thus powerless to change one kind of animal into another. Now some evolutionists are saying the same thing, asserting that natural selection has made no significant contribution at all to the general overall course of evolution. They are saying that there must be some other mechanism at work in evolution. This is outright heresy in the halls of Darwinism.

Thus, Stephen Jay Gould entitled his recent account of one of these schools of thought "A Threat to Darwinism."[1] It should be understood that these investigators are unabashed evolutionists, but they are rejecting one of the basic tenets of Darwin and of the modern neo-Darwinian

*Part I found in Impact Article No. 42, Acts & Facts Vol. 5, No. 12, December, 1976.

theory, the idea that natural selection is the main driving force of evolution. In his article Gould points out that a significant number of evolutionists are maintaining that most genetic variations (assumed by evolutionists to have arisen by mutations) that have become established are neutral and thus transparent to natural selection. That is (for example), when variants among protein molecules are compared with one another, many, and even most, seem to have no advantage or disadvantage when compared to the others. They are thus selectively neutral; they are transparent to natural selection. Natural selection then has nothing to do with the establishment of most genetic variations, it is asserted. These mutations have become established by random, accidental processes; for example, by "genetic drift." Thus a few individuals may be accidentally cut off somehow from the bulk of the population, carrying with them only a fraction of the total gene pool. The high degree of inbreeding within this small population then concentrates and enhances these genetic traits and a variant form of the species rapidly surfaces. "Neutralists," as advocates of this theory are called, believe that many repetitions of this process, along with continued mutations to replenish the gene pool, have been responsible for the evolutionary origin of all living things. "Selectionists" vigorously dispute this contention.

Creationists insist that at best such a process could only produce variants within an established kind and could never produce new and novel structures, and, furthermore, *no* random process, genetic drift, mutations, or otherwise could produce millions of complex creatures from a single-celled organism in three billion years, or even in millions times three billion years.

A frontal attack on the neo-Darwinian selection theory by Steven M. Stanley appeared recently in the prestigious *Proceedings of the National Academy of Science.*[2] Stanley maintains that "Gradual evolutionary change by natural selection operates so slowly within established species that it cannot account for the major features of evolution."[3] Stanley is thoroughly impressed by the apparent sudden

appearance (on a geological time scale) in great diversity
of various types of animals citing, for example, the Cambrian "explosion" of a great variety of highly complex
creatures; the "rapid evolutionary origin" of lung-fishes
(Dipnoi); and the sudden appearance, or "radiation," of
the 32 orders of mammals. He maintains that the neo-
Darwinian model of gradualistic change by natural selection cannot account for such rapid origins.

Stanley believes that evolution has occurred by abrupt,
random production of new species. He offers no explanation whatsoever how a species may abruptly, at random,
produce new species. Assuming evolution to be a fact, and
maintaining that the fossil record clearly contradicts the
neo-Darwinian theory of gradual change through small
mutations and natural selection, he simply assumes then
that evolution must have occurred rapidly by "random
speciation events." Thus, beginning with a single-celled
organism (however that arose in the first place) several
billion years ago, Stanley suggests that some sort of blind,
random, speciation process must have produced what we
have today, because all other suggested ideas are incapable
of explaining the overall process of evolution and the
actual facts of the fossil record.

In place of slow adaptation through natural selection,
Stanley wishes to postulate a more rapid evolutionary process, and he replaces natural selection with the idea that
some lines led to more and perhaps better things simply
because one species happened to randomly produce more
new species than did others. This is rather analogous to the
fact that one who purchases a thousand tickets in a lottery
has a better chance of winning the prize than one who
purchases a single ticket.

Stanley points out that if his theory is correct, neo-
Darwinism, accepted by the vast majority of evolutionists,
is incorrect. He states, "If most evolutionary changes occur during speciation events and if speciation events are
largely random, natural selection, long viewed as the process guiding evolutionary change, cannot play a significant role in determining the overall course of evolution."[4]

He even goes so far as to say that "The reductionist view that evolution can ultimately be understood in terms of genetics and molecular biology is clearly in error."[5] If what Stanley says is true, the theory of evolution, actually devoid of any real evidence from the fossil record to support it, is devoid even of a theoretical framework.

Even if it is assumed that the processes of chance mutations and natural selection are at work, these processes could never have produced millions of complex species (or a single complex species for that matter) from a single-celled organism. Thus, Dr. Murray Eden, an evolutionist, rejects the neo-Darwinian theory of random chance mutations with natural selection. He has asserted:

> It is our contention that if "random" is given a serious and crucial interpretation from a probabilistic point of view, the randomness postulate is highly implausible and that an adequate scientific theory of evolution must await the discovery and elucidation of new natural laws—physical, physico-chemical and biological.[6]

Eden calculates that this assumed process could produce only relatively slight changes in three billion years and would, in fact, require billions of times longer to produce man and other complex species from a single-celled organism.

If natural selection is a relatively powerless force, then by Sir Julian Huxley's own admission, evolution would be impossible. Huxley, referring to calculations of H.J. Muller, states that the chances of getting a horse from a single-celled organism by mutation but without natural selection is one chance out of one thousand to the millionth power.[7] That number is one followed by three million zeroes, a number so large it would take three large volumes of 500 pages each just to print. Clearly, Huxley is saying that getting a horse by mutation but without natural selection would be flatly impossible. But, he declares, it has happened, thanks to natural selection!

Natural selection is evidently Huxley's god, for nothing less could convert an impossibility into a certainty. But, as Eden and other mathematicians have acknowledged, mutation with natural selection can work no miracles. Furthermore, it is manifestly evident that if, as Stanley asserts, natural selection is such an impotent force it has had no effect on the general overall course of evolution, then indeed evolution is impossible. It would require a miraculous force, let alone a relatively impotent force, to overcome odds of one out of a thousand to the millionth power. Belief in evolution indeed requires an incredible faith.

Furthermore, even though the odds against getting a horse from a single-celled organism by naturalistic processes are incredibly impossible, the odds against getting the first living cell from an inanimate physico-chemical world would be immensely greater. Even the most "primitive" living thing would have required hundreds of different kinds of complex molecules, perhaps as many as ten thousand, no one really knows.[8] In addition to these complex molecules, many very complex structures, such as membranes, the mitochondria or energy "factories," ribosomes, some sort of organized genetic material, and numerous other structures would have been required for the functioning of living things. Finally, all of this must be coordinated in time and in space in a highly specific and complex manner. The jump from the molecular to the cellular is a jump of fantastic dimensions, requiring a much greater increase in order and complexity than the origin of a horse from a single-celled organism.

Huxley states that the odds against getting a horse is impossibly high without natural selection. Whether or not natural selection can actually overcome the impossible odds against getting a horse from a single-celled organism, *it is certain that natural selection could have been of no help in overcoming the most impossible odds of all—the odds against obtaining a living cell by naturalistic processes from inanimate inorganic material.*

Whatever may be said about the operation and efficacy of natural selection in the living world, it is impossible for natural selection to function in the absence of living things. Natural selection is being defined currently as differential reproduction. There can be no differential reproduction in an inanimate world because there is no such thing as a self-replicating molecule on the face of the earth, nor is any even conceivable. Replication not only requires encoded information such as that found in the DNA that makes up the genetic material, but chemical energy of a highly specific type, the necessary sub-units or building blocks, and highly specific catalysts such as enzymes. Other factors found in the cytoplasm of cells are required for the replication of DNA molecules, and the whole is extremely sensitive to the immediate environment. In other words, practically the entire cell is involved in the replication of DNA as well as the production of protein molecules and other complex structures.

There could be no selection of any kind in an inanimate environment. For example, hydrogen peroxide, highly toxic to living cells, is a metabolic product of cellular activity. We therefore possess an incredibly efficient enzyme for catalyzing the breakdown of hydrogen peroxide. This enzyme, catalase, has a turnover rate of several billion per minute. Because of the high toxicity of hydrogen peroxide, our cells require an exceedingly efficient enzyme to catalyze its decomposition. We certainly couldn't survive without this enzyme. If, however, such a molecule somehow should have arisen by chance against impossible odds in the primordial ocean, the primordial ocean couldn't have cared less. Who or what was to determine that a molecule that could decompose hydrogen peroxide was to be preferred over the infinite number of other protein molecules that supposedly could have arisen in the primordial ocean?

As a matter of fact, even though the many metabolic activities found within a living cell are absolutely indispensable for its existence, and these activities are in turn almost totally dependent upon enzymes, the existence of enzymes before living things existed would have been disastrous. Let us suppose that a proteolytic enzyme, that is, an enzyme that catalyzes the hydrolysis or breakdown of protein, somehow arose in the hypothetical "primordial soup" of the primeval world. Its origin would have been totally disastrous, for it would have happily set about catalyzing the rapid destruction of all protein in sight, and soon there would be no protein left. Similarly, RNases would destroy all the RNA, DNases would break down all the DNA, deaminases would deaminate all amines, decarboxylases would decarboxylate all carboxylic acids, etc. How could such substances be "selected for" when their presence outside of the regulated environment of a living cell would have been destructive?

By no stretch of the imagination, then, could natural selection have had anything to do with the origin of life. What was the incredibly powerful force operating within the naturalistic world that managed to overcome the fantastically impossible odds against getting the first living cell? There simply was none, and thus the origin of life by naturalistic, mechanistic process is totally impossible.

REFERENCES

1. S.J. Gould, "A Threat to Darwinism," *Natural History Museum,* December, 1975, pp. 8-9.
2. S.M. Stanley, "A Theory of Evolution Above the Species Level," *Proceedings National Academy of Science,* vol. 72, pp. 640-650 (1975).
3. S.M. Stanley, *ibid.,* p. 646.
4. S.M. Stanley, *ibid.,* p. 648.
5. S.M. Stanley, *ibid.,* p. 650.
6. M. Eden, "Inadequacies of Neo-Darwinian Evolution as Scientific Theory," in *Mathematical Challenges to the Neo-Darwinian Theory of Evolution,* P.S. Moorhead and M.M. Kaplan, Wistar Institute Press, Philadelphia, 1967, p. 109.
7. J. Huxley, *Evolution in Action,* The New American Library, New York, 1953, pp. 45-46.
8. Van Rensselear Potter, "Biothics," *Perspectives in Biology and Medicine,* Autumn, 1970, p. 139.

No. 44, February, 1977
ON THE ORIGIN OF LANGUAGE
Les Bruce, Jr.*

In the Western world the study of language began as a philosophical inquiry into origins.[1] The Greeks (Third and Fourth Century B.C.) initiated the study of language essentially to explain its origin. The conventionalists hypothesized that the relationship between the form of language (i.e., primarily the sounds and words) and meaning was essentially arbitrary, a convention of society. The naturalists hypothesized that the form of a word (i.e., its sounds) had a natural association with its referent in the real world. Only certain sound combinations (words or parts of words), however, were directly associated as an imitation of an object, its sound or an idea directly associated as an imitation of an object (e.g., kookaburra).

In an effort to explain how most of language, which is not so directly relatable to meaning, derived from an onomatopoeic beginning, the discipline of etymology began. Through studying the derivational history of words (etymology) the naturalists intended to demonstrate that the origin of all of language was ultimately relatable to words which directly reflected the meanings of their referents.

The first philosophical forum on language eventually developed into a discussion on the regularity of language patterns. Two basic theoretical positions emerged as explanatory frameworks for language, that which opted for irregularity and that which insisted that language was essentially regular. From the pre-eminence of the latter position it became popular to explain the irregularities of language on the basis that language somehow became corrupted with improper usage through time; this theoretical

---

*The author is a member of the Summer Institute of Linguistics and the Wycliffe Bible Translators; he is presently a candidate for the degree of Ph.D. in the discipline of linguistics. He has also served as a visiting Professor of Linguistics at Christian Heritage College. He wishes to thank his colleagues who have offered critical comments on earlier drafts of this article, especially David Thomas, also of the Summer Institute of Linguistics.

position regarded the older forms of language to be the purer forms.

By the Nineteenth Century there was a severe reaction to the highly speculative nature of the philosophizing about the original language of man which had characterized much of the study of language up until then. The interest was still historical, but the goal was not so idealistic. It was a romantic era of a rediscovery of the national past; the mother tongues of nations and families of nations rather than the mother tongue of the whole human race became the focus of attention. The romantic nationalism was a definite influence, but perhaps a more basic cause of the more realistic goal was the reaction to previous unscientific speculations. The felt need was to take a more scientific approach by analyzing empirical data. Thus was ushered in the period of systematic comparison of languages for the purpose of reconstructing the historical past.

During the Nineteenth Century largely under the leadership of German scholars an impressive amount of detailed scholarly work was done. Building on Sir William Jones' discovery that Sanskrit was genetically related to Latin and Greek and other European languages as well, these early historical linguists began to develop principles of language comparison. The availability of historical data not only made possible advances in the reconstruction of the original Indo-European language[2] (proto Indo-European), it also enabled linguists to describe the processes of change by which the proto-language developed into the diversity of the many Indo-European languages.

The German based "neo-grammarian" school is known for its contribution to the study of sound change in the last quarter of the Nineteenth Century. The neo-grammarians, through meticulous analysis of historical text material, demonstrated the striking regularity of sound change. Hermann Paul (1846-1921), the foremost theoretician of the neo-grammarians, identified convenience as the central mechanism of sound change; within the framework of convenience he categorized three types of sound changes under the mode of "mispronunciation."[3] Leonard Bloomfield

(1887-1949) was an early American structuralist who extended the neo-grammarian position with greater detail. He catalogued the mechanisms of sound change as two types: stabilizing vs. deteriorating or simplifying mechanisms. He documented at least three stabilizing changes characterized as re-formation and compensatory processes. In the simplifying category Bloomfield documented no less than eleven processes of sound change.

Detailed documentation by the neo-grammarians of various processes of language change, especially those of sound change, contributed greatly to the statement of two basic principles of language change, (1) the process of streamlining and (2) the process of restructuring. Martinet, one of the most eminent historical linguists in the Twentieth Century, is credited with formulating these two principles of language change. He refers to the restructuring process, which maintains adequate communication, as being in conflict with the streamlining process which manifests (in language) the human tendency toward reducing effort to a minimum.

> Linguistic evolution may be regarded as governed
> by the permanent conflict between man's com-
> municative needs and his tendency to reduce to a
> minimum his mental and physical activity. Here
> as elsewhere, human behavior is subject to the
> law of least effort. (Martinet 1964:167).

The law of least effort effects a relentless streamlining of the status quo, reducing complexity and redundancy, which in turn eventually leads to restructuring adjustments in the various systems of language to help maintain an acceptable level of communication. The restructuring principle could be termed the law of conservation of communication.

It would be misleading to imply that Hermann Paul was not interested in the origin of language; the question of origin certainly interested Paul as it still does linguists today. The essential difference between modern linguistics (the past 175 years) and that of the two previous millennia is that linguistics has moved from the purely philosophical realm to that of the empirical sciences. Linguists are still intrigued with the question of origins but their speculations on the origin of language must be based on observable facts about language.

Two important basic principles of language must be mentioned, the streamlining effect of least effort and the compensatory maintenance of communication, or restructuring; two observations that relate to these are worth noting.

a. Primitive languages: No group of human beings today, even those living in a stone-age culture, speak what could be conceived of as a primitive language. Furthermore, no known language in all of history was in any sense primitive. Elgin remarks, "The most ancient languages for which we have written texts—Sanskrit, for example—are often far more intricate and complicated in their grammatical forms than many contemporary languages." (Elgin 1973:44). This, of course, is no surprise to us if the inevitable processes of simplification observable today have consistently been operating for all or most of human history (this is in itself of course indeterminate, but we can at least conclude that simple material cultures do not imply simple languages).

b. Creativity of language: The vocabulary may be considered to be the most creative area of language, and even here, "For the most part, people tend to re-adapt existing lexical material rather than create entirely new material." (Langacker 1967:186). Apart from re-adapting and extending existing vocabulary items from within a particular language, words or parts of words are commonly borrowed from other languages. A language seldom exhibits creativity in the sense of inventing new and unique forms.

The English pronoun system illustrates the two basic principles in action today. The oldest English pronoun system distinguished three numbers (singular, dual, plural) for each of 1st, 2nd, and 3rd persons. Today standard English distinguishes only singular and plural. The previously "extravagant" system has been streamlined by neutralizing the difference between duality and plurality. In addition, with the 2nd person "you" the singular-plural distinction has been lost, resulting in unacceptable ambiguity (ineffective communication) at times. (One of the first times I asked the girl who is now my wife for a date I ended up taking a whole carload of people on an outing because she wasn't sure whether I meant "you-singular" or "you-plural;" I was too embarrassed to expressly exclude everyone else who was there at the time. As far as I was concerned, that was an unacceptable ambiguity!) The restructuring presently going on in English to remedy this situation involves adding particles from elsewhere in the grammar into the pronoun system. A new 2nd-person-plural pronoun is being formed in the northeastern United States by adding the normal noun pluralizer "s" to the pronoun "you" resulting in the plural "yous" (pronounced the same as "ewes"). The much-publicized "Southern dialect" has restructured the system in another way. A phrase-level quantifier "all" has been added in a contracted form of "you-all" resulting in "y'all." In both cases the restructuring process is clearly adaptive rather than innovative.

Many linguists, apparently including Martinet, believe that the two opposing principles equalize each other. Langacker states, "Just as there are no primitive languages, there are no 'corrupt' languages. Languages change, but they do not decay" (Langacker 1973:17). This is a difficult point to verify. Support for this claim seems to have been well documented in a historical review of the sound system of Spanish. While sounds have changed, the number of distinctive features in the system have remained fairly constant; from the viewpoint of information processing the overall process of change has not altered the potential for communication. Many of Bloomfield's examples of simplification due to sound change appear to affect syntactic categories and vocabulary. The loss of noun case endings in English is a case in point. The relative complexity of communication potential of the resulting system is difficult to evaluate. While the case ending functions of identifying subjects, objects, etc. have been shifted to another level in grammar (word order on the clause level now usually identifies the subject and object) it is difficult to judge how the two systems compare in efficiency of communication. Some questions to be asked would be, "What happened to previous functions of word order in clauses?," "Is word order now overloaded with the jobs of case-role encoding and the indicating of old and new information in a discourse?," "Is focus involved?"

Language is fantastically complex. Its built-in means of combining and recombining (nesting) of its various levels has suggested to many leading linguists that language is theoretically infinite though not practically so in everyday usage. It almost sounds too complex to be able to detect any significant leveling out of language any more than one could detect by observation that the sun is burning itself out.

As far as I am aware no linguist seriously purports that the restructuring process of language overrides the streamlining process resulting in a qualitative positive development of language. If we decide that language did originally develop, possibly evolving from animal communication, we can only do so assuming evolution to be a universally valid principle. This type of *a priori* reasoning was the basic fallacy of pre-Nineteenth Century "speculative grammar" which was pre-scientific in the modern sense of the word.

Furthermore, the observable data neither indicate that such a period of pre-historic development even existed, nor do they suggest a cause of the subsequent state of equilibrium or process of simplification that would have to have come into operation at some time after such a pre-historic development. Noam Chomsky, one of the most prominent linguists of this century, has indicated that human language and animal communication are not even comparable entities, they are so different.

Either the streamlining and restructuring processes balance each other or the streamlining process is gradually reducing language to a limited system of over-generalities. Either human languages have always existed with essentially the potential they exhibit now or they once exhibited greater potential for precise communication than they do now.

Labov, a prominent contemporary socio-linguist, comments on these two processes in his effort to understand the place of language in an evolutionary framework:

> It is plain to most linguists that the "destroy and rebuild" theory of linguistic evolution is equivalent to claiming that the whole process is dysfunctional. For the systematic part is the destructive one, and the analogical re-shaping seems to be making the best of a bad job. And if the principle of least effort is the evil genius behind the destruction, we can only look at language change as a kind of massive testimony to original sin. (Labov 1973:245)

In the remainder of his thesis Labov does not provide any relevant alternative to the dysfunctional role of language change. He does not deny that language change results in diversification of languages and not in overall complexity or adaptive radiation. He rather looks for functional evolutionary result in the development of human society. Thus he suggests that language diversity provides relative cultural isolation, maintaining cultural pluralism which presumably promotes the evolution of human society. But he cannot provide a functional role for language change purely within the development of language. Language development seems to be dominated by a dysfunctional (non-evolutionary) process.

Conclusion

Regardless of how we might attempt to fit language into the broader picture, looking at language by itself there is no evidence that language is the product of any positive developmental process. Language is in a state of consistent change which at best seems to maintain a state of equilibrium.

REFERENCES

1. The Indian tradition antedates the work of the Greeks. Panini (Fourth Century B.C.) culminated the work of his predecessors with a grammatical description of Sanskrit which has been acclaimed as being the most detailed and comprehensive grammar ever done. The Indians were more interested in an accurate accounting of Sanskrit rather than answering philosophical questions.
2. Work in the Nineteenth Century was based essentially on the classical languages (Latin and Greek) and the then-oldest-attested Indo-European language, Sanskrit. Hittite was identified as an older Indo-European language subsequent to the uncovering of Hittite inscriptions in the 1870's about 150 kilometers east of Ankara, Turkey. Hittite became extinct by 1200 B.C.
3. Mispronunciation or changed pronunciations were caused by convenience not to be confused with laziness, neglect, or some natural ease of pronunciation of individual sounds. Instead, mispronunciation is an effect involving the assimilation of sounds and the influence of the symmetry (pattern pressure) of the entire sound system. These changes were not considered to be deteriorative in the sense of "corrupting" language as linguists of earlier periods had suggested.

BIBLIOGRAPHY

1. Bloomfield, Leonard, 1933. *Language.* New York: Henry Holt and Company, Inc. June, 1958 edition.
2. Elgin, Suzette H. 1973. *What is Linguistics?* Englewood Cliffs, New Jersey: Prentice-Hall, Inc.
3. Greenberg, Joseph (ed.), 1966. *Universals of Language* (2nd ed.). Massachusetts: The M.I.T. Press.
4. Ivic, Milka, 1965. *Trends in Linguistics* (translated by Muriel Hapell). The Hague: Mouton & Co.
5. Langacker, Ronald W., 1967. *Language and Its Structure.* New York: Harcourt Brace, and World, Inc.
6. Labov, William, 1973. "The Social Setting of Linguistic Change," *Current Trends in Linguistics.* T.A. Sebeok (ed.), V. II, Paris: Mouton.
7. Lyons, John, 1968. *Introduction to Theoretical Linguistics.* London: Cambridge University Press.
8. Martinet, Andre, 1960. *Elements of General Linguistics* (translated by Elisabeth Palmer, 1964. London: Faber and Faber). Originally published by Max Leclerc et Cie, Proprietors of Librairie Armand Colin.
9. Paul, Hermann, 1970. *Principles of the History of Language* (translated from 2nd edition by H.A. Strong). College Park: McGroth Publishing Company.
10. Wilson, Clifford, 1978. *Monkeys Will Never Talk . . . Or Will They,* San Diego, Creation-Life Publishers.

No. 45, March, 1977
CAN YOU . . . RECOGNIZE BIAS IN HISTORY CONTENT?
Mary Stanton, Ed.D.*

The Golden Horde swept across hills and valleys from Mongolia like a swarm of locusts attacking fields of ripened grain. Animal skin clothing blended each Tartar into one being with his lightning-swift horse. Strong men cowered behind barricaded mosques praying to Allah for protection of their women and children. Christians filled churches and prayed to God for deliverance from "The Scourge of Heaven." Surely, Genghis Khan and his Horde were beasts from the underworld, using churches and mosques as stables and prostitute houses. No good thing escaped their touch. Could these Tartars have served any purpose in History?

Yes, indeed they did. While their pagan conduct cannot be condoned, the Khans' Golden Horde stopped the ravaging worldwide thrust of Islam, organized quarreling tribes of India and prepared the foundation for modern Turkey.

In this brief thought out of the book of History, we learn that *teleology* is one of the building blocks for reconstructing human conduct in the past. It seems that there are three foundational concepts on which history content has been built: the *being of God,* the *nature of origins,* and *purposefulness* or teleology. By way of these three concepts, bias enters into the content because each of them has two sides facing each other—but separated by a wide range in differences. The two sides are in contradistinction to each other according to the author's choice of content.

Since historians now have an exhaustless reservoir of material about most people who lived on earth, they must select content information for their books. Who determines the guidelines of choice and on what basis is selection

---

*Dr. Mary Stanton is an educator, archaeologist, and historian. She is co-author of the new ICR-sponsored textbook on world history, *Streams of Civilization,* which incorporates the recommendations in this article.

made? Ultimately, the historian's value systems and philosophy of life will determine text book content. Therefore, in spite of objectivity goals, personal belief colors the content.

Consider the two sides of each core concept in History. God is defined within the Judaeo-Christian framework as One who has revealed Himself through nature's orderliness; through prophets and human conscience; through the written Word and Jesus, the Living Word; and through history which lays the foundation for our study of history content. If History and the Bible are two of God's media for revelation, the Bible is to be respected as historical truth.

In contradistinction to this teaching, history content may represent God as a humanistic or man-made concept evolving through time and may insist that every people has the right to conceive of deity (deities) according to their choosing because there are no absolutes. The secular-humanistic concept teaches that the Bible "contains the word of God" but it is man's record of his own times as he understood them.

However, archaeology has never uncovered a civilization which did not believe in deity and life after death. The closer archaeological historians have come to Mt. Ararat, the more they have discovered that man's belief in Jehovah-God concurs with the Biblical record.

Concerning the second concept, that of origins, the Judaeo-Christian records declare that in the beginning God was the Creator of a perfectly designed, completed universe. In contradistinction to this revelation, secular/humanist history teaches that man is the product of evolution over a period of three to five million years (according to Leakey's latest estimate). Principles of basic evolution appear through history content so that it is essential to define its many-sided teaching.

Evolution . . . as found in most history content is a combination of Darwinian and contemporary thought: (1) emergence of *Homo sapiens* out of a series of lower primate groups; (2) survival of the fittest through natural selection but which is also applied to social life and business; (3) race is a sub-species of man; (4) development of monotheism from nature gods (animism) to polytheism, to one power over others as illustrated by the Hebrew tribal deity, Yahweh. Buettner-Janusch have defined evolution today as (1) change in genetic composition; (2) change in morphological differentiation; (3) progressive diversification. The changes are through mutation, adaptation, and natural selection.

While Biblical historians do not deny that changes are everywhere in progress, they teach that changes are a part of the original, internal, planned structuring by God.

By way of illustration, the first unit in most history textbooks is a study of Archaeology and its contribution to History. But Pre-history also appears in this unit and students see pictures of Australopithecines (southern or African ape-like) as the first men—rather than Adam, Eve, and the rest of the original family.

The Ice Ages are usually discussed in the first unit of the secular/humanist history as evidence for uniformitarian basis of man's emergence. The Biblical explanation of ice masses says, "They are the results from the Noahic Flood catastrophe." Nothing is said in Humanist history books about the perfectly human elements found even beneath the Australopithecines.

The Institute for Creation Research in San Diego has provided the reading public with extensive scientific literature on this subject. Qualified men of science have established the error of this philosophy.

A Word of Warning . . . to history students and teachers: The content of the first unit in any Humanist oriented history will reveal the philosophy and value systems for the rest of the textbook.

The third concept controlling history content is teleology which says that there is a cause and effect relationship between all events or situations. The changes have been a logical result of law-principles at work throughout every part of the universe where God is in control of His Creation. (Daniel 2:19-22 and/or I Sam. 2:2-9).

In contradiction to God's control with purposefulness, is the secular/humanist position teaching students that man is the consequence of his own doing through man's trial-and-error life style.

Whereas the migration-dispersion of people out of the Mesopotamian Valley can be followed with a high degree of accuracy through pottery types, jewelry, burial customs and language, most textbooks tend to ignore this evidence and start the ape-like man in the first unit and then jump into a well developed civilization arriving out of nowhere— as for example, the Sumerians at the northern end of the Persian Gulf. Students are intrigued by the brilliant sciences, trade, religion, and architecture that miraculously appear in Sumer, ancient Egypt and the Indus River Valley.

More bold evolutionists teach parallel cultural evolution in several river valleys. The similarity of culture patterns is explained by teaching that each group looked around themselves for ways to modify nature to satisfy basic needs (such as making pottery out of clay). According to secular/humanists, these culture items were developed independently and any likeness to one another was purely coincidental.

Africa has suffered the most from non-Christian history which has pictured non-human primates evolving into *Homo sapiens* around the Olduvai Gorge or out of the monkey-dominated jungles. The ancient and brilliant civilizations of Ethiopia and North Africa are usually ignored as are the migrations of their cultures southward.

Western civilizations did not originate with Greece and Rome. In giving credit to whom credit is due, the Greeks adopted the Hebrew/Phoenician language and passed it along to the Romans; they copied the Egyptian architecture with its massive columns and the frieze decor. Greek political scientists quite probably based their ideas for democracy and government organization upon the ancient Sumerian bicameral legislature and Persian division of powers.

Upon all of the previous elements used in government, the Romans fashioned their empire that enclosed the Levant and Mediterranean shores. According to Biblical history, all of these governments were a part of God's design creating "the fulness of times" for the coming of His Christ during the time when the Roman Empire controlled the "Middle of the Earth"—a teaching denied by Humanism.

With increasing clearness, authors of recent history textbooks have been giving Judaism, Jesus Christ, and the Church a more Biblical matrix. We commend them for this changed attitude. However, one area of history continues to be treated with a preponderance of humanist bias. That is the Byzantine Era. Most historians continue to make Rome the first center of the Church, to give credit to Rome for establishing the solid foundation of Christianity and for spreading the Gospel during the first centuries after Pentecost.

Much more emphasis needs to be placed on the Biblical-Historical order of the emerging Church. According to the Bible (Dr. Luke's book of Acts), the first Church Council was held in Jerusalem with James as the head; then Antioch became the center for the Church's missionary thrust. Hebrew and Christian History has received more accurate treatment since archaeologists such as William Albright of the School of Antiquities at Johns Hopkins University declared that no part of the Bible has been disproven by the science of Archaeology.

Out from Church centers in Alexandria, Egypt; in Syria and Palestine; in Asia Minor and Greece, the Coptic and Orthodox Churches established local assemblies and commissioned missionaries to carry the Gospel throughout Africa, Asia, and Eastern Europe particularly.

God chose the able Emperor Constantine to provide a degree of security in a world of paganism. Orthodox leaders were directed by Constantine to assemble major world councils at Ephesus, Nicea, or Constantinople for the express purpose of confirming Christian faith. By the time of Justinian's reign, Constantinople was the strong voice for Christianity. During this period of history known as the Byzantine Era, distinctive Church architecture was designed, schools and seminaries in universities were established, and regular Councils were called to settle doctrinal disputes. Representatives from Church assemblies in and around Rome attended the councils with their interpreters because all business was conducted in the Greek language.

Over the Byzantine Bridge crossed Orientalism to become Occidentalism. The cumbersome cuneiform and Semitic languages were exchanged for phonetic alphabetic script and speech. History was divided into B.C. and A.C. by Byzantine scholars who also established the Hebrew seven-day week.

Western law, not only in the Church, but also in society, is based on Justinian's Christian code of ethics. Byzantine missionaries carried the schools as well as the Gospel into Eastern Europe thereby instilling Christian value systems in society as well as bringing the message of salvation to the individual. One of their greatest contributions to the people where Christianity went was the two-pronged work of putting languages into writing and then translating the Bible into all of the languages. Missionaries from Orthodox churches established hundreds of literate communities.

While the more glaring biases in history content appear in ancient and medieval times, modern history has not escaped the humanists' pens. The Puritan-Pilgrim ethic and education have been distorted. Fundamental Christians have faced ridicule when actually they were the bulwark against German Criticism (known by many names such as the Graf-Wellhausen School of Theology, the J-E-D-P Analysis) and kept the light of the Gospel of Christ burning brightly. Fundamentalist believers started Christian radio stations and Gospel programs; established Bible schools and strong Biblical seminaries; and they applied archaeology to Biblical studies to confirm the Word of God in the midst of pseudo-scientific attacks. The position and influence of Fundamentalists has finally been acknowledged as a positive force in our society when the Gallup Poll published its results in September, 1976. According to that poll, at least 34% of the United States electorate claim to be "born again" and follow the tenets of evangelical Christianity. But what will historians say about them?

In spite of humanist attacks upon evangelical Christianity around the world, Bible-believers have taken a stand against non-Christian textbooks in West Virginia. Biblically oriented books are being written on a thoroughly academic level to counteract the humanist philosophies in History and other subject areas.

Remember Paul's defense of history as revelation: "God who made the world and all it contains, who is Lord of heaven and earth, . . . He has made from one person every nation of men to settle on the entire surface of the earth, definitely appointing the preestablished periods and the boundaries of their settlements, . . . " (from *The Modern Language Bible,* Acts 17:22-26).

No. 46, April, 1977

EBLA: ITS IMPACT ON BIBLE RECORDS

Clifford Wilson, M.A., B.D., Ph.D.*

The new findings at Ebla are possibly the most significant discovery yet made so far as they relate to the background of early Bible times. The impact on some areas of Biblical knowledge will indeed be startling.

**Where Ebla is Located . . . And
The Work Begins**

Tell Mardikh—the ancient Ebla—is on the main road to Aleppo in Northern Syria, being not quite half way between Hamath and Aleppo. It is nearer to Aleppo than to Hamath. There is a mound and a small village about one kilometer off the highway. Professor Paolo Matthiae of the Rome University has been excavating there since 1964, but his work was not spectacular until 1968 when

*Dr. Clifford Wilson is an archaeologist, linguist, and Bible scholar. He has a Ph.D. in Psycholinguistics from the University of South Carolina and is a member of the faculty at Monash University in Australia.

his team produced a statue dedicated to the goddess Esh-tar, and bearing the name of Ibbit-Lim, a king of Ebla. This endorsed the positive identification of the city. The kingdom of Ebla had previously been known in Sumerian, Akkadian, and Egyptian texts, and the excavators had good clues when they began digging in this 50-feet high mound. Now their hopes were bright for the future.

In the 1975 season some 15,000 tablets were recovered. To bring the report up to date, the excavators recently reported (with a smile!) that 1976 was a poor season— only 1,600 tablets were found! One tablet stated that the city had a population of 260,000.

Professor Giovanni Pettinato, also of the University of Rome, is the epigrapher working on the tablets, and some of what follows stems from his reports, both in the *Biblical Archaeologist* of May, 1976, and in public lectures and discussions at the University of Michigan in November 1976. Professor Matthiae also lectured at that time, and both professors were most cooperative in two days of lectures, discussion, and question and answer sessions. It was this writer's privilege to participate in these public functions as well as in more private meetings with the archaeologists and with a number of leaders in the field of Biblical archaeology and Semitic studies.

What The Tablets Are All About

It is probable that the 17,000 tablets so far recovered are not from the major royal archives, but are rather a collection of records that were kept near the central court. Here the provisions were stored, tribute was collected, and apprentice scribes did their copying from the tablets which they would take temporarily from the royal archives themselves. A wide variety of tablets were copied, and this is of tremendous importance, for it means that today we have a wide range of these copied tablets available for study.

The two rooms where the main body of 15,000 tablets were recovered were close to the entrance to the palace. If the royal archives themselves are found as excavation proceeds, the potential for the study of Bible backgrounds and ancient history is tremendous.

As Professor Pettinato has pointed out, these are the sorts of tablets that scholars dream about, but rarely find. Personal names are included, and in one text alone 260 geographic names have been given. Other texts give lists of animals, fish, birds, professions, and names of officials.

There are a number of historical texts which can be tied in with other known records, such as those of the city of Marik, coming down to the time of Narim Sin who eventually defeated the Eblahites decisively. It appears that the city was defended by mercenaries rather than by its own army. Professor Pettinato conjectures that this is probably the reason why Akkad finally prevailed over Ebla.

The tablets would appear to date to the last two generations of the city, somewhere about 2300 B.C.—possibly 100 years earlier. The final destruction was about 2250 B.C.

There are literary texts with mythological backgrounds, incantations, collections of proverbs, and hymns to various deities. Rituals associated with the gods are referred to, many of these gods being known in Babylonian literature of a later period. These include Enki, Enlil, Utu, Inana, Tiamut, Marduk, and Nadu. The god of the city of Kish is also referred to.

Most of the tablets deal with economic matters, tarrifs, receipts, and other commercial dealings. However, other matters such as offerings to the gods are also dealt with.

The city was in contact with other cities all over the Near East. One of the interesting illustrations of this comes from the list of nations given to messengers as they traversed certain routes, with the names of the cities given. There are lists of towns in their geographic regions, and even lists of the towns that are subject to Ebla. Biblical towns known in later times are included, such as Ashdod and Sidon.

Vocabulary Lists in Two Languages

There are syllabaries of grammatical texts, making it

possible to go from one language to another. There are
no less than 114 Sumerian Eblahite vocabularies, these
being the first such lists recovered from any ancient site.
One of these vocabulary tablets contains nearly 1,000
translated words, and it has 18 duplicates.

It has long been known that scribes in Assyria copied
tablets from Babylonia, but it is now established that
scholars in Mesopotamia had also copied some of their
tablets from the Syrian libraries.

When the first tablets were found, it was soon realized
that this city used a very ancient language in the North
West Semitic group which was previously unknown. Professor Pettinato labeled this "Paleo-Canaanite." In layman's terms, this means "ancient Canaanite." At the close
of this article in *Biblical Archaeologist* Professor Pettinato
tells us:

> The pronominal and verbal systems, in particu-
> lar, are so clearly defined that one can properly
> speak of a Paleo-Canaanite language closely
> akin to Hebrew and Phoenician.

These Ebla tablets are written in a Sumerian script, with
Sumerian logograms adapted to represent Akkadian words
and syllables. About 1,000 words were recovered initially
(hundreds more later) in vocabulary lists. The words are
written out in both Sumerian logograms and Eblaic syl-
lable-type writing. These offered an invaluable key to the
interpretation of many of the Ebla texts.

The vocabularies at Ebla were distinctively Semitic: the
word "to write" is k-t-b (as in Hebrew), while that for
"king" is "malikum," and that for "man" is "adamu."
The closeness to Hebrew is surprising.

It is relevant to note that some of the tablets deal with
judicial proceedings. There are elaborations as to the
penalties incurred when a person is injured, and there are
details about various trials. Some of these points make
foolish the former criticisms against the possibility of the
existence of a Mosaic law-code. Here is a civilization about

1,000 years earlier than that of Moses, and in writing it gives all sorts of details about the administration of justice. It is clearly a highly developed civilization, with concepts of justice and individual rights to the fore. To suggest that Moses could not have dealt with such cases is ludicrous.

Some tablets deal with case law, and the law code of Ebla must now be recognized as the oldest ever yet found. In dealing with the penalties for injuries, distinction is made according to the nature of the act. An injury caused by the blow of a hand merited a different penalty from one caused by a weapon such as a dagger. Differing penalties are prescribed for various offenses.

There is elaborate discussion of case law, with varying conditions recognized for what at first sight might seem to be the same crime. In the case of a complaint involving sexual relations, if the girl was able to prove that she was a virgin and that the act was forced on her, the penalty against the man was death. Otherwise he would pay a fine that varied according to circumstances. It is remarkably like Deuteronomy 22:22-30, supposedly very late according to liberal scholarship.

In the public lecture series referred to above, Professor David Noel Freedman pointed out that about 17,000 tablets and significant fragments have been found at this site, and they date to approximately 2400 B.C. to 2250 B.C. This would be about four times the grand total of all tablets found, dating to that period, from all other sites. The nearest in magnitude for the number of tablets would be Mari, dating several hundred years later.

Personal Names and Places in the Tablets

A number of personal names in the Ebla documents are very similar to names used at later times in the Old Testament. One such name is Michael (mi-ka-ilu) which means, "Who is like El?" A related form, also in the Ebla texts, is *mi-ka-ya* which is well-known in the Bible, with the *ya* ending replacing the *el*. Other names are e-sa-um (Esau), da-'u-dum (David), sha-'u-lum (Saul), and Ish-ma-

Il (Ishmael), this last meaning "Il (El—God) has heard me."

Other examples given by Professor Pettinato are En-na-ni-Il which gave over to En-na-ni-Ya (Il/Ya has mercy on me); A-dam-Malik (man of Milik); 'il-ha-il (Il is strength); Eb-du-Ra-sa-ap (Servant of Rasaph; Ish-a-bu (A man is the father); Ish-i-lum (A man is the god); I-sa-Ya (Ya has gone forth); I-ad-Da-mu (The hand of Damu); and Ib-na-Ma-lik (Milik has created). Hebrew scholars recognize remarkable similarities to later Hebrew in the Old Testament, and Professor Pettinato himself states, in the *Biblical Archaeologist* referred to above, "Many of these names occur in the same form in the Old Testament, so that a certain interdependence between the culture of Ebla and that of the Old Testament must be granted."

Hebrew Words Akin to Ebla Words

At Ebla, the king has the Sumerian title "en," and according to the vocabulary lists already mentioned, the Paleo-Canaanite equivalent is "Malek." This is virtually the same as the Hebrew word for "king" in the Old Testament "melek." The elders of the kingdom were the "abbu," remarkably close to "abba" (father) of the Old Testament. At many points the similarity to Old Testament Hebrew is very close.

Man's search for the true God and for spiritual truth is shown by some of the personal names at Ebla. "Mi-ka-Ya," meaning "Who is like Ya?" replaced "Mi-Ka-Il," meaning "Who is like Il (El)?" "En-na-ni-Ya" meant, "Ya has mercy on me." Re-i-na-Adad," telling the world that "Adad (a god) is our shepherd," reminds the Christian of Psalm 23 where the ultimate of that searching for divine leading and protection is found as the psalmist exclaims, "*The Lord* is *my* shepherd."

Professor Pettinato discusses the names of some of the gods attested at Eber, including "Il/El of the Ugaritic texts," and tells us that "from Eber on, Il was substituted for by Ya . . . it appears evident that under Ebrum a new development in West Semitic religious concepts took place that permitted the rise of Ya. It would be more correct to see it as renewed acknowledgment of Yahweh. Dagan of the Old Testament is well-known, being associated with several places already known to scholars, including "Dagan of Canaan." This indicates that the term "Canaan" was known much earlier than previously believed.

One aspect of special interest to Bible students is that a number of Old Testament cities are referred to. There are cities that were previously known in 1st and 2nd Millennium records, but now they are referred to in these 3rd Millennium B.C. tablets. There is Salim, possibly the city of Melchizedec, Hazor, Lachish, Megiddo, Gaza, Dor, Sinai, Ashtaroth, Joppa, and Damascus. Of special interest is Urusalima (Jerusalem), this being the earliest known reference to this city.

Although a city called Salim is referred to in the tablets, there is no indication just what its geographic location is. It is referred to separately from Urusalima (Jerusalem), and this would indicate that the two cities are separate.

Two of the towns mentioned are Sodom and Gomorrah. Here we are transported back to about 2300 B.C., and we find that these towns were regularly visited, being on the route of the King's Highway that ran down from Damascus. There are actually references to five "cities of the Plain" (to use the Biblical term at Genesis 14:2), and these were Sodom, Gomorrah, Admah, Zeboiim, and Zoar. We are told in that same verse that an earlier name for Zoar was Bela.

Another of the towns referred to is Carchemish, and Professor Pettinato made the point that the prophet Isaiah (at Isaiah 10:9) has a remarkable knowledge of this name, as shown in the text preserved at Isaiah 10:9. This preserves the ancient name of the god "Chemosh," the Moabite god known in later Bible times.

There is a creation record remarkably similar to the Genesis account. There are dealings with Hittites long before Abraham purchased the Cave of Machpelah from the Hittites of his time—it is not so long since it was argued there were no Hittites so early. There are treaties and covenants similar to those in Exodus, and for the protection of society there are laws that point towards the concept of justice so prominent in Exodus. There are ritualistic sacrifices long before those of Leviticus, and before the Canaanites from whom some critics claimed the Hebrews borrowed them. There are prophets proclaiming their message long before the nevi'im (prophets) of the Old Testament, though the Old Testament's superiority in the realms of ethics, morality, and spiritual values stands unchallenged. The Old Testament records have that indefinable something that is different. Metaphorically, they bear within them the imprint of the finger of God.

The story has only just begun and there will be echoes from Ebla for generations to come. It is at least thought-provoking that findings such as those at Ebla consistently support the Bible as a thoroughly acceptable record. To this writer it is far more than a wonderful history text: it is God's Word of Truth, His revelation of Himself in the Person of His Son.

(The foregoing material is taken from Dr. Clifford Wilson's new book *EBLA TABLETS: Secrets of a Forgotten City,* published by Creation-Life Publishers, San Diego, CA 92115. Publication date: April, 1977, Price: $1.95.)

No. 47, May, 1977
NOAH'S ARK GOES TO HOLLYWOOD
John D. Morris, M.S.*

The search for Noah's Ark has many years been a source of fascination and intrigue for millions. The story has such appeal that the news media had always been anxious to report any news dealing with the Ark. These accounts have not always been factual or favorable, but they have been well circulated.

*John D. Morris is Field Scientist of I.C.R. He has completed work for his M.S. in Geological Engineering, and has authored two books on the search for the Ark.

The first major splash was in 1883 when Turkish avalanche investigators claimed a discovery of the Ark. The world press so twisted and turned this story, however, and made such a sport of it, that those inclined to accept it were intimidated.

In 1940 the second major story hit the American public. The fictional account of Vladimar Roskovitsky was printed and reprinted in newspapers, magazines, books, tracts, etc. in spite of the fact that the author of the story claimed it was mostly false, built on only the barest of details supplied by the families of two of the deceased members of the reported Russian expedition.

During the '40s, the Ark continued to be in the news, with Air Force personnel claiming sightings from the air, a Kurdish peasant finding it by accident, and several expeditions raising support and making plans.

Fernand Navarra, the French climber, had his day in the spotlight when he displayed to the world an ancient piece of handtooled wood that he removed from a crevasse in the ice cap of Mt. Ararat. Later, in 1969, he returned with a team from SEARCH INC. and discovered other small pieces of wood in a nearby location.

In this decade, the publicity has been of a different sort. There have been numerous expeditions with many participants, most of whom consistently lecture and write on the subject, and few in this country are not aware to some degree that the search is current. Since 1972 ten books have been written on the subject, all of which have been good sellers. These books have varied in viewpoint, content, and accuracy, but are all reasonably factual.

The Institute for Creation Research has always maintained a strictly ethical, legal, and moral stand in its expeditions and its publications have strived for precise accuracy even though truth may not make such exciting reading. It is in that light that some of the more recent well known and circulated items must be discussed.

Satellite Photos

The first of the major news stories of this decade was

the report on February 21, 1974, that a NASA satellite known as the Earth Resources Technology Satellite (ERTS, now known as LANDSAT) had photographed Noah's Ark from an altitude of 450 miles. The news was repeated in virtually every newspaper and on every radio and television station.

Unfortunately, when examined by photographic experts, the object in question turned out not to be the Ark. It was many times too large and not at all in the area under consideration as the possible resting place of the Ark. NASA experts agree that the Ark, even if fully exposed, and under optimal conditions, would likely not be visible. In any case, they are certain that this object, located at about 6,000 feet elevation, is not the Ark.

Holy Ground Mission Changing Center

Several years ago a small group of people established a commune in rural east Texas and formed a unique cult under the leadership of Tom Crotser, and began their "ministry of restoration." They feel that many major Old Testament relics, artifacts, dwelling places, etc. must be restored before Christ can set up His Kingdom on earth. They claim a special anointing of God to do this work, while espousing doctrines far removed from mainline Christianity.

They believe that one of the major remains that must be restored in their program is Noah's Ark, and they have been actively searching since 1971. In 1974, they returned from Mt. Ararat, actually claiming to have found the Ark, and produced a lone picture which has since enjoyed wide circulation, showing primarily what is claimed to be "the planking on the side" of the Ark.

However, their messianic complex has perhaps justified, in their thinking, actions which others would find questionable, so that at least some of their statements are open to question. They have consistently used the material of others, claiming it was their own, and drawn false conclusions from it. For example, the intriguing picture of the "unidentified object," taken by the Archaeological Research Foundation in 1966, which shows an unusual but unidentified Ark-like formation in the distance, has now appeared without permission in many newspapers and personal pictures sponsored by the Mission and used as proof that they have found the Ark.

Their 1974 photo has been claimed as a telephoto of the Ark, taken from 2,000 feet away. The photograph is far out of focus and shows a mountainous region and an unusual rock formation. However, very sharp and distinct lines appear on the picture running parallel along the formation. However, any photographer knows that in a telephoto taken from 2,000 feet, if anything is in focus, everything should be in focus. But in this picture, the only thing that does appear sharply is the supposed "planking," which is the only proof offered by the Mission to substantiate their claim of seeing "the planking on the side" of the Ark. CIA representatives have scrutinized the picture, as they do everything on the subject, and labeled it as an amateurish job of retouching.

Noah's Ark: Movie Star

In the past three years, two feature length movies have been produced detailing the search for Noah's Ark. Both of these films are interesting and informative, and an effort in both was made to be fair to the Biblical concept of a global flood in Noah's day, but numerous errors were present that confused the issue.

"The Ark of Noah"

The first of the two movies resulted from an illegal expedition in August of 1974, led by film producer Bart LaRue, of Jannus of Hollywood. LaRue and his crew literally bribed their way up the mountain, climbing at night to avoid detection whenever possible. Much of the movie details these bribes and calls attention to the corruption within the Turkish government. As a result, Bart LaRue was banned from Turkey and is under peril of arrest and prosecution if he returns. In fact, when the writer of this article was in Turkey in May of 1975, several times he was detained for questioning and once arrested for several hours, until it was definitely ascertained that he had no connection with LaRue or with any of the other illegal groups that had surreptitiously climbed the mountain looking for the Ark, (including the Holy Ground Mission).

Before launching his expedition, LaRue contracted with SEARCH INC. for all of their archival material. Much of the footage in his film stemmed from expeditions in the sixties launched by the Archaeological Research Foundation and later SEARCH INC. itself. This footage supplemented some rather dramatic shots of the glacier where Navarra and SEARCH found wood in 1955 and 1969 respectively.

LaRue's film has not been successful in commercial theatres. It was somewhat upstaged by the second movie, which benefited from a massive advertising budget. La Rue's movie is now playing (in an abbreviated version) in churches around the country. It contains some of the background research into past sighting, into the folklore and symbolic place names of the Ararat area, and shows the political problems and physical dangers encountered. Black and white movies of Navarra and his wood taken in 1955 precede the SEARCH 1969 discovery and LaRue's expedition. Also included is a rather interesting study of the Flood and Flood geology although this is not entirely compatible with the Biblical Flood model as understood by the Institute for Creation Research. Deleted from the original feature length version are some of the many statements of Turkish corruption and details of the supposed bribes.

In its present form it is neither particularly Christian nor creationist, but it does contain worthwhile information.

"In Search of Noah's Ark"

Publicity on its grandest scale resulted from the second feature length movie, which currently is playing across the country. Produced by Sun Classic Pictures, Inc., a subsidiary of the Schick Razor Company, the movie is said to have cost about one-half million dollars to produce and five million dollars to advertise; however, the movie is expected to gross thirty million dollars.

The Sun Classic emphasis is in family-oriented pictures, although it is not a Christian organization as such. Several years ago, this company conducted a nationwide survey to determine what subjects people were interested in, and the number one subject was the search for Noah's Ark! Plans were laid to produce a dramatized documentary detailing the past sightings, current research, technical features of the Ark and Flood, culminating in the Navarra and SEARCH finds, much as Bart LaRue's film had done.

After the script had been written and production started, problems arose and Sun Classic hired Dave Balsiger, a California advertising man thoroughly familiar with the facts of the search, to check the script accuracy. Balsiger, a ghost writer for Fernand Navarra's book *Noah's Ark: I Touched It,* recognized serious problems in the original script. Balsiger was acquainted with the work of the personnel of the Institute for Creation Research, and frequently consulted this writer and other ICR scientists as he rewrote major portions of the script. The final product suffered somewhat in the hands of editors and advertising men who were more interested in a sensational movie than in strict factuality but, all things considered, the movie has had an overall positive effect, in informing people of the search and of the fact that serious scientific investigators are involved.

Unfortunately, a number of historical, Biblical, and scientific errors did creep in. Because so many people have mistakenly assumed that ICR is responsible for the film, some of these errors should be noted.

The pre-flood geography, meteorology, and other conditions implied in the film included a curious mixture of local-flood concepts (as put forward by Biblical skeptics for decades) along with various speculative concepts of astral catastrophism. This, of course, involves a number of significant differences with a straightforward rendering of the Genesis account and resulting logical deductions therefrom.

The Bible indicates that it had never rained before the Flood, yet in the movie Noah and his family were already familiar with rain, snow, thunder and other storms. Most Biblical creationists feel that the water canopy of Genesis was made up of invisible water vapor, with uninhibited views of the stars and with no clouds. But the movie, in its reenactment of the building of the Ark, and collecting of the animals, showed both cloudy days and sunny days, and then rehearsed the concept of a canopy made of ice crystals, translucent but not transparent, which was supposedly precipitated by an astral near-miss, causing the Flood. This latter model, of course, seems a clear contradiction with Scripture, and has thus raised many unnecessary questions.

If the Flood story in the Bible is to be regarded as sober history, then we should not expect to recognize any pre-Flood geography. The surface of the globe would have been totally restructured. All of the fossil-bearing sedimentary rock would have been laid down at this time, in places many miles thick. Certainly, we have no justification for placing the Garden of Eden or Noah's pre-Flood home in the Mesopotamian valley, but the movie does just that. In the same breath the film speaks of 60,000 feet of Flood strata in India and a few feet of supposed "Flood" silt at Ur of the Chaldees. The wood found by Navarra (white oak) is said to have come from the fertile crescent, since that same type of wood grows there now, but the fact is that thousands of feet of Flood-lain strata underlie the present river valley.

In reenacting the Flood story, the movie varied from the Biblical version in a few details, such as the sending out of doves, the rainbow, chronology, and others, but in essence the story was correct. The footage showing the destruction due to advancing Flood waters is especially dramatic. Equally interesting are the construction methods used and the stability studies of an Ark model in a hydraulic testing facility.

Once the movie leaves the more historic areas, serious

errors and unproved assumptions are introduced. The Navarra wood is discussed at length and an effort is made to establish its ancient vintage. First the carbon-14 dates, which don't agree with the estimated date of the Flood, are explained away. Attention turns, then, to highly subjective and unreliable techniques based on uniformitarian principles that would not be accurate if the catastrophe which they are trying to demonstrate is indeed history. Four methods, the degree of lignite formation, gain in wood density, cell modification, and degree of fossilization, all yielded older dates but these were rather uncertain estimates, and in fact are rejected by most scientists. The Navarra wood remains highly questionable in origin, and Navarra's claim to have found the Ark is at best premature.

The climax of the movie is the presentation of all possible positive data, with very little regard for the canons of true evidence, including the unusual geologic formation photographed in 1959 from the air 50 miles to the south of Mt. Ararat and known without a doubt not to be the Ark. In addition, the ERTS photograph discussed earlier is studied in detail in a very impressive piece of footage in a NASA laboratory. The sensors located a spot on the photo that possessed a different reflectivity than any other spot on the mountain. Unfortunately, since the spot was at about the 5,000 foot level, it could not be the Ark, and in all likelihood was the new tin-roofed schoolhouse in the village of Ahora, on the lower slopes of the mountain.

To prove its bold statement that the Ark has been found, the movie showed both the "unidentified object" taken by the Archaeological Research Foundation in 1966 and the obviously-retouched Holy Ground Mission photo. In both cases the director and producer were aware that neither photo should be considered as proof of anything. And since these two "pictures of the Ark" were at different locations, a broken-Ark theory was postulated, with half of the Ark in two separate locations. However, there are *four* sites actually mentioned in this film, the Navarra site, the NASA spot, the "unidentified object," and the Mission photo, and all four are distinct and widely separated, and furthermore, none are in the places specified in the movie.

These differences may seem trivial, but the fact remains that the Ark has not yet been rediscovered, and the search must go on. The Institute for Creation Research is presently approaching the proper Turkish authorities in an effort to overcome the negative publicity of the past few years and to launch a serious investigation once again.

No. 48, June, 1977
CIRCULAR REASONING
IN EVOLUTIONARY GEOLOGY
Henry M. Morris, Ph.D.

Creationists have long insisted that the main evidence for evolution—the fossil record—involves a serious case of circular reasoning. That is, the fossil evidence that life has evolved from simple to complex forms over the geological ages depends on the geological ages of the specific rocks in which these fossils are found. The rocks, however, are assigned geologic ages based on the fossil assemblages which they contain. The fossils, in turn, are arranged on the basis of their assumed evolutionary relationships. Thus the main evidence for evolution is based on the assumption of evolution.

A significant development of recent years has been the fact that many evolutionary geologists are now also recognizing this problem. They no longer ignore it or pass it off with a sarcastic denial, but admit that it is a real problem which deserves a serious answer.

The use of "index fossils" to determine the geologic age of a formation, for example, is discussed in an interesting way in an important recent paper by J.E. O'Rourke.

These principles have been applied in *Feinstratigraphie,* which starts from a chronology of index fossils, and imposes them on the rocks. Each taxon represents a definite time unit and so pro-

vides an accurate, even "infallible" date. If you
doubt it, bring in a suite of good index fossils,
and the specialist without asking where or in
what order they were collected, will lay them out
on the table in chronological order.[1]

That is, since evolution always proceeds in the same way
all over the world at the same time, index fossils representing a given stage of evolution are assumed to constitute
infallible indicators of the geologic age in which they are
found. This makes good sense and would obviously be the
best way to determine relative geologic age—if, that is, we
knew infallibly that evolution were true!

But how do we know that? There is such a vast time
scale involved that no one can actually observe evolution
taking place.

That a known fossil or recent species, or higher
taxonomic group, however primitive it might
appear, is an actual ancestor of some other species or group, is an assumption scientifically un-
justifiable, for science never can simply assume
that which it has the responsibility to demonstrate . . . . It is the burden of each of us to demonstrate the reasonableness of any hypothesis
we might care to erect about ancestral conditions,
keeping in mind that we have no ancestors alive
today, that in all probability such ancestors have
been dead for many tens of millions of years, and
that even in the fossil record they are not acces-
sible to us.[2]

There is, therefore, really no way of proving scientifically any assumed evolutionary phylogeny, as far as the fossil
record is concerned.

Likewise, paleontologists do their best to make
sense out of the fossil record and sketch in evolutionary sequences or unfossilized morphologies

without realistic hope of obtaining specific verification within the foreseeable future.[3]

It would help if the fossil record would yield somewhere
at least a few transitional sequences demonstrating the
evolution of some kind of organism into some other more
complex kind. So far, however, it has been uncooperative.

The abrupt appearance of higher taxa in the fossil
record has been a perennial puzzle . . . . If we
read the record rather literally, it implies that organisms of new grades of complexity arose and
radiated relatively rapidly.[4]

Transitions are well documented, of course, at the *same*
levels of complexity—within the "kinds," that is—but
never into "new grades of complexity." *Horizontal*
changes, however, are not really relevant to the measure of
geologic time, since such changes occur too rapidly (e.g.,
the development of numerous varieties of dogs within
human history) to be meaningful on the geologic time
scale, and are reversible (e.g., the shift in the population
numbers of the peppered-moth of England from light-
colored to dark-colored and back again).
    Thus *vertical* evolutionary changes in fossils are essential
to real geologic dating, but they are impossible to prove.
They must simply be assumed.
    The dating of the rocks depends on the evolutionary
sequence of the fossils, but the evolutionary interpretation
of the fossils depends on the dating of the rocks. No won-
der the evolutionary system, to outsiders, implies circular
reasoning.

The intelligent layman has long suspected circular
reasoning in the use of rocks to date fossils and
fossils to date rocks. The geologist has never
bothered to think of a good reply, feeling the
explanations are not worth the trouble as long as
the work brings results. This is supposed to be
hard-headed pragmatism.[5]

The main "result" of this system, however, is merely the widespread acceptance of evolution. It is extremely inefficient in locating oil or other economically useful deposits. Perhaps, however, geologists feel that, since biologists had already proved evolution, they are justified in assuming it in their own work. But biologists in turn have simply assumed evolution to be true.

> But the danger of circularity is still present. For most biologists the strongest reason for accepting the evolutionary hypothesis is their acceptance of some theory that entails it. There is another difficulty. The temporal ordering of biological events beyond the local section may critically involve paleontological correlation, which necessarily presupposed the non-repeatability of organic events in geologic history. There are various justifications for this assumption but for almost all contemporary paleontologists it rests upon the acceptance of the evolutionary hypothesis.[6]

And, as far as "ordering of biological events beyond the local section is concerned," O'Rourke reminds us again that:

> Index fossils . . . are regarded as the features most reliable for accurate, long-distance correlations.[7]

As mentioned earlier, more and more modern geologists are now recognizing the existence of circular reasoning in their geological methodologies. Among these, in addition to those already cited, is Dr. Derek Ager, current president of the British Geological Association.

> It is a problem not easily solved by the classic methods of stratigraphical paleontology, as obviously we will land ourselves immediately in an impossible circular argument if we say, firstly

that a particular lithology is synchronous on the evidence of its fossils, and secondly that the fossils are synchronous on the evidence of the lithology.[8]

In another article, Dr. Ager, who is also Head of the Geology Department at Swansea University, notes the problem involved in trying to use minor differences in organisms (that is, what creationists would call horizontal changes, or variations) as time markers.

We all know that many apparent evolutionary bursts are nothing more than brainstorms on the part of particular paleontologists. One splitter in a library can do far more than millions of years of genetic mutation.[9]

It would seem that this would lead to great uncertainty in the use of extinct marine organisms (about whose intraspecific variability while they were living we know nothing whatever) as index fossils.

Another geologist who has recognized the circulatory problem is Dr. Ronald West, at Kansas State University.

Contrary to what most scientists write, the fossil record does not support the Darwinian theory of evolution because it is this theory (there are several) which we use to interpret the fossil record. By doing so, we are guilty of circular reasoning if we then say the fossil record supports this theory.[10]

Still another comment on the circular reasoning process involved in developing paleontological sequences appears in an important symposium paper.

The prime difficulty with the use of presumed ancestral-descendant sequences to express phylogeny is that biostratigraphic data are often used in conjunction with morphology in the initial evaluation of relationships, which leads to obvious circularity.[11]

In view of such admissions from many leading evolutionists, it is clear that there neither is, nor can be, any *proof* of evolution. The evidence for evolution is merely the assumption of evolution.

The most extensive recent discussion of the circular reasoning problem in evolutionary geology is the paper by O'Rourke.[12] Although he attempts to explain and justify the process as being based on induction from observed field data, he does admit many important problems in this connection. With respect to the geologic column and its development, he says:

> Material bodies are finite, and no rock unit is global in extent, yet stratigraphy aims at a global classification. The particulars have to be stretched into universals somehow. Here ordinary materialism leaves off building up a system of units recognized by physical properties, to follow dialectical materialism, which starts with time units and regards the material bodies as their incomplete representatives. This is where the suspicion of circular reasoning crept in, because it seemed to the layman that the time units were abstracted from the geological column, which has been put together from rock units.[13]

The fiction that the geological column was actually represented by real rock units in the field has long been abandoned, of course.

> By mid-nineteenth century, the notion of "universal" rock units had been dropped, but some stratigraphers still imagine a kind of global biozone as "time units" that are supposed to be ubiquitous.[*]

Behind all such assumed time units must be the doctrinaire assumption of evolution, which is the basic component of materialism.

> The theory of dialectic materialism postulates matter as the ultimate reality, not to be questioned . . . . Evolution is more than a useful biologic concept: it is a natural law controlling the history of all phenomena.[15]

And if physical data in the field seem in any case to contradict this assumed evolutionary development, then the field data can easily be reinterpreted to correspond to evolution! This is always possible in circular reasoning.

> Structure, metamorphism, sedimentary reworking and other complications have to be considered. Radiometric dating would not have been feasible if the geologic column had not been erected first . . . . The axiom that no process can measure itself means that there is no absolute time, but this relic of the traditional mechanics persists in the common distinction between "relative" and "absolute" age.[16]

In this exposition, O'Rourke thus decries the common reliance on an implicit circular argument which he attributes to the assumption of dialectic materialism, and urges his colleagues to deal pragmatically with the actual stratigraphic rock units as they occur in the field, in confidence that this will eventually correlate with the global column built up gradually by similar procedures used by their predecessors.

He does recognize, however, that if the actual physical geological column is going to be used as a time scale, it is impossible to avoid circular reasoning.

> The rocks do date the fossils, but the fossils date the rocks more accurately. Stratigraphy cannot

avoid this kind of reasoning if it insists on using only temporal concepts, because circularity is inherent in the derivation of time scales.[17]

REFERENCES

1. J.E. O'Rourke, "Pragmatism versus Materialism in Stratigraphy," *American Journal of Science*, Vol. 276, January 1976, p. 51.
2. Gareth V. Nelson, "Origin and Diversification of Teleostean Fishes," *Annals, New York Academy of Sciences.* 1971, p. 27.
3. Donald R. Griffin, "A Possible Window on the Minds of Animals," *American Scientist*, Vol. 64, September-October 1976, p. 534.
4. James W. Valentine and Cathryn A. Campbell, "Genetic Regulation and the Fossil Record," *American Scientist*, Vol. 63, November-December, 1975, p. 673.
5. J.E. O'Rourke, *op cit*, p. 48.
6. David G. Kitts, "Paleontology and Evolutionary Theory," *Evolution* Vol. 28, September, 1974, p. 466.
7. J.E. O'Rourke, *op cit*, p. 48.
8. Derek V. Ager, *The Nature of the Stratigraphic Record* (New York, John Wiley & Sons, 1973) p. 62.
9. Derek V. Ager, "The Nature of the Fossil Record," *Proceedings of the Geological Association*, Vol. 87, No. 2, 1976, p. 132.
10. Ronald R. West, "Paleontology and Uniformitarianism," *Compass*, Vol. 45, May 1968, p. 216.
11. B. Schaeffer, M.K. Hecht and N. Eldredge, "Phylogeny and Paleontology," Ch. 2 in *Evolutionary Biology*, Vol. 6 (edited by Th. Dobzhansky, M.K. Hecht and W.C. Steere; New York Appleton-Century-Crofts, 1972) p. 39.
12. J.E. O'Rourke, *op cit;* pp. 47-55.
13. *Ibid*, p. 49.
14. *Ibid*, p. 50.
15. *Ibid*, p. 51.
16. *Ibid*, p. 54
17. *Ibid*, p. 53.

No. 49, July, 1977

FROM EVOLUTION TO CREATION:
A PERSONAL TESTIMONY
Dr. Gary Parker

[Ed. Note: The following is condensed from four radio talks, now available in booklet form through Creation-Life Publishers. Dr. Parker, member of Phi Beta Kappa and recipient of two nationally competitive fellowship awards, received his doctorate in biology with a cognate in geology in 1973. A recent addition to the staffs of ICR and Christian Heritage College, Dr. Parker chairs the new Life

Science Department for the college, which offers a major in biology including courses in genetics, anatomy and physiology, ecology, biosystematics, microbiology, cell biology and biochemistry, and strong support courses in physical sciences.]

Moderator: Dr. Parker, I understand that when you started teaching college biology you were an enthusiastic evolutionist.

Yes, indeed. The idea of evolution was very satisfying to me. It gave me a feeling of being one with the huge, evolving universe continually progressing toward grander things. Evolution was really my religion, a faith commitment and a complete world-and-life view that organized everything else for me, and I got quite emotional when evolution was challenged.

As a religion, evolution answered my questions about God, sin, and salvation. God was unnecessary, or at least did no more than make the particles and processes from which all else mechanistically followed. "Sin" was only the result of animal instincts that had outlived their usefulness, and salvation involved only personal adjustment, enlightened self-interest, and perhaps one day the benefits of genetic engineering.

With no God to answer to, no God with a purpose for mankind, I saw our destiny in our own hands. Tied in with the idea of inevitable evolutionary progress, this was a truly thrilling idea and the part of evolution I liked best.

Did your faith in evolution affect your classroom teaching?

It surely did. In my early years of teaching at both the high school and college levels, I worked hard to convince my students that evolution was true. I even had students crying in class. I thought I was teaching objective science, not religion, but I was very consciously trying to get students to bend their religious beliefs to evolution. In fact, a discussion with high school teachers in a graduate class I was assisting included just that goal: encouraging students to adapt their religious beliefs to the concept of evolution!

I thought you weren't supposed to teach religion in the public school system.

Well, maybe you can't teach the Christian religion, but there is no trouble at all in teaching the evolutionary religion. I've done it myself, and I've watched the effects that accepting evolution has on a persons's thought and life. Of course, I once thought that effect was good, "liberating the mind from the shackles of revealed religion" and making a person's own opinions supreme.

Since you found evolution such a satisfying religion and enjoyed teaching it to others, what made you change your mind?

I've often marveled that God could change anyone as content as I was, especially with so many religious leaders (including two members of the Bible department where I once taught!) actually supporting evolution over creation. But through a Bible study group my wife and I joined at first for purely social reasons, God slowly convinced me to lean not on my own opinions or those of other human authorities, but in all my ways to acknowledge Him and to let Him direct my paths. It is a blessed experience that gives me an absolute reference point and a truly mind-stretching eternal perspective.

Did your conversion to Christianity then make you a creationist?

No, at least not at first. Like so many before and since, I simply combined my new-found Christian religion with the "facts" of science and became a theistic evolutionist and then a progressive creationist. I thought the Bible told me *who* created, and that evolution told me *how*.

But then I began to find scientific problems with the evolutionary part, and theological problems with the theistic part. I still have a good many friends who believe in theistic evolution or progressive creation, but I finally had to give it up.

What theological problems did you find with theistic evolution?

Perhaps the key point centered around the phrase, "very good." At the end of each creation period (except the second) God said that His creation was good. At the end of the sixth period He said that all His works of creation were very good.

Now all the theistic evolutionists and progressive creationists I know, including myself at one time, try to fit "geologic time" and the fossil record into the creation periods. But regardless of how old they are, the fossils show the same things that we have on earth today—famine, disease, disaster, extinction, floods, earthquakes, etc. So if fossils represent stages in God's creative activity, why should Christians oppose disease and famine or help preserve an endangered species? If the fossils were formed during the creation week, then all these things would be very good.

When I first believed in evolution, I had sort of a romantic idea about evolution as unending progress. But in the closing paragraphs of the *Origin of Species,* Darwin explained that evolution, the "production of higher animals," was caused by "the war of nature, from famine and death." Does "the war of nature, from famine and death" sound like the means God would have used to create a world all very good?

In Genesis 3, Romans 8 and many other passages, we learn that such negative features were not part of the world that God created, but entered only after Adam's sin. By ignoring this point, either intentionally or unintentionally, theistic evolutionists and progressive creationists come into conflict with the whole pattern of Scripture: the great themes of Creation, the Fall, and Redemption—how God made the world perfect and beautiful; how man's sin brought a curse upon the world; and how Christ came to save us from our sins and to restore all things.

With the Scriptures so plain throughout, are there still many Christians who believe in theistic evolution or progressive creation?

Yes, there are. Of course, I can't speak for all of them, but I can tell you the problems I had to overcome before I could give up theistic evolution myself. First, I really hate to argue or take sides. When I was a theistic evolutionist I didn't have to argue with anybody. I just chimed in smiling at the end of an argument with something like, "Well, the important thing is to remember that God did it."

Then there is the matter of intellectual pride. Creationists are often looked down upon as ignorant throw-backs to the nineteenth century or worse, and I began to think of all the academic honors I had, and to tell you the truth, I didn't want to face that academic ridicule.

Finally, I, like many Christians, was honestly confused about the Biblical issues. As I told you, I first became a creationist while teaching at a Christian college. Believe it or not, I got into big trouble with the Bible Department. As soon as I started teaching creation instead of evolution, the Bible Department people challenged me to a debate. The Bible Department defended evolution, and two other scientists and I defended creation!

That debate pointed out how religious evolution really is, and the willingness of leaders to speak out in favor of evolution makes it harder for the average Christian to take a strong stand on creation. To tell you the truth, I don't think I would have had the courage, especially as a professor of biology, to give up evolution or theistic evolution without finding out that the bulk of scientific data actually argues *against* evolution.

In that sense, then, it was really the scientific data that completed your conversion from evolution, through theistic evolution and progressive creation to Biblical, scientific creationism?

Yes, it was. At first I was embarrassed to be both a creationist and a science professor, and I wasn't really sure what to do with the so-called "mountains of evidence" for evolution. A colleague in biology, Allen Davis, introduced me to Morris' and Whitcomb's famous book, *The Genesis Flood*. At first I reacted strongly against the book, using all the evolutionist arguments I knew so well. But at that crucial time, the Lord provided me with a splendid Science Faculty Fellowship award from the N.S.F., so I resolved to pursue doctoral studies in biology, while also adding a cognate in geology to check out some of the creationist arguments first hand. To my surprise, and eventually to my delight, just about every course I took was full of more and more problems in evolution, and more and more support for the basic points of Biblical creationism outlined in *The Genesis Flood* and Morris' later book, *Scientific Creationism.*

Can you give us some examples?

Yes indeed. One of the tensest moments for me came when we started discussing uranium-lead and other radiometric methods for estimating the age of the earth. I just knew all the creationists' arguments would be shot down and crumbled, but just the opposite happened.

In one graduate class, the professor told us we didn't have to memorize the dates of the geologic system since they were far too uncertain and conflicting. Then in geophysics we went over all of the assumptions that go into radiometric dating. Afterwards, the professor said something like this, "If a fundamentalist ever got hold of this stuff, he would make havoc out of the radiometric dating system. So, keep the faith." That's what he told us, "keep the faith." If it was a matter of keeping faith, I now had another faith I preferred to keep.

Are there other examples like that?

Lots of them. One concerns the word paraconformity. In *The Genesis Flood,* I had heard that paraconformity was a word used by evolutionary geologists for fossil systems out of order, but with no evidence of erosion or overthrusting. My heart really started pounding when paraconformities and other unconformities came up in geology class. What did the professor say? Essentially the same thing as Morris and Whitcomb. He presented paraconformities as a real mystery and something very difficult to explain in evolutionary or uniformitarian terms. We even had a field trip to study paraconformities that emphasized the point.

So again, instead of challenging my creationist ideas, all the geology I was learning in graduate school was supporting them. I even discussed a creationist interpretation of paraconformities with the professor, and I finally found myself discussing further evidence of creation with fellow graduate students and others.

What do you mean by "evidence of creation?"

All of us can recognize objects that man has created, whether paintings, sculptures, or just a Coke bottle. Because the pattern of relationships in those objects is contrary to relationships that time, chance, and natural physical processes would produce, we know an outside creative agent was involved. I began to see the same thing in a study of living things, especially in the area of my major interest, molecular biology.

All living things depend upon a working relationship between inheritable nucleic acid molecules, like DNA, and proteins, the chief structural and functional molecules. To make proteins, living creatures use a sequence of DNA bases to line up a sequence of amino acid R-groups. But the normal reactions between DNA and proteins are the "wrong" ones, and act with time and chance to disrupt living systems. Just as phosphorus, glass, and copper will work together in a television set only if properly arranged by human engineers, so DNA and protein will work in productive harmony only if properly ordered by an outside creative agent.

I presented the biochemical details of this DNA-protein argument to a group of graduate students and professors, including my professor of molecular biology. At the end of the talk, my professor offered no criticism of the biology or biochemistry I had presented. She just said that she didn't believe it because she didn't believe there was anything out there to create life. But if your faith permits belief in a Creator, you can see the evidence of creation in the things that have been made (as Paul implies in Rom. 1:18-20).

Has creationism influenced your work as a scientist and as a teacher?

Yes, in many positive ways. Science is based on the assumption of an understandable orderliness in the operation of nature, and the Scriptures guarantee both that order and man's ability to understand it, infusing science with enthusiastic hope and richer meaning. Furthermore, creationists are able to recognize *both* spontaneous *and* created (i.e., internally and externally determined) patterns of order, and this opened my eyes to a far greater range of theories and models to deal with the data from such diverse fields as physiology, systematics, and ecology.

Creationism has certainly made the classroom a much more exciting place, both for me and my students. So much of biology touches on key ethical issues, such as genetic engineering, the ecological crisis, reproduction and development, and now I have so much more to offer than just my own opinions and the severely limited perspectives of other human authorities. And, of course, on the basic matter of origins, my students and I have the freedom to discuss *both* evolution *and* creation, a freedom tragically denied to most young people in our schools today.

Creationists have to pay the price of academic ridicule and occasional personal attacks, but these are nothing compared to the riches of knowledge and wisdom that are ours through Christ! I only wish that more scientists, science teachers, and science students could share the joy and challenge of looking at God's world through God's eyes.

No. 50, August, 1977

**CONSIDERATIONS REGARDING A
MODEL FOR EXPERIMENTAL PSYCHOLOGY**

Paul D. Ackerman, Ph.D.*

The present paper will discuss some basic considerations in formulating a Biblical creation model for experimental psychology. As a first step, it will be useful to examine in a somewhat oversimplified way the current state of experimental psychology as it operates under the general evolution model. At the heart of the evolutionary viewpoint is

*Doctor Ackerman received his Ph.D. in Social Psychology from Kansas State University in 1968. He is Assistant Professor of Psychology at Wichita State University.

the assumption that the universe, including its psychological life forms, is the result of a strictly materialistic process involving vast amounts of time and random changes. If one assumes the validity of this "time plus chance" explanation, it becomes very difficult to believe that present natural phenomena are as complex as they might superficially appear. To put it another way, the evolutionist is logically inclined to assume that underlying the apparent complexity of the universe there must be a very basic simplicity. Thus from the evolutionists' perspective, if scientists are going to explain the thoughts and actions of psychological organisms, they must search for simple, economical explanations of the apparently complex behaviors in which they engage. This leads them to adopt an approach to scientific investigation and explanation which is called "reductionism."[1] The psychologist attempts to explain the very complex things people do—such as speaking, problem solving, remembering, and so forth— in terms of relatively simple mechanisms.

In contemporary experimental psychology, dominated almost exclusively by the evolutionary model, one can identify two broad reductionist camps. In one camp may be called biological reductionists, those who attempt to explain the activity of intelligent creatures in terms of genetic make-up, hormone balances, brain cell activity, and more complex instincts and brain functioning patterns. These psychologists believe that the seemingly infinite complexity and variety of intelligent activity observed in nature can be reductionistically explained in terms of relatively more simple and yet still highly complex biological mechanisms.

Opposed to the biological reductionist camp are those in the environmental reductionist camp. Environmental reductionists are also evolutionary in orientation, but they feel uncomfortable with the level of biological complexity posited by the biological reductionists. They prefer a still simpler biological component with more weight given to environmental factors in explaining the complex activities of people and animals. Emphasis is given to such factors as stimulus/stimulus, stimulus/response, and response/reward histories, along with more abstract environmental dimensions such as education, cultural background, and so forth.

A simple analogy will illustrate the difference between these two views. Suppose that a group of scientists was called in to examine some mysterious and advanced model of airplane that had landed in their country for unknown reasons. As the scientists comb over the aircraft, they develop two opposing concepts as to how it is flown. Some scientists focus on the cockpit with its complex instruments and control stick and come to the conclusion that it is flown manually. But other scientists become intrigued with a complicated computer located in the interior of the craft, and as a result become convinced that the plane is flown by means of an "automatic pilot." The ensuing argument between the "manual control" and "automatic pilot" proponents is somewhat analogous to the nature vs. nurture argument in psychology. The "manual control" view illustrates the environmental camp, and the "automatic pilot" view illustrates the biological camp. In this analogy the manual controls represent the relatively simple biological component posited by the environmental reductionist. Thus, the plane must be directed by outside environmental forces (i.e., the pilot) if it is to fly successfully. The "automatic pilot" on the other hand represents the more complex biological component posited by the biological reductionist. To a much greater degree the plane with an automatic pilot is guided on the basis of internal forces and relatively independent of outside environmental ones.

A Creationist Model

In contrast to the above views it is possible to formulate a creation or design model for experimental psychology. An event which took place in connection with the recent Mars landing program provides an excellent illustration for such a model. First of all, no one supposes that the two

Viking spacecrafts evolved. We all know that a great deal of energy and intelligence went into their design and construction. When they reached Mars, an interesting thing happened to one of them. A switch malfunctioned, and an important mechanical arm could not be moved. The project scientists, however, did not throw up their hands in despair as one might expect. Rather, they began studying the problem and eventually succeeded in bypassing the faulty switch, thus allowing the arm to work properly. Now one might say to himself, "How can this be possible? If a house light switch is faulty it must be replaced. One could not bypass it from the next room, let alone from millions of miles away in space." The answer is simple. The Houston scientists were able to bypass the faulty switch because highly intelligent designers had planned for these and many other contingencies in advance. In other words, the spacecraft was not simply designed to operate on the surface of Mars. It was designed to include a wide range of alternative modes of operation in the event of mechanical failure. It was, in effect, *overdesigned*. The concept of "overdesign" or "contingency design" could be useful in formulating a viable scientific creation model for experimental psychology. If the "mechanical" body a person lives in were designed by an infinitely intelligent creator, scientists might expect to find evidence of overlapping and redundant systems similar to those in the Mars vehicle. This would allow alternate modes of operation in the event of the failure of one or more key psychological or biological systems.

There are convincing data from experimental psychology as well as everyday experience pointing directly and powerfully to just such a conclusion. Psychological organisms, including man, demonstrate a remarkable combination of extremely efficient and economical organization on the one hand, and incredible potential for functional flexibility on the other. Biological reductionists have tended to appreciate only the first of these characteristics while environmental reductionists have tended to recognize only the latter.

Current Situation in Psychology

Returning to the description of the current state of psychology, the reader may recall the analogy of the scientists examining the aircraft. One group believes the plane is flown manually (environmental control) and the other that it is flown by automatic pilot (biological control). Of course the fact is that the plane has both capabilities, so in a sense both groups are right in their positive claims and wrong in their opposition to the opponent's position. Now what happens as these two groups battle with each other? Each side makes dramatic claims which the opponent denies. The "automatic pilot" group provides evidence that the plane can be safely and accurately flown even with the pilot blindfolded. The "manual operation" group, on the other hand, puts on an impressive demonstration of acrobatic flying using the manual controls. Both sides are embarrassed and puzzled at accomplishments by the opponents. In a sense, this is the state of affairs in psychology today.

Two of the most prominent examples are the following. Contrary to the expectations of environmentalists, the biological reductionists point to accumulating evidence that human beings grow almost automatically into their language ability. With minimal training and apparently haphazard learning conditions, they are able to master the language with remarkable ease and regularity. On the other hand, contrary to the expectations of biological reductionists, the environmentalists continue to demonstrate and uncover evidence for the incredible capacity and flexibility organisms have for learning. They are fond of demonstrating that supposedly fixed biological sequences of behavior acquisition can be altered or reversed by certain training procedures. The teaching of reading to preschool age children is one dramatic example.

But the flaw in modern psychology goes deeper than simply two opposing sides having part of the truth and not realizing the opponent's share of it. The fact is that both sides, being wedded to the evolutionary model, fail to do justice to even those areas where they happen to be—in a sense—correct. The level of complexity and richness of design (i.e., overdesign) goes far beyond current evolutionary/reductionist theories. The result is, as a colleague recently put it, that practice is constantly outstripping theory. Nonpsychologists are constantly doing things that the experts say are impossible. The only reason they even try to do them is either because they are unaware of expert opinion or for some reason choose to ignore it.

Examples From The Environmentalist Camp

Perhaps the most dramatic recent environmental example concerns a young student at De Paul University. This illustration was recently reported in the National Press by Ronald Kotulak of the Chicago Tribune.[2] In 1953, in order to save a youngster's life from the effects of a severe brain malfunction, surgeons removed the entire left half (or hemisphere) of his brain. Biologically oriented experts, viewing this case in the light of a considerable body of sound scientific evidence that the crucial brain centers for speech and language functions are located in the left hemisphere, predicted that young man would never be able to speak or use language in a normal manner. But as Kotulak reports, "Ever since the operation (the young man) has been dumbfounding the medical profession. Doctors who examine him shake their heads in disbelief." By the age of nine his intellectual capacity was measured in the dull-normal range. By the age of 21, his verbal IQ scores had risen to the bright-normal range. Finally, tests at age 26 showed him to be scoring in the superior range for verbal intelligence. Again to quote Kotulak, "Everything science knows about the brain says it's impossible for (this young man) to be doing as well as he is. Pages of medical textbooks will have to be ripped out and rewritten."

Another dramatic case is that of a young mongoloid child named Nigel Hunt. When Nigel was only two-weeks-old his parents were told by experts that no matter how much love and care they gave him he would always be an idiot. Nothing they could do would alter that fact. Fortunately for Nigel, his parents refused to believe the experts. With great patience, the boy's mother worked with her growing child. Making a game out of it, she spelled out words phonetically as soon as he could talk. Her devotion was rewarded, for by the time Nigel started to school his parents were told that, "no child in his primary school could read better." As Nigel grew older his astounding accomplishments continued. He taught himself to type using his father's typewriter, and then at age 17, became the first mongoloid to write a book, an autobiography entitled, *The World of Nigel Hunt*.[3] Cases such as these highlight an exciting potential for a creation oriented science of psychology.

Examples From The Biological Camp

While the above cases speak to what can be accomplished through experience and training, the following examples show the capacity of animals and humans to attain mature functioning with minimal learning requirements. Examples illustrating this biological preparedness are not difficult to find. Bird migration is one dramatic and well-known instance. A more recently documented illustration can be found in the work of psychologist, Gene Sackett.[4] He experimented with infant monkeys and found evidence that they have an innate ability to recognize (in terms of visual preference) their own species as well as react appropriately to certain social cues. For instance, two- to four-month-old monkeys that had never seen another monkey nevertheless showed signs of fear when exposed to pictures of an angry and threatening adult monkey. Similar evidence for human babies has been shown by Frantz[5] and Ball.[6]

One famous researcher in this area, T.G.R. Bower, has reported the results of some fascinating and excellent laboratory research on the development of visual perception in six- to eight-week-old babies.[7] Many of Bower's results are startling to any reductionist view of man. To quote Bower regarding the results from one of his experiments, "This finding seems very important, since it is a blow not only against the idea (common to nativists and empiricists) that perception of simple variables is in some way developmentally earlier than perception of complex variables."[7]

Conclusion

What Bower has stated is a specialized version of the basic preconception underlying virtually all of modern science, including psychology. It is the evolutionary, reductionistic assumption that simple things precede and are more basic than complex things. Against this idea is the Biblical assertion, "In the beginning God . . . . " A creationist psychology need not abandon the search for underlying mechanisms as method, but only the belief that reductionism is *the route* to basic truth. The discovery of efficient and economical underlying mechanisms can greatly enhance man's understanding and control over nature, and the search for such mechanisms would continue to be an integral part of science. But additionally, a creationist science could infuse a new optimism that the creation contains numerous built-in but as yet undiscovered potentialities for dealing with man's most troublesome problems. Psychologists might come to realize a whole new range of possibilities in terms of service to their fellow man and reduction of human suffering. The possibilities in the area of mental retardation and brain damage are particularly exciting. How many more children like Nigel Hunt or the boy with severe brain damage might be blessed? What possibilities might be uncovered if experimental psychologists were taught to suspect the presence of and search for designed, backup capability. What excitement and adventure to begin to discover and appreciate the Creator's marvelous "overdesign."

REFERENCES

1. *Webster's New Collegiate Dictionary* defines reductionism as "a *procedure*

or theory that reduces complex data or phenomena to simple terms."
(Emphasis added) No criticism of reductionism as a procedure is intended.

2. *The Wichita Eagle*, November 8, 1976.
3. Hunt, N. *The World of Nigel Hunt*. New York: Garrett, 1967.
4. Sackett, Gene P., "Monkeys Reared in Isolation with Pictures as Visual Input: Evidence for an Innate Releasing Mechanism," *Science*, 1966, Vol. 154, pp. 1468-1473.
5. Frantz, R.L., "The Origin of Form Perception," *Scientific American*, 1961, Vol. 204, pp. 66-72.
6. Ball, W., and Tronick, E., "Infant Responses to Impending Collision: Optical and Real," *Science*, 1971, Vol. 171, pp. 818-820.
7. Bower, T.G.R., "The Visual World of Infants," *Scientific American*, 1965, Vol. 215, pp. 80-92.

No. 51, September, 1977

THE RELIGION OF EVOLUTIONARY HUMANISM AND THE PUBLIC SCHOOLS

Henry M. Morris, Ph.D.

The modern creationist movement and the resistance of secular educators to this movement have brought into clear focus one very important fact. Our American public schools and secular universities are controlled by the religious philosophy of evolutionary humanism. Furthermore, through its pervasive influence on the graduate schools and the textbook publishers this powerful concept has had significant impact even on most Christian schools.

Resistance to the proposed teaching of theistic creationism as an alternative to evolutionism commonly masquerades under the supposed authority of "science." The recent anti-creationist manifesto of the American Humanist Association proclaims the following:

> There are no alternatives to the principle of evolution, with its "tree of life" pattern, that any competent biologist of today takes seriously . . . . Evolution is therefore the only view that should be expounded in public-school courses on science.[1]

That evolution is *not* science, however, has not only

been clearly demonstrated by the many modern publications of creationist scientists[2] but also is frequently recognized even by evolutionist scientists. For example, Loren Eisely says:

> With the failure of these many efforts, science was left in the somewhat embarrassing position of having to postulate theories of living origins which it could not demonstrate. After having chided the theologian for his reliance on myth and miracle, science found itself in the unenviable position of having to create a mythology of its own: namely, the assumption that what, after long effort could not be proved to take place today had, in truth, taken place in the primeval past.[3]

In fact there are now many evolutionists who recognize that the "theory of evolution" is really a tautology, with no predictive value.

> I argue that the "theory of evolution" does not make predictions, so far as ecology is concerned, but is instead a logical formula which can be used only to classify empiricisms and to show the relationships which such a classification implies . . . . these theories are actually tautologies and, as such, cannot make empirically testable predictions. *They are not scientific theories at all.*[4]

Even the writer of the Foreword of the 1971 edition of Darwin's *Origin of the Species,* himself a distinguished evolutionary biologist, has frankly recognized that evolution is simply a belief.

> [The theory of evolution] forms a satisfactory faith on which to base our interpretation of nature.[5]

Evolution is thus admittedly not scientifically testable, even though it is taught very dogmatically in most public schools. However, educators insist that creationism and theism must be excluded from education on the ground that they are not scientific!

This rejection is often emphatic and even slanderous. Dr. Preston Cloud of the University of California at Santa Barbara, for example, becomes quite melodramatic.

> Religious bigotry is abroad again in the land
> . . . . Although the creationists may be irration-
> al, . . . they have proven themselves to be skill-
> ful tacticians, good organizers and uncompro-
> mising adversaries . . . . And anyone who has
> studied their benign manner in public debate,
> their tortured logic and their often scurrilous
> expression in books and tracts for the faithful,
> has little difficulty in visualizing creationist po-
> lemicists, given the opportunity, in the role of
> Pius V himself.[6]

This is not the language of objective science, of course, but of religious emotion. Dr. Cloud failed to mention that he had himself participated in such a debate on his own campus, before an audience composed mainly of university students, the large majority of whom had voted after the debate that the creationists had a better *scientific* case than the evolutionists. As a matter of fact, a common complaint at the debate was that the evolutionists had not presented a consistent scientific case at all, while the creationists had dealt *only* with science.

If creationists are, as Cloud declares, "bigots," he should recognize that there are other bigots also. One of the nation's top scientists has charged:

> One of the most astonishing characteristics of
> scientists is that some of them are plain, old-
> fashioned bigots. Their zeal has a fanatical, ego-
> centric quality characterized by disdain and in-

> tolerance for anyone or any value not associated
> with a special area of intellectual activity.[7]

The fact is, however, that creationists are not attempting
to oust evolutionary humanism from the public schools,
but only to obtain a fair hearing for theistic creationism
as an alternative. Both concepts involve faith and neither
is scientifically testable in the ultimate sense.

> A hypothesis is empirical or scientific only if it
> can be tested by experience . . . . A hypothesis
> or theory which cannot be, at least in principle,
> falsified by empirical observations and experi-
> ments does not belong to the realm of science.[8]

Although the author of the above statement is a leading
evolutionary biologist, it is obvious that his definition
would exclude evolution, no less than creation, from the
realm of science. In fact, a creationist might legitimately
argue that evolution actually has been tested, *and disproved,* since it has never been observed in action and
since it contradicts the scientific law of increasing entropy
or disorder. One must, therefore, not only believe in evolution without evidence, but in spite of the evidence.
Evolutionists walk by faith, not by sight!

Furthermore, not only is evolution taught in the schools
as a scientific dogma, but as basic in all the social sciences
and humanities as well. It is, in fact, a complete world-
view, purporting to explain the origin, development, and
meaning of all things.

> The place of biological evolution in human
> thought was, according to Dobzhansky, best
> expressed in a passage that he often quoted from
> Pierre Teilhard de Chardin. "[Evolution] is a
> general postulate to which all theories, all hypo-
> theses, and all systems must henceforward bow
> and which they must satisfy in order to be think-
> able and true. Evolution is a light which illumi-

nates all facts, a trajectory which all lines of thought must follow."[9]

Theodosius Dobzhansky, the subject of the eulogy from which the above quotation was taken, was a church member and claimed to be a creationist, but he meant by this that the wonderful process of natural selection had "created" all things!

> Dobzhansky was a religious man, although he apparently rejected fundamental beliefs of traditional religion, such as the existence of a personal God and of life beyond physical death . . . . Dobzhansky held that, in man, biological evolution had transcended itself into the realm of self-awareness and culture. He believed that mankind would eventually evolve into higher levels of harmony and creativity. He was a metaphysical optimist.[10]

Until his death, Dobzhansky had been probably the world's leading spokesman for evolution.

> From today's perspective, Dobzhansky appears as perhaps the most eminent evolutionist of the twentieth century.[11]

His influence on the nation's schools has been profound, to say the least, and he is typical of practically all leaders of evolutionary thought.

Evolution as a complete system of life and meaning has, in fact, dominated intellectual thought and the teachings in the colleges since at least the last quarter of the nineteenth century.

> . . . after a generation of argument, educated Americans in general came to accept the fact of evolution and went on to make whatever intellectual adjustments they thought necessary.[12]

Once it came to be accepted by the intellectuals, the religious liberals quickly, and typically, followed along. The most influential of these was the famous Henry Ward Beecher.

> Darwinian evolutionary science presented little or no challenge to Beecher's doctrinal beliefs, for Beecher's Christianity was already far removed from Biblical literalism into a vague poetic emotional realm of edifying thoughts, elevated feelings and joyful noises unto the Lord.[13]

Beecher published his *Evolution and Religion* in 1883, and its arguments are still being repeated almost verbatim by theistic evolutionists today. Very quickly after that, evolution began to dominate the public schools.

> In a nation that was undergoing a tremendous urban, industrial and technological revolution, the evolutionary concept presented itself to intellectuals as the key to knowledge. And beyond that, the technical needs of industry called for a revolution in higher education away from the traditional classical and moral orientation and toward the sciences . . . which were reclassifying man and society in evolutionary terms. In general the concept of education from kindergarten to graduate school was reoriented from the teaching of a fixed body of knowledge to the teaching of methods of inquiry to be applied to the continually changing facts of existence.[14]

This trend, of course, was tremendously accelerated under the influence of John Dewey and his disciples in the first half of the twentieth century, leading finally to the complete dominance of the public schools by naturalistic evolutionism and secular humanism at the present time.[15]

It was not always thus in our country or in our public

schools, however, and it is certainly in conformity with American constitutionalism to seek to return the schools to their intended character and purpose.

> The American nation had been founded by intellectuals who had accepted a world view that was based upon Biblical authority as well as Newtonian science. They had assumed that God created the earth and all life upon it at the time of creation and continued without change thereafter. Adam and Eve were God's final creations, and all of mankind was descended from them. When Jefferson, in his old age, was confronted with the newly developing science of geology, he rejected the evolutionary concept of the creation of the earth on the grounds that no all-wise and all-powerful Creator would have gone about the job in such a slow and inefficient way.[16]

Jefferson's argument, of course, is perfectly valid today. The "god" of evolution (in the rationale of de Chardin and the other leaders of theistic evolutionary thought) is certainly not the God of the Bible, the omnipotent and omniscient God of orthodox Judaism and Biblical Christianity. Evolutionary humanism in our schools is not only a religion, but is a religion which opposes Judaism, Christianity, and the Bible in no uncertain terms.

> In cultures such as ours, religion is very often an alien form of life to intellectuals. Living as we do in a post-Enlightenment era, it is difficult for us to take religion seriously. The very concepts seem fantastic to us . . . . That people in our age can believe that they have had a personal encounter with God, that they could believe that they have experienced conversion through a "mystical experience of God," so that they are born again in the Holy Spirit, is something that attests to human irrationality and lack of sense of reality.[17]

With this type of attitude dominating the thinking of modern leaders in education, it is not surprising that there is so much resistance to allowing creationism to be returned to the schools. Neither is it surprising that a humanistic and atheistic religious philosophy in the schools has generated an amoralistic attitude in society, increasing in influence with each emerging generation. A remarkable testimony has been published by Aldous Huxley, one of the most influential writers and philosophers of our day, grandson of evolutionist Thomas Huxley, brother of evolutionist Julian Huxley, and one of the early advocates of a "drug culture" and sexual permissiveness.

> I had motives for not wanting the world to have meaning; consequently assumed it had none, and was able without any difficulty to find satisfying reasons for this assumption . . . . The philosopher who finds no meaning in the world is not concerned exclusively with a problem in pure metaphysics; he is also concerned to prove there is no valid reason why he personally should not do as he wants to do . . . . For myself, as no doubt for most of my contemporaries, the philosophy of meaninglessness was essentially an instrument of liberation. The liberation we desired was simultaneously liberation from a certain political and economic system and liberation from a certain system of morality. We objected to the morality because it interfered with our sexual freedom.[18]

The following conclusions are clearly justified by the facts at hand: (1) A system of evolutionary humanism dominates our public schools and this system has produced devastating results in the moral and social realms; (2) neither the philosophy of humanism nor the evolutionary philosophy on which it is based is "scientific," in any proper sense of the term, though both are materialistic and essentially atheistic; (3) the system of evolutionary humanism is, therefore, merely a religious philosophy, a "non-theistic religion," as claimed by the American Humanist Association itself; (4) all the known facts of science (as well as the facts of human experience) correlate with belief in special creation and a personal Creator much better than belief in evolution and humanism correlate with those facts; (5) consequently, the "creation model," and its implications in all fields, should be taught equally and fairly with the "evolution model" in the public schools. All serious-minded and fair-minded parents, teachers, and school administrators are urged to work diligently to that end.

REFERENCES

1. American Humanist Association, "A Statement Affirming Evolution as a Principle of Science," *The Humanist,* January-February, 1977, Vol. XXXVII, p. 4. This manifesto was prepared by a committee composed of Bette Chambers (A.H.A. president), Isaac Asimov, Hudson Hoagland, Chauncy Leake, Linus Pauling, and George Gaylord Simpson and signed by 163 others, most of whom are prominent humanistic educators— including psychologists Carl Rogers and B.F. Skinner, left-wing philosopher Corliss Lamont, anthropologist Sol Tax, and others.

2. For example, see *Scientific Creationism* (Ed. by Henry M. Morris; San Diego, Creation-Life Publishers, 1974, 277 pp.) Also note that the Creation Research Society has approximately 550 members, all with graduate degrees in science from accredited universities.

3. Loren Eisely, *The Immense Journey* (New York: Random House, 1957), p. 199.

4. R.H. Peters, "Tautology in Evolution and Ecology," *American Naturalist,* Vol. 110, No. 1, 1976, p. 1. Emphasis his.

5. L. Harrison Matthews, "Introduction to *Origin of Species*" (London, J.M. Dent, 1977), p. xii.

6. Preston Cloud, "Scientific Creationism. A New Inquisition," *The Humanist,* Vol. XXXVII, January-February, 1977, p. 67.

7. Philip H. Abelson, "Bigotry in Science," *Science,* Vol. 144, April 24, 1964, p. 373.

8. Francisco J. Ayala, "Biological Evolution: Natural Selection or Random Walk?" *American Scientist,* Vol. 62, Nov.-Dec., 1974, p. 700.

9. Francisco Ayala, " 'Nothing in Biology Makes Sense Except in the Light of Evolution. Theodosius Dobzhansky, 1900-1975," *Journal of Heredity,* Vol. 68, No. 3, 1977, p. 3.

10. *Ibid.,* p. 9.

11. *Ibid.,* p. 6.

12. Gilman M. Ostrander, *The Evolutionary Outlook, 1875-1900,* (Clio, Michigan, Marston Press, 1971), p. 2.

13. *Ibid.,* p. 39.

14. *Ibid.,* p. 2.
15. See the writer's new book, *Education for the Real World* (San Diego: Creation-Life Publishers, 1977, pp. 47-105) for further documentation on the capture and current domination of the public schools by these systems.
16. Gilman M. Ostrander, *op cit,* p. 1.
17. Kai Nielsen, "Religiosity and Powerlessness: Part III of 'The Resurgence of Fundamentalism,' " *The Humanist,* Vol. XXXVII, May-June, 1977, p. 46.
18. Aldous Huxley, "Confessions of a Professed Atheist," *Report: Perspective on the News,* Vol. 3, June, 1966, p. 19.

No. 52, October, 1977
THE IMPACT OF EVOLUTION ON THE SOCIAL SCIENCES

John N. Moore, M.S., Ed.D.[*]

Very possibly no other author in the nineteenth century influenced human thought all around the world more than Charles Darwin when he published his two books: *The Origin of Species* and *The Descent of Man.* The "lineage" of Darwinism in scholarly thinking is brought out in two excellent and recent reference works: *The Comparative Reception of Darwinism,* edited by Thomas F. Glick[1] and *Darwin in America (The Intellectual Response, 1865-1912)* by Cynthia Eagle Russett.[2] Darwinism was later replaced by Neo-Darwinism which has been replaced by the Modern Synthetic Theory of Evolution. In fact, today, the evolutionary viewpoint is so broadly applied that one can speak most accurately of Total Evolutionism, as including Stellar Evolution, Molecular Evolution, Organic Evolution, and Societal (or cultural) Evolution.

However the broadened viewpoint of Total Evolutionism that has developed in a little over a century from Darwinism is without any significant repeatable empirical data from naturally occurring events. On the contrary evolutionists must speak glowingly and write ingeniously about numerous *supra*-natural concepts; such as, "big bang" explosion of a dense particle, spontaneous generation of living substance, mountain building due to move-

*Author John N. Moore is Professor of Natural Science at Michigan State University.

ment of dry rock masses, division of one land mass into existing continents, and new physical traits through mutational changes. All of these ideas are totally without any empirical support from studies of naturally occurring events of the magnitude involved in such concepts. Yet the circumstantially grounded megaevolutionary point of view involving Total Evolutionism is *the* world view that has been adopted by influential scholars in every major academic discipline of human thought. Evolution is the *supreme* over-riding point of view or world view adopted in every major academic discipline by the intelligentsia around the world.

The full range of research in the history of ideas substantiates that selected indoctrination among the intellectuals of the world has increased ever since publication of Charles Darwin's, *The Origin of Species,* in 1859. Darwin did not "invent" evolution, but his book *seemed* to provide support for a point of view, a world outlook that was just what the intelligentsia of his day wanted. What Darwin wrote was evidently just what the "mainstream" of academia in England, and subsequently in nation after nation, were waiting for.

Darwin's initial turning from belief in special creation of all living things (since he had actually been taught the "Fixity of species" concept, as his teachers evidently were not aware of changes in the thinking of Linnaeus) came while he was on board the H.M.S. Beagle on a voyage around the world. He studied very thoroughly the two volume work on geological changes authored by Charles Lyell, he studied "on the spot" geologic features of South America and the Galapagos Islands in the Pacific Ocean, and he read a book on food consumption and human population by Thomas Malthus.

All of these factors were synthesized in Darwin's thinking in such a manner that he discarded his *belief* in special creative acts of God as an origin of living things. Darwin replaced that belief with his own *belief* that competitive interactions of many variations of living things in natural environments resulted over great lengths of time in changes

of organisms—some becoming extinct and others producing new varieties that presumably became new kinds of
organisms. He called his imagined process "natural selection". When his explanation of this presumed means
whereby changes of living things (megaevolution) came
about on the earth was read by his contemporaries, such
as Herbert Spencer, they adopted the phrases, "survival
of the fittest," or "struggle for existence," when they
thought about Darwin's ideas. Victorian Englishmen knew
much about wars, disease, famines, and weather conditions, and this idea was easily understood.

Evidently most of the scholars attracted to Darwin's
ideas were unpracticed in the close study of Genesis of the
special creative acts of God regarding origin of heaven and
earth and all that is therein. Evidently they were not personally "armed" with the unchanging and unchangeable
answers about ultimate origin in the Bible; hence, most
English scholars were "susceptible" and became confused
by the various speculative ideas and imaginations of Darwin and his followers. They were vulnerable to so-called
naturalistic, non-supernatural ideas.

Victorian Englishmen were easily persuaded that some
"natural selection" of living things occurred analogously
to domestic organisms, about groups of human beings
with "class" status, about nations competing in world
economics, and about naval and land warfare. *But Darwin never established scientifically that natural selection
was a means whereby evolution (megaevolution) occurred.*
He only published a lengthy series of persuasively presented arguments. And no scientist has been able to study
scientifically the origin of any new *kinds* of organisms. Yet
the megaevolutionary point of view is adopted completely
in all the major academic disciplines that comprise human
knowledge!

The colossal scope of this "selected" indoctrination can
be understood by tracing acceptance of the "struggle for
existence" or "survival of the fittest" concepts in fields
other than biology. This "lineage" is presented diagram-
matically in the accompanying "flowchart" of Darwin's

influence. Some details of this broad acceptance of evolutionary thinking by specialists in social studies and humanities as well as science are given in this paper and a second paper to be published later.

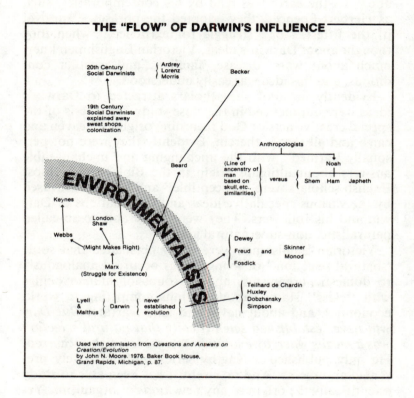

THE "FLOW" OF DARWIN'S INFLUENCE

Used with permission from *Questions and Answers on Creation/Evolution* by John N. Moore. 1976. Baker Book House, Grand Rapids, Michigan, p. 87.

Economics

Karl Marx was a prime leader among the intelligentsia of the world who utilized Darwin's concept of "natural selection", or "struggle for existence." Marx wrote his associate Friedrich Engels that he considered Darwin's ideas about competition of living things in the natural environment to be relevant to what Marx reasoned was a warfare or struggle of classes of human beings. Marx and Engels wrote most explicitly of competition between a working class and a bourgeoisie class. For Marx the concept of "struggle for existence" became translated into "class warfare".[3]

Then as the acceptance of the idea is traced into other countries, the concept of "might makes right" seemed to be sanctioned from the writings of Darwin, and the thinking of Marx. In Germany, Darwinism and Marxism were broadly adopted. These two isms can easily be identified as basic to the superman concept of Nietzsche and the superior Aryan race concept of Hitler.

In fact dictatorial actions of Hitler, Mussolini, Lenin, Stalin, Kruschev, and current U.S.S.R. leaders as well, have all been sanctioned supposedly by Darwin's "natural selection" through the "struggle for existence" and the "survival of the fittest". The Fascist axis nations were believed by their leaders to be most worthy of survival; similarly, the Communist nations—either U.S.S.R. and its satellites of the 1970's, or China, Viet Nam and other Communist Asian nations—are claimed by their own theoreticians to be most worthy of survival. Empirical evidence is abundant that coexistence with Communist nations does not occur. The nations of Esthonia, Latvia, Ukrania, Bessarabia, and Tibet are mute evidence to this point.

Particularly in England the Fabian Socialists, under the leadership of Sidney and Beatrice Webb, interjected the "struggle for existence" concept into a political, ballot box frame of reference. Fabian Socialists thought in terms of "social evolution" that seemed to be a consistent extension of supposed biological evolution. Of course there have been multiple extensions of Marx's thinking regarding his presumption of class warfare, as can be traced in the works of John Maynard Keynes and his American followers as democratic socialism became established in the United States after 1932. Repeatedly, Darwin's evolutionary thinking has become a root sanction

for State government to intervene for the survival of what
is "best", according to the reasoning of the elite few
(Fabian Socialist, Communist, and Democratic Socialists)
for the "benefit" of the many (ordinary citizens).

Political Science

Impact of evolutionary thinking in political science can
be traced, similar to the force of such thinking in economics, through analyzing the positions taken by those
who were influenced by and became followers of Karl
Marx, either directly or indirectly, such as Carl Becker
and many, many others.[*] Becker continued the use of
Marxian ideas, and influenced several decades of graduate
students by his evolutionary thinking, which was oriented
along the struggle for existence line in modern society,
until he recognized the logical consequences of that thesis
(in the form that might makes right) when he learned of
the savage, cruel rape of Europe by Hitler's minions.
That there are really no philosophical differences between
Fascist Germany and Communist Russia can be documented quite easily by tracing acceptance of Marxism by
Lenin and the eventual development of Bolshevism and
Leninism. The thinking of the leaders of the U.S.S.R. is
rooted deeply in an evolutionary outlook.[5]

American History

The impact of evolutionary thinking in American history
can also be traced in the form of acceptance of the thinking of Karl Marx. The concept of struggle for existence
which Marx found in Darwin's book, *The Origin of
Species,* was used by Marx to support and excuse his thesis
of class warfare. Society was the context for the struggle
for survival of "class" human beings. Then in American
history this relationship of struggle for existence and supposed class warfare was applied by Charles A. Beard[6]
when he wrote regarding passage of the Constitution of
the United States of America.

According to Beard, passage of the Constitution in each

of the thirteen colonies was the result of class warfare, wherein the landed gentry and noblemen were for the Constitution and farmers and the poor and indigent were against the Constitution. Thus Beard's ideas were a basis for selected indoctrination indirectly in Darwinian struggle for existence from the time Beard's ideas were published in 1913 until some forty years later when Beard's thesis of class warfare in the colonies was shown to be completely invalid by the research and analysis of actual colonial records of voting practices and land ownership by two independent investigators, Robert Brown[7] and Forrest McDonald.[8] They accomplished the research that Beard *never* completed!!

In a later article, the impact of evolutionary thinking on the humanities and on education in general will be outlined.

REFERENCES

1. Austin: University of Texas Press, 1974.
2. San Francisco: W.H. Freeman and Company, 1976.
3. Zirkle, Conway. 1959. *Evolution, Marxian Biology, and the Social Scene.* Philadelphia: University of Pennsylvania Press; and Selsam, H. 1959. "Charles Darwin and Karl Marx," Mainstream 12 (6): 28 and 36. June.
4. Brown, Robert E. 1970. *Carl Becker on History and the American Revolution,* East Lansing, Michigan: *The Spartan Press.*
5. Zirkle, *Op. Cit.*
6. Beard, Charles A. 1913. *An Economic Interpretation of the Constitution of the United States.* N.Y.: The Macmillan Company. See also Robert E. Brown 1956. *Charles Beard and the Constitution* (A Critical Analysis of "An Economic Interpretation of the Constitution"). Princeton, N.J.: Princeton University Press.
7. Brown, Robert E. 1955. *Middle-Class Democracy and the Revolution in Massachusetts,* 1671-1780. Ithaca, N.Y.: Cornell University Press for The American Historical Association; and Robert E. Brown and B. Katherine Brown 1964. *Virginia 1705-1786: Democracy or Aristocracy?* East Lansing, Michigan: Michigan State University Press.
8. McDonald, Forrest. 1958. *We the People* (Economic Origins of the Constitution). Chicago: The University of Chicago Press.

No. 53, November, 1977
THE IMPACT OF EVOLUTION
ON THE HUMANITIES AND SCIENCE
John N. Moore, M.S., Ed.D.

In a previous article *(Acts & Facts,* October, 1977), the effects of evolutionary thinking on economics, political science, and the study of American history were outlined.

Literature

The novels of Jack London, the plays of George Bernard Shaw, and even the poetry of Alfred Tennyson contain a seemingly convincing basis for belief in the "evolution" of humankind.[1] Tennyson had expressed an evolutionary viewpoint actually some time before Darwin's book appeared in 1859. But the writings of these "greats" of literature, and authors of other *belles lettres* as well, were strongly instrumental in adding to the impact of Darwin's second book, *The Descent of Man,* in converting nineteenth century intellectuals to acceptance of the concept of the so-called evolution of human beings.

Actually both London and Shaw were English socialists and followers of the thinking of the Fabian Society, which came into existence due to the work and effort of Beatrice and Sidney Webb, who in turn were followers in England of Karl Marx. Thus the "web" of selected indoctrination and inter-relationship of propagandists for an evolutionary viewpoint or world outlook can be extended. And both London and Shaw used their literary works to present Marxian socialistic views as most plausible and to illustrate the struggle for existence concept. London especially popularized the "red tooth and claw" phrase through the struggles he wrote about in *White Fang* and *The Call of the Wild.* The latter book has been repopularized by way of television dramatization in the late 1970's. Continued use of evolutionary thinking by novelists can be shown in the works of Veblen, Norris, Dreiser, and Michener, whose *Centennial* is a *par excellence* example of misapplication of "historical" geology in early chapters.

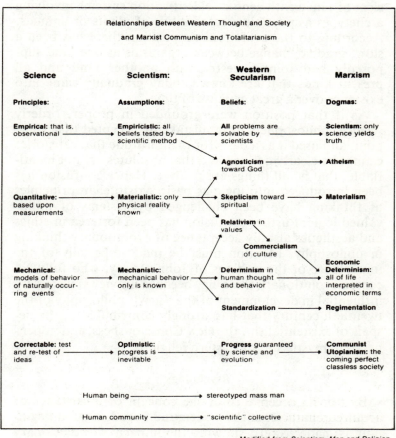

Relationships Between Western Thought and Society
and Marxist Communism and Totalitarianism

Science	Scientism:	Western Secularism	Marxism
Principles:	**Assumptions:**	**Beliefs:**	**Dogmas:**
Empirical: that is. observational	**Empiricistic:** all beliefs tested by scientific method	**All** problems are solvable by scientists	**Scientism:** only science yields truth
		Agnosticism toward God	**Atheism**
Quantitative: based upon measurements	**Materialistic:** only physical reality known	**Skepticism** toward spiritual	**Materialism**
		Relativism in values	
		Commercialism of culture	
Mechanical: models of behavior of naturally occurring events	**Mechanistic:** mechanical behavior only is known	**Determinism** in human thought and behavior	**Economic Determinism:** all of life interpreted in economic terms
		Standardization	**Regimentation**
Correctable: test and re-test of ideas	**Optimistic:** progress is inevitable	**Progress** guaranteed by science and evolution	**Communist Utopianism:** the coming perfect classless society

Human being ⟶ stereotyped mass man

Human community ⟶ "scientific" collective

— Modified from *Scientism, Man and Religion*
by D.R.G. Owen. 1952
Philadelphia: The Westminster Press.

Philosophy

In philosophy the impact of evolutionary thought can be traced through the increasingly broad application of criticism of nineteenth century classification systems involving archetypes as possible created kinds of plants or animals. According to the evolutionist's position there has been a slow, gradual change between organisms as one kind supposedly had joint ancestry with another kind and all present kinds that are known today gradually came into existence over a great expanse of time.

As if that position were grounded in proper, orderly science, philosophers have mistakenly accepted that viewpoint and used it as a basis for their attitude that categories cannot be clearly defined and that absolutes are not identifiable, that is, all things are relative. Hence confusion has been introduced into logic as basic Aristotelian principles of thinking have been challenged by systems of multivalued logic. Further confusion has been fostered in ethics and aesthetics also by acceptance of evolutionary thinking in philosophy. Mention must be made especially of the importance of the writings of John Dewey, who fully accepted evolutionary thinking, because his views[2] were very influential in development of the "new" philosophy of the twentieth century that has strongly contributed to the despair of existentialism, the New Consciousness, and "openness" to mysticisms of Eastern religions.[3]

Psychology

By tracing acceptance of the concept of inheritance of acquired characteristics by Sigmund Freud, a good beginning is made toward showing the impact of evolutionary thinking in psychology and psychiatry. In the late edition of his book, *The Origin of Species,* Darwin utilized the concept of inheritance of acquired characteristics fostered by Lamarck, who believed that characteristics acquired during the lifetime of an individual were transmitted somehow to offspring. Though this idea is now fully discredited and completely rejected by leading biologists and geneticists, when Freud accepted the idea, he gave significant impetus to the environmentalist inclination so prominent in psychology. According to environmentalists, an individual's behavior is the consequence of the environment in which growth and development have occurred. Today, B.F. Skinner, and also Robert Ardrey, Konrad Lorenz, and Desmond Morris, reflect broad acceptance of the environmentalist approach which is based upon the unscientific idea of an evolutionary origin of humankind.[4]

Science

In the multiple sub-fields of the scientific discipline the impact of evolutionary thought has been almost complete. The influential writings of such leaders as the late Julian Huxley, Theodosius Dobzhansky, and Pierre Teilhard de Chardin in support of the infusion of evolutionary thinking into all facets of biology and associated sciences still have great impact in the training programs of young scientists and in the mass communications media as well. In addition to their influence, G.G. Simpson still serves as a strong guide to almost ubiquitous application of evolutionary thought.

However, weaknesses and deficiencies in Darwinism, Neo-Darwinism, and even the modern synthetic "theory" of evolution have been published by scientists[5] in every decade since *The Origin of Species* was published in 1859. Yet such criticisms have not been included to any significant extent in science textbooks. Actually specific impetus inaugurated in the 1960's to expand and augment the teaching of evolutionary origins in the secondary schools in the United States has really been an important cause in the 1970's for the development of creationism teaching, that is, explanation of the scientific basis or support of the creation account of origins.[6]

Education

The "prime mover" of modern education, John Dewey, showed a broad acceptance of Darwinism in his extensive writings. He viewed the human being as an "evolved" creature that was slowly improving physically and mentally. According to Dewey, the environment in which schooling occurred was most important. Because Dewey stressed an evolutionary outlook in many if not all of his books, and since several generations of educators have followed Dewey's thinking in one form or another, *environmentalism* has become a strong viewpoint in the development of educational principles and policies in the public schools in the United States. The human being has been treated as an intelligent animal developing as a consequence of interaction with the environment, as a "survivor" by use of its wits.[7]

Theology

Finally, even the modern-day study of theology has been largely controlled by evolutionary ideas. Wherever acceptance of the Graff-Wellhausen "hypothesis" regarding criticism of Biblical texts can be shown, then evidence is gained for broad impact of evolutionary thinking. According to that view the Bible content has "evolved." A most influential spokesman for the view of "evolution" of the Bible was Harry Emerson Fosdick.[8] He wrote extensively on the theme that man's worship of God "evolved" from the worship of a sun god and moon god, to a mountain god and river god, to a crop god, to a tribal god, to an Omnipotent God. Actually polytheistic worship has been a degenerate derivation of ancient, initial monotheism in all groups of peoples on the earth as can be shown by reference to outstanding present-day scholarship.[9] The whole position of higher criticism and form criticism of the twentieth century is rooted in an evolutionary viewpoint.

REFERENCES

1. Conner, Frederick W. 1949. *Cosmic Optimism* (A Study of the Interpretation of Evolution by American Poets from Emerson to Robinson). Gainesville, Florida: University of Florida Press; Leo J. Henkin 1940.

Darwinism in the English Novel. N.Y.: Corporate Press, Inc.; Bert J. Loewenberg 1964. *Darwinism: Reaction or Reform?* N.Y.: Holt, Rinehart and Winson; Stow Parsons (Editor) 1956. *Evolutionary Thought in America,* N.Y.: George Braziller, Inc.; Georg Roppen 1956. *Evolution and Poetic Belief.* Oslo, Norway: Oslo University Press; Lionel Stevenson 1963. *Darwin Among the Poets.* N.Y.: Russell and Russell. See also Zirkle, Conway 1959. *Evolution, Marxian Biology and the Social Scene.* Philadelphia: University of Pennsylvania Press, especially Chapter 10, "Marxian Biology in the Communist World."

2. See various Dewey books such as *Reconstruction in Philosophy* (1920) and *The Quest for Certainty* (1929).

3. Schaeffer, Francis A. 1968. *Escape from Reason.* Chicago: Inter-Varsity Press; and James W. Sire 1976. *The Universe Next Door* (A Basic World View Catalog). Downers Grove, Illinois: Inter-Varsity Press.

4. Skinner, B.F. 1971. *Beyond Freedom and Dignity.* Toronto, N.Y. Bantam Books, N.Y.: Vintage Books; Robert Ardrey 1970. *The Social Contract.* N.Y.: Atheneum and *African Genesis.* 1962. N.Y.: Atheneum; Konrad Lorenz 1966. *On Aggression.* N.Y.: Harcourt, Brace and World; Desmond Morris 1967. *The Naked Ape.* London: Cape. See Francis A. Schaeffer 1972. *Back to Freedom and Dignity.* Downers Grove, Illinois: Inter-Varsity Press in which he responds to the Skinner Book as well as to Jacques Monod's 1971 *Chance and Necessity.* N.Y.: Knopt and to Francis Crick's 1966 *Of Molecules and Men.* Seattle: University of Washington Press.

5. An accumulative computerized bibliographic compilation is available for one dollar upon request to Dr. Moore. These materials were gathered while using six research grants from Michigan State University over twelve years under the title, "Library Search for Representative Statements by Scientists on Organic Evolution, Natural Selection, and Related Topics since 1859".

6. Books published by Creation-Life Publishers, such as *Origins: Two Models* by Richard Bliss; *Streams of Civilization,* Vol. One. *Ancient History to 1572 A.D.* by Albert Hyma and Mary Stanton; *Scientific Creationism* by Henry M. Morris, Editor; or *Biology: A Search for Order in Complexity* Edited by John N. Moore and Harold S. Slusher. 1974. Grand Rapids, Michigan: Zondervan Publishing House.

7. White Morton. 1943. *The Origins of Dewey's Instrumentalism.* N.Y.: Columbia University Press. Among many books by John Dewey see his *Essays in Experimental Logic* (Chicago: University of Chicago Press, 1916) and *Logic: The Theory of Inquiry* (N.Y.: Henry Holt & Co., 1938). See also Zirkle, *Op. Cit.,* Reference 1.

8. McDowell, Josh. 1972 *Evidence That Demands A Verdict* (Historical Evidence for the Christian Faith). San Bernardino: Campus Crusade for Christ, International. Also excellent on the Graff-Wellhausen thesis is Oswald T. Allis, 1943. *The Five Books of Moses.* Philadelphia: Presbyterian and Reformed Publishing Company; and Clifford Wilson, 1977. *Ebla Tablets: Secrets of a Forbidden City.* San Diego: Master Books.

No. 54, December, 1977
ALBERT SZENT-GYORGYI'S THEORY OF SYNTROPY AND CREATIONISM

Jerry Bergman, Ph.D.*

Creationists have often discussed the principle of increasing entropy (the second law of thermodynamics), or the pervasive tendency for organized forms of matter to gradually disintegrate into lower and lower levels of organization. A city, if it were deserted would eventually disintegrate. The metal in the city would rust, the mortar in the buildings would crack, the wood would rot, etc. In time, less and less differentiation would exist until, if the area were a closed system (no new energy was brought in to rebuild the city), all of the molecules would be evenly distributed within a given area. Diffusion, the tendency for molecules to distribute themselves throughout an area, would occur.

For example, if a bottle of perfume opened up in a sealed room, the perfume molecules, although at first concentrated in the bottle, will gradually spread outward from the bottle until the number of molecules per cubic centimeter found in the perfume bottle also will be found in all areas of the room itself (Anthony, 1963, pp. 35-36). Likewise, diffusion always results, if enough time elapses, in an even scattering of solute particles among solvent molecules. Given enough time, even solid objects break down and diffuse. Rocks, land, and other solid objects are worn down by the movement of water, solid particles are moved by wind and by the growth of plants, to name a few of the more common methods.

Entropy also applies to energy. Energy diffuses until it is equally dispersed. For example, if a hot piece of metal is dropped into a bucket of water in time it will lose its

---

*The Author. Dr. Jerry Bergman is Assistant Professor of Psychology at Bowling Green State University in Ohio. His Ph.D. is from Wayne State University in Detroit, majoring in Educational Psychology and Evaluation and Research. He has authored several books and many articles in his field.

heat to the water until the metal and water are the same temperature. In time the water will lose its heat to the air until the water becomes the same temperature as that inside the room. The room, in turn, loses it sheat to the outside rooms, (McCormick, 1965, pp. 288-289). This diffusion would theoretically continue until the energy is equally dispersed throughout the universe. Even in energy transformations directed by man, some energy is forever lost. As in all energy transformations, there is a "tendency for some of the energy to be transformed to non-reversible heat energy" (Morris, 1963, p. 33).

However in the life process we commonly find what seems to be a decrease of entropy occuring. Living organisms cause increased organization, both in their own world and sometimes even in the world around them, reducing diffusion and in essence working to oppose the universal tendency toward energy and matter equilibrium. On the basis of the evolutionary hypotheses it is then postulated that a process of self-transformation has occurred, resulting in the conversion of a primordial disordered state, via increasing complexity, to a highly ordered state, and eventually the evolution from amoeba to mammal, and from mammal to man.

A main difference between amoeba and man is increased complexity, requiring some mechanism to counteract the second law of thermodynamics. In other words, there must exist something, a "force", to counteract the universal movement towards equal distribution of all matter and energy.

One attempt to deal with this was proposed by Albert Szent-Gyorgyi. Szent-Gyorgyi, an eminent scientist born in Hungary in 1893, was educated at the University of Budapest and Cambridge. He has the unique distinction of being awarded two Nobel Prizes for his scientific research (1937 and 1955). Szent-Gyorgyi is now the Director of Research at the Institute for Muscle Research in Massachusetts and has written a number of books on his research.

Szent-Gyorgyi postulates that there exists what he calls

the "principle" of *syntropy* or "negative entropy." Realizing that entropy is a universal "force" which causes organized forms to gradually disintegrate into lower and lower levels of organization, he pictures the world as, in essence, a great machine running down and wearing out. The concept of syntropy postulates the existence of the opposite force, a force which causes living things to reach "higher and higher levels of organization, order and dynamic harmony." (Vargiu, 1977, p. 14). The basic problem as stated by Szent-Gyorgyi is "that there is some basic difference between the living and the non-living . . . as scientists we cannot believe the laws of the universe could lose their validity at the surface of our skin," pointing out that the law of entropy, for some reason, seems not to prevail in living systems.

Although entropy is increasing, another force obviously is also operating. Thus we have the problem of the tendency for the world to gradually disintegrate into lower and lower levels of organization and the converse fact that "putting things together in a meaningful way . . . is one of the basic features of nature" (p. 19, 1977). The contrast between entropy in the non-living world and syntropy in the living world is discussed by Szent-Gyorgyi as follows:

> Inanimate nature stops at the low level organization of simple molecules. But living systems go on and combine molecules to form macromolecules, macromolecules to form organelles (such as nuclei, mitochondria, chloroplasts, ribosomes, and membranes) and eventually put these all together to form the greatest wonder of creation, a cell, with its astounding inner regulations. Then it goes on putting cells together to form "higher organisms" and increasingly more complex individuals . . . at every step, new, more complex and subtle qualities are created, and so in the end we are faced with properties which have no parallel in the inanimate world . . . (p. 15-16, 1977).

In postulating his theory of syntropy, Szent-Gyorgyi, perhaps unintentionally, brings forth one of the strongest arguments for creationism—the fact that a body organ is useless until it is completely perfected. The hypothesized law of "survival of the fittest" would generally select against *any* mutations until a large number of mutations have already occurred to produce a complete and functional structure; after which natural selection would then theoretically select for the organism with the completed organ. This difficulty is summed up by Szent-Gyorgyi:

> . . . "Herring gulls" have a red patch on their beak. This red patch has an important meaning, for the gull feeds its babies by going out fishing and swallowing the fish it has caught. Then, on coming home, the hungry baby gull knocks at the red spot. This elicits a reflex of regurgitation in mama, and the baby takes the fish from her gullet. All this may sound very simple, but it involves a whole series of most complicated chain reactions with a horribly complex underlying nervous mechanism of the knocking baby and that of the regurgitating mother. All this had to be developed simultaneously, which, as a random mutation, has the probability of zero. I am unable to approach this problem without supposing an innate "drive" in living matter to perfect itself (p. 18-19, 1977).

Syntropy is similar to earlier theories which have been termed "vitalism" (Morris, 1966, p. 34; and Szent-Gyorgyi, 1977, p. 19). Consequently Szent-Gyorgyi's theory has been criticized as being little more than a variation of vitalism.

All non-living "organisms" wear away until they "break" through use, called "normal wear". A new car progressively wears out and eventually the car has to be replaced. Even if a car is not used, it rusts, rots, and decays from just sitting. The use of any mechanical unit causes the unit's eventual destruction. But use[1] of living organisms, in time, causes them (unless other factors intervene, as illness) to *build up,* to become stronger (DeVries, 1970), actually improve themselves as the physical fitness advocates today have abundantly stressed. Inactivity, though, causes organisms to decay, tear down, and in time "break down." If an arm were put in a plaster cast for several years, it would "wither away," becoming thin, emaciated, weak, and useless. One of the major problems for living organisms is not activity but inactivity. The aging process is a different factor, evidently the accumulation of misuse, disease, stress, etc. Activity, in most cases, slows down the normal aging process. Thus use *tears down* nonlife, but *builds up* life.

Szent-Gyorgyi states he plans to spend the rest of his life working on the above problem, because he feels, in essence, the present evolutionary mechanism is inadequate, i.e.:

> . . . most biological reactions are chain reactions. To interact in a chain, these precisely built molecules must fit together most precisely, as the cog wheels of a Swiss watch do. But if this is so, then how can such a system develop at all? For if any one of the specific cog wheels in these chains is changed, then the whole system must simply become inoperative. Saying it can be improved by random mutation of one link . . . [is] like saying you could improve a Swiss watch by dropping it and thus bending one of its wheels or axles. To get a better watch all the wheels must be changed simultaneously to make a good fit again (p. 18, 1977).

Thus the problem. The solution Szent-Gyorgyi proposes (for which there is little direct empirical evidence) is that there must be an "innate force" in all living things which functions to improve the organism. However, Szent-Gyorgyi's concept of syntropy could just as logically and effectively be replaced by the creation hypothesis.

The concept of syntropy, while it does help explain some of the serious gaps in the theory of evolution, is still an appeal to a "natural" physical entity to explain the living world. If syntropy exists, it would seem possible to locate the organ or structures that causes syntropy to occur. The mechanism could be a single organ in the body similar to the hypothalmus, which directs body activity in a unified fashion, or it could be found in each individual cell. If it exists in individual cells, there likewise must be some outside mechanism of the cells, to coordinate this "drive to perfect itself" and make the body cells cooperate together. Otherwise individual cells would strive independently to perfect themselves, evolving in different directions, and in time cause disharmony and dysfunction in the organism.

The most important problem, though, is accounting for the cause or origin of this hypothesized drive. Can a "natural" means be found to explain the existence of this drive in all organisms as hypothesized? Could the natural selection hypothesis account for it? Is it hypotheisized all organisms have the syntropy mechanism? If it was clearly beneficial, presumably evolution would consistently select against those organisms lacking syntropy. Yet if an animal or a plant is fully adapted to its environment there would be no need for syntropy, (i.e. it would only be needed until the organism reached a high level of adaptation). Beyond this it would seem that the drive would, if it continued to make changes, cause the organism, in time, to become less adapted to the environment. Once adaptation is achieved, the drive must somehow stop, or risk doing harm to the organism as environmental changes would require very limited readaptation. As most "low level" organisms are highly adapted to their environment, we could ask what causes some organisms to continue to "try to perfect themselves" so that they reach much higher levels of development? Do all animals seek to change in the direction of man? If so, why have most animals fallen far short? Has this "drive" failed in most animals?

Any drive to perfect an organism would not produce results in a single organism, but would express itself only through a number of generations. As this would not confer any survival benefits to the individual organism, the evolutionary theory would dictate that it would not confer any advantage, and thus could not generally have a selection advantage. The drive would have to cause a change primarily in the gametes or sex cells. Changes in the gametes could not be accomplished unless such changes would benefit a possible future organism. The drive is toward improvement, not random changes. How could the structure which is responsible for syntropy know specifically what changes to make to improve the whole organism? Does this structure experiment by trial and error and if so, what process of feedback does it utilize?

Syntropy clearly helps to account for a number of realities the evolutionary hypothesis cannot explain, but as noted above, there are a number of serious questions which mitigate against the theory. At present the concept of syntropy is primarily metaphysical, similar to Freud's ego, id, and super-ego constructs. Importantly, though, the need to develop a concept such as syntropy clearly illustrates that scientists realize that there are serious problems with the theory of evolution, problems which are often ignored. The recognized need for the syntropy concept illustrates that the difficulties which have been stressed by creationists for some time are increasingly being recognized by evolutionists in the various evolutionary schools of thought. And once a serious examination of these problems is undertaken, scientists may begin to search for concepts which fit the facts much more adequately than the evolutionary hypothesis.

BIBLIOGRAPHY

1. Anthony, Catherine Parker, 1963. Textbook of Anatomy and Physiology, St. Louis: The C.V. Mosby Co.
2. DeVries, Herbert A. "Physiological Effects of an Exercise Regimen Upon Men Aged 52 to 88" *Journal of Gerontology* 1970.
3. McCormick, W. Wallace. 1965 *Fundamentals of College Physics,* New

York: The Macmillan Co.
4. Morris, Henry M. 1963. *The Twilight of Evolution,* Grand Rapids, MI: Baker Books. Szent-Gyorgyi, Albert. 1977. "Drive in Living Matter to Perfect Itself," *Synthesis* I, Vol. 1, No. 1, pp 14-26.
5. Szent-Gyorgyi, Albert. 1972. *The Living State: With Remarks on Cancer,* New York: Academic Press.
6. Vargiu, James. 1977. Editor of *Synthesis 1,* (Introduction to article by Szent-Gyorgyi, p. 14). Vol. 1, No. 1.